Conventional Wisdom, Parties, and Broken Barriers in the 2016 Election

Conventional Wisdom, Parties, and Broken Barriers in the 2016 Election

Jennifer C. Lucas, Christopher J. Galdieri, and Tauna Starbuck Sisco

LEXINGTON BOOKS
Lanham • Boulder • New York • London

Published by Lexington Books
An imprint of The Rowman & Littlefield Publishing Group, Inc.
4501 Forbes Boulevard, Suite 200, Lanham, Maryland 20706
www.rowman.com

Unit A, Whitacre Mews, 26-34 Stannary Street, London SE11 4AB

British Library Cataloguing in Publication Information Available

The hardback edition of this book was previously catalogued by the Library of Congress
as follows:

Library of Congress Cataloging-in-Publication Data Available

ISBN 978-1-4985-6661-2 (cloth : alk. paper)
ISBN 978-1-4985-6663-6 (pbk. : alk. paper)
ISBN 978-1-4985-6662-9 (electronic)

Contents

List of Figures

List of Tables

Introduction

Breaking the Conventional Wisdom in 2016

Jennifer Lucas, Christopher Galdieri, and Tauna Sisco

Well before the first primary votes of the 2016 election cycle were cast, it was clear that the election had the potential to break long-standing demographic barriers in American politics. The candidacy of Hillary Rodham Clinton held the potential to lead to the first nomination of a female candidate by a major political party and the first election of a woman to become president of the United States. Nor was Clinton the only potential "first" to seek the presidency in 2016. Across both party's nomination contests, an array of candidates sought to break religious, ethnic, and racial barriers within their parties or for the nation at large. From that perspective, part of the story of 2016 is why some barriers or glass ceilings were broken and why others held for at least one more election cycle.

Other aspects of the election held the prospect of breaking historical precedents. Donald Trump sought to become the first person to win the presidency despite never holding any political or military position, and was the first such candidate to win a major party's nomination since Wendell Willkie won the Republican nod in 1940. Hillary Clinton sought to become the first Democrat elected to succeed a Democratic president in American history. Republican voters chose their candidate from one of the largest fields in presidential campaign history, while Democrats chose from one of the smallest. And Republicans managed to break Democrats' long-standing hold on key states in the industrial Midwest, while Democrats failed to balance those losses with inroads into the south and southwest despite massive investments of time, money, and effort. From this perspective, part of the story of 2016 is about why some historical trends were broken, while others were not.

Furthermore, there were many unconventional aspects to the 2016 primary and general elections. Perhaps most readily observed by pundits and amateurs alike is that Trump carried several states that were expected to be solidly in the

Democratic column. Instead, what had been strongly Democratic states in the previous six elections went Republican against nearly all expectations. Which voters shifted their partisan allegiances, and which voters didn't turn out to vote on Election Day? Did those voters who were supposed to be a firewall for Clinton lose her support? And who did Trump bring into the Republican coalition? This book begins by deconstructing voter coalitions and behavior, and attempts to identify whether the 2016 results were significantly different from recent elections, or whether the conventional wisdom mainly held, but small shifts produced big results in the Electoral College. In other words, did 2016 voters defy the conventional wisdom in political science?

Perhaps more surprisingly were the nomination processes for the two parties in 2016. Democrats had a surprisingly hard-fought battle between Senator Bernie Sanders and former Secretary of State Hillary Clinton. Though Clinton was the frontrunner, Sanders had enough support for a more ideologically liberal agenda that the nomination contest lasted until the final primaries in June. For the Republican Party, the nomination process was even more divisive, with the candidate least beholden to the party establishment winning a large enough plurality of votes in enough primaries to win the nomination. With "never Trump" rallying cries gaining attention throughout the entire campaign, and Trump's lack of traditional Republican stances on issues like trade, foreign policy, and taxes, the party was divided throughout the campaign but ended up with Republican majorities in both the House of Representatives and Senate, and Trump in the White House. Several Republican incumbents survived strong challengers, especially in states where Clinton underperformed, helping to solidify unified government for at least the following two years. How then did the nomination process compare to previous election cycles? Did endorsements and intra-party politics play out in the same way? Or did Trump's candidacy signal something new in the way modern candidates are chosen? While this may seem like an abstract question, it would fundamentally change American politics if a flood of celebrity candidates follows Trump in 2020 and beyond.

And other breakage in the election held darker implications. The nomination of Trump, despite his scandal-tarred past, absence of political experience, and lack of support from elite Republican Party actors, indicates that the GOP has lost control of its nomination process. The strength of Senator Bernie Sanders' challenge to Hillary Clinton for the Democratic nomination, despite her extensive support among the elite ranks of the party, suggests that the tension apparent in 2016 between Democratic leadership and some of the voters that party relies on could continue through subsequent election cycles. For the fifth time in American history, and the second time in five elections, the winner of the popular vote did not win in the Electoral College, an outcome that upends the traditional linkage between public preferences and electoral and policy outcomes. Exacerbating matters is the magnitude of Trump's popular vote loss; while Al Gore's popular vote victory in 2000 was just half a million votes out of 105 million cast, Hillary Clinton led Trump by nearly 3 million votes when all was said and done. This surprising result led many political scientists to question whether 2016 truly marked a major turning point in American elections as portrayed in the media—a break from the conventional wisdom—or whether it was really the exception that proved the rule. This book takes up the question of internal party politics in a time of intense partisan polarization, examining the ways in which 2016 revealed important changes in the party nomination process and the ability of elites to control it.

While Trump's victory did not occur in a vacuum, the ways in which the presidential election might have influenced congressional elections are also up for debate. While some Republican incumbents did seem to benefit from Trump coattails, Trump's outsider status and lack of deep connection to the Republican establishment may have complicated congressional elections. For example, an Access Hollywood video surfaced in which Trump was heard making disrespectful sexual remarks about women. How did congressional candidates respond to this, and how did it play out in Senate races across the country? On the other hand, with Trump playing up his credentials as a plain-spoken outsider, did incumbent members of Congress push back against that idea or try to embrace it? How did Trump's outsider politics effect down-ballot races? Finally, this book also examines a vitally important topic that received less attention than it should have in 2016: election administration. While there were significant concerns about voter wait times and discrimination in previous elections, did we hear less about this because progress was made? Or did the many other storylines of 2016 simply swamp coverage of this important issue?

This book aims to answer the above questions, and put the conventional wisdom to the test. One vital way to ensure strong theories in political science is to put them to rigorous testing in new contexts. Therefore, in this book, political scientists examine previous theories and trends in light of the 2016 election to determine the extent to which 2016 undermined or supported those theories. While in some areas it seems as though 2016 was really just what would have been predicted, in others, this election and the new president pose significant challenges to mainstream theories in political science.

We divide the book into four sections: voting trends and voter demographics, political parties, congressional elections, and election administration. The voting trends and voter demographics section examines whether there were major voting shifts in 2016, the reasons traditionally blue states like Michigan and Wisconsin flipped to red, and why Latinos did not provide the boost Clinton needed to win. The section on political parties examines theories set out in the path-breaking *The Party Decides* to analyze whether party elites are still the driving force in presidential elections in light of Trump's lack of support from traditional party leaders, particularly during the Republican primary election. The final chapter in this section looks at one particularly important cause of the undermining of the party system: conspiracy theories, and the way they were mobilized in 2016. The third section looks at the link between the Trump presidential candidacy and the 2016 congressional elections. Boatright and colleagues examine the impact of Trump's gendered comments on Senate elections. Considering the importance of "outsider" rhetoric at the presidential level, the next chapter asks whether this outsider rhetoric was deployed by congressional candidates, and surprisingly find that it was not just challengers but long-time members of Congress who ran as "outsiders." Finally, in the last two presidential contests, election administration, including long voter wait times and discrimination, were of significant interest. However, we heard less about this in 2016. The last chapter examines whether election administration actually improved in 2016, or whether attention to these problems were lost in the surprising outcome.

How did the conventional wisdom fare? As Brewer and Powell note in chapter 1, on the surface the use of social media grew, expectations and limitations of what a presidential candidate can (and cannot) do expanded, a female candidate got closer to the White House than ever before, and many seemingly solid blue states turned red. However, looking at voting trends shows more support for predicted trends than one might expect, especially the lasting effects of partisan polarization, even with shifting coalitions within the parties. Instead, it appears that Democrats were slightly more likely to stay home and Republicans slightly more likely to show up to vote. They note that many differences between voter groups from 2008 to 2016 were fairly small. On the other hand, education had an important impact. Brewer and Powell demonstrate that voters with no college education switched from supporting Obama to supporting Trump by seven points. Similarly, they note that the rural/urban divide among voters was particularly potent in 2016.

This is echoed in Chad Kinsella's chapter, which focuses on the so-called "Blue Wall," a series of states, especially in the Midwest, which many thought to be an impregnable failsafe for Secretary Clinton even if Trump were to outperform his polling in several battleground states. Several of these states voted Republican for the first time in several decades, and he compares the political geography of the 2008 and 2016 presidential elections. Kinsella also notes the importance of the rural/urban split in 2016, with the largest drops in the Democratic vote coming in rural counties in Kentucky, West Virginia, and the Midwest. This likely explains Democrats losing control of the Kentucky legislature for the first time in almost 100 years. On the other hand, Trump did not perform as well as previous Republican candidates in southern states, while many suburban counties trended increasingly Democratic.

Therefore, while the Electoral College secured Trump's victory, there are concerning trends for both parties as they look to shore up votes for 2020.

With the death of Justice Antonin Scalia in 2016, few issues bled over from congressional politics to the presidential election as did the question of who would replace Scalia. With Republican Senators refusing to vote on President Obama's nominee to fill the vacancy, it was clear the next president would do so. Trump claimed that his victory was significantly due to the public's opinion of the Court. McMahon shows that a Clinton win would likely have shifted the swing justice from Justice Kennedy to Justice Breyer—a major ideological shift. He also demonstrates that many issues on the Court's recent agenda, including health care, gun rights, campaign finance, and same-sex marriage, were a driving force in the campaign and especially the debates. Exit poll data backs this up, as evangelical voters did not abandon Trump over his personal indiscretions and accusations of sexual assault and harassment, but instead stayed with him because of the importance of appointing the next justice, as did over 20 percent of voters who said it was the most important issue for them. These trends among evangelicals are especially notable in the "Blue Wall" states discussed by Kinsella. On the other hand, many of these trends were not too different from recent previous elections.

The next three chapters discuss groups of voters more in-depth, focusing on ethnicity, age, gender, and voters motivated by anger and contempt. Atiya Stokes-Brown shows that while Latinos were a heralded part of the Obama coalition and a quickly growing subgroup, Latinos did not prove to be the firewall that would protect a Clinton victory. She notes there are several reasons for this, including the Clinton campaign failing to reach out to the Latino community as effectively as Obama had, state voter identification laws that may have discouraged some Latino voters, and religious and racial diversity among Latinos. Rickenbach and Ossoff also demonstrate that while age and gender are important themselves, when you look at the two simultaneously, an interactive effect emerges. Middle-aged and older men were more likely to vote for and felt more favorable toward Donald Trump than younger men. In addition, middle-aged and older women were less likely to vote for and reported less favorability toward Hillary Clinton than younger women. As you would expect, female voters were more likely to report being bothered by Trump's treatment of women, and were more likely to be scared of the prospect of him as president. Male voters reported feeling more scared of Clinton as president but were not particularly excited about Trump. Finally, Mattes, Roseman, Redlawsk, and Katz showed respondents negative television ads from the campaign to ascertain whether they made people feel anger or contempt or both. While both candidates were perceived negatively, they found that those who felt contempt after viewing an ad had more negative opinions, while anger at an ad improved opinions of the candidates.

The next section of the book examines the role of political parties in 2016, a topic of great concern to many activists and partisans. Collens and Wanless examine the issue of endorsements, which in previous elections have been strong indicators of winning the nomination. In particular, the theory in *The Party Decides* was put to the test in 2016. They note that elite endorsements may have been diminished in their effectiveness, especially with a large Republican field and no clear consensus alternative to Trump, and with a lack of enthusiasm for Clinton. Their analysis of survey data indicates that those who were least trusting of elites were more likely to support Trump or Sanders for their respective partisan nominations. The 2016 election may undermine conventional wisdom about the importance of endorsements.

Since the early 1900s, and especially since the 1970s, America's major political parties have been moving in the direction of internal party democracy, embracing primaries and other means for rank-and-file voters to have a say in nominations and other aspects of party governance. They have particularly developed a system of primary debates between candidates seeking presidential nominations. Masket and Azari examine the modern history of presidential primary debates and the evolution of the rules and norms that now govern them. While presidential primary debates have become steadily more an established, institutionalized part of the presidential nomination process, the parties have developed these debates without clear definitions of who may participate in them. Thus the debates, designed in part to mitigate against the nomination of an unpopular candidate hostile to key party goals, ended up perversely facilitating such a nomination in 2016.

Finally, to get some sense of how Trump was able to overcome the party establishment and mobilize non-traditional voters, Atkinson, DeWitt, and Uscinski show that conspiracy theories played a more prominent role and were used very differently—particularly by elites—in 2016 when compared to prior elections. With Trump's first forays into presidential politics focusing on birtherism and the false conspiracy theory that Obama was not born in the United States, it is not surprising that his campaign was able to mobilize and organize voters by deploying conspiracy theories as signals. They also argue that conspiracy theories in 2016 were different from other conspiracy theories, because they were concentrated among like-minded people rather than spread more broadly, as rumors are often traditionally spread. This is certainly a clear example of the unconventional nature of the 2016 election.

The next section of the book analyzes the extent to which the presidential candidates influenced congressional elections. Chapp, Hofrenning, Benning, and Zielske investigate whether Trump's outsider rhetoric could also be found in House elections. Surprisingly, they find that 2016 was not particularly different from the previous election in the deployment of outsider rhetoric. While it would seem that incumbents would not be able to claim outsider status, they are almost as likely to claim to be outsiders. Those claiming to be outsiders in 2016 were not just riding the Trump bandwagon, but were playing to what they think will win in their district.

Similarly, Boatright, Sterling, and Tatar also examine the influence of the presidential elections on congressional elections, but they find a greater effect in Senate races. Their content analysis of campaign advertising documents how the use of gender stereotypes in the presidential campaign corresponded to the use of these stereotypes in Senate elections. Senate ads responded to the presidential campaign, with candidates and their allies seeking to distance themselves from some of Trump's more offensive sexist remarks. They also demonstrate that there are some important differences depending on whether a woman was running in the Senate race, which perhaps reinforces the need for more women in office. Overall, these chapters indicate that there is mixed evidence about the extent to which presidential politics shaped congressional races.

Finally, Fine and Stewart update readers about an important topic: election administration. Voter confidence in elections is extremely important to the legitimacy of the electoral process. Particularly with Trump hedging whether he would support a duly elected President Clinton during the election, and concerns about foreign hacking of elections, these concerns were a topic of significant discussion in 2016. When it comes to increasing voter confidence through decreasing wait times, the two areas studied in this chapter have both made improvements after the Presidential Commission on Election Administration's recommendations from 2012. Their results show that concerns about the integrity of the electoral process may be a lasting result of the 2016 election.

Each chapter that follows begins by laying out the conventional wisdom (what political science theories say about the topic), and then analyses whether 2016 supported or undermined that theory. On balance, it appears that 2016 did not have the earth-shattering effect on many of the fundamental trends documented by political scientists in the modern era. While the bells and whistles gave the appearance of a significant departure from the norm throughout the campaign process, in many ways these chapters indicate that the conventional wisdom should not be discarded so quickly.

Each of these chapters were originally presented at the American Elections conference held at Saint Anselm College, in Manchester, New Hampshire in March 2017. We are indebted to the college, our departments, the administrative staff and colleagues for their support for the conference. This book would not have been possible without them.

Part I

VOTING DEMOGRAPHICS: DID VOTER TRENDS FOLLOW THE CONVENTIONAL WISDOM?

Chapter 1

Targeting the Vote

Constituency Appeals and Group Voting in the 2016 Presidential Election

Richard J. Powell and Mark D. Brewer

VOTING IN THE 2016 ELECTION

In the early stages of the 2016 presidential election, conventional wisdom held that the election would almost certainly be a continuation of long-simmering partisan battles.[1] In fact, the most likely scenario seemed to be a showdown Democrat Hillary Clinton and Republican Jeb Bush, a continuation of the political prominence of the Bush and Clinton families that stretched back decades. Of course, other scenarios seemed possible, especially on the Republican side in which a number of experienced politicians prepared to run, most notably Senators Marco Rubio, Rand Paul, and Ted Cruz, and experienced governors Chris Christie and John Kasich. Nearly everyone expected Hillary Clinton to cruise to an easy victory for her party's nomination.

Of course, this is not what happened. On the Democratic side, Clinton faced a remarkably strong challenge from the most unlikely of rivals, Senator Bernie Sanders, a 74-year-old, little-known, self-described democratic socialist from Vermont. And even more unusually, the Republicans deviated from any previously known political script to nominate Donald Trump, the New York businessman with no prior experience in elective office or military service, and a past filled with controversy.

In terms of the deeper political dynamics, conventional wisdom provided a set of clear expectations. By 2016, American politics had become polarized along partisan lines to an extent not seen in over a century. Recent elections had seen fewer and fewer persuadable voters as Democrats and Republicans proved exceptionally loyal to their own party. Even most independents, about one-third of electorate, mostly comprised "closet partisans" who rarely strayed in their vote choices. Thus, candidates and their campaigns focused on two main strategies: motivating their own partisans to turn out on election day and making appeals to an ever-smaller percentage of the electorate that was considered persuadable. To do so, political professionals increasingly made use of sophisticated "micro-targeting" techniques, aided by the evolving tools of big data and social media.

In addition, a fairly uniform set of norms and expectations had developed on how candidates should conduct themselves that included a modicum of civility, professionalism, and evidence-based appeals. Conventional wisdom assumed that candidates would be punished by voters if they strayed too far from these expectations. In the early days of the Republican nomination, conventional wisdom held that Donald Trump's insurgent campaign would certainly collapse under the weight of his controversial statements and norm-challenging behaviors. Once it became apparent that Trump would win the nomination, conventional wisdom coalesced around the idea that Hillary Clinton would easily prevail in the general election. That expectation dominated until well into the evening of Election Day.

As we discuss in this chapter, and throughout this book, the 2016 presidential election upended conventional wisdom in unprecedented ways, especially concerning norms of how political figures are expected to behave and the boundaries of acceptable forms of campaign rhetoric. However, in some deeper ways, conventional wisdom fared better. Once the dust settled on the election, it became clear that partisan polarization was as strong as ever. In terms of the winning coalition, Trump's victory can be explained by the durability of polarization as most Republicans "came home," combined with some additional support among white working-class voters. As we discuss below, most divisions within the electorate reflected long-term trends underway well before 2016, with some hints of important new developments. Trump rallied Republicans, despite the persistent misgivings of the "Never-Trump" Republicans. As shown in Table 1.1, he won a slightly lower percentage of Republican votes than Romney had in 2012 (88% to 93%), but Republican turnout was higher than it had been in 2012, yielding a net gain of 0.4 percent of the vote once turnout was taken into consideration.[2] On the Democratic side, Clinton performed worse that than Obama had in 2012, garnering 89 percent of the Democratic votes. However, the proportion of the electorate that was Democratic dropped by 2 percent over 2012 and 3 percent over 2008. In other words, many Democrats simply stayed home, perhaps due to Clinton's email scandal or then-FBI director James Comey's announcement that the FBI had reopened its investigation into the scandal shortly before the election. In the end, partisan polarization seemed to override all of the highly unusual noise of this campaign.

In at least two other respects, conventional wisdom held up fairly well in the 2016 campaign. Political observers have long noted the unlikelihood of a political party winning three or more consecutive presidential elections.

The victories of Harry Truman in 1948 and George H.W. Bush in 1988 are the only times this has occurred in the post–World War II era. Throughout the campaign, Trump's unconventional behavior distracted pundits from some of the deeper patterns in American electoral politics. In this chapter we subject these strains of conventional wisdom to deeper analysis, especially the voting behavior of key demographic groups in the electorate and the campaign appeals that candidates utilized to reach those groups.

RACE/ETHNICITY

In recent elections, making appeals to voters based on race and ethnicity has been a critical campaign strategy for presidential candidates. Race and ethnicity have been important factors in recent presidential elections, a trend that continued in 2016, albeit in very different ways. As the campaign unfolded, conventional wisdom held that Hillary Clinton would do very well with critical minority groups due to her skillful use of data analytics combined with Donald Trump's frequent controversial comments about key racial and ethnic groups.

As a reference point, we can begin by looking at white voters. For all the talk about Trump's appeal to white voters in 2016, Clinton only suffered a net decline of 0.7 percent among whites as compared to Obama in 2012. However, the aggregate total obscures largely off-setting but significant changes among sub-groups of white voters. Clinton performed much better than Obama with college-educated whites, while performing worse with non-college-educated whites, especially men. Trump, in particular, struck a deep chord with rural and blue-collar white voters who had long felt that dominant elites in American politics had disregarded their interests. They were particularly attracted to Trump's hard-hitting rhetoric on immigration and international trade (Carswell 2016).

Before turning to the key groups of Hispanics and blacks, it is important to note that a range of racial and ethnic groups have been important to the electoral strategies of the two main parties in recent elections. In 2016, Clinton performed better with Asian voters (65%) than Obama in 2008 (62%), but did not match his total with that group in 2012 (73%). Even as Asians have been moving away from Republicans over the past several election cycles, Asians are not monolithic in their voting behavior. Americans of Indian origin, for example, have tended to be more supportive of Republicans than other Asians. As a result, the Trump campaign made numerous appeals to this group (Bump 2016; Decker 2016).

We now turn our attention to two groups that have received considerable attention in studies of electoral behavior, Hispanics, and blacks.

Table 1.1 Voting Trends in 2008, 2012, and 2016 Presidential Elections

Net Effect on the Two-Party Vote 2012 to 2016	Change in Two-Party Democratic Vote Share from 2012 to 2016	Change in Share of Voters from 2012 to 2016	Social Group	2016			2012			2008		
				Clinton	Trump	Share of Voters	Obama	Romney	Share of Voters	Obama	McCain	Share of Voters
			Sex									
-1.1	-2.3	0	Men	41	52	47	45	52	47	49	48	47
0.7	1.3	0	Women	54	41	53	55	44	53	56	43	53
			Race and Ethnicity									
-0.7	-0.4	-1	White	37	57	71	39	59	72	43	55	74
-1.2	-2.2	-1	Black	89	8	12	93	6	13	95	4	13
0.5	-2.2	1	Latino/Hispanic	66	28	11	71	27	10	67	31	9
0.6	-3.1	1	Asian	65	27	4	73	26	3	62	35	2
			Sex and Race									
-0.9	-2.7	0	White Men	31	62	34	35	62	34	41	57	36
0.5	2.4	-1	White Women	43	52	37	42	56	38	46	53	39
-0.1	-2.5	0	Black Men	82	13	5	87	11	5	95	5	5
-1.0	-1.1	-1	Black Women	94	4	7	96	3	8	96	3	7
0.0	0.0	0	Latino Men	63	32	5	65	33	5	64	33	4
-0.2	-3.4	0	Latino Women	69	25	6	76	23	6	68	30	5
			Education									
-4.4	-5.7	-3	No College Degree	44	51	50	51	47	53	53	46	56
0.0	-4.8	3	Some College	43	51	32	49	48	29	51	47	31
3.0	4.7	3	College	49	44	32	47	51	29	50	48	28
0.8	4.4	0	Postgrad	58	37	18	55	42	18	59	40	17
			Type of Community									
-2.3	-4.0	-4	Rural	34	61	17	39	59	21	53	45	21
1.5	1.0	2	Suburban	49	49	49	48	50	47	51	48	49
1.5	0.6	2	Urban	60	34	34	62	36	32	63	35	30

Religious Tradition

Protestant (all)	-1.1	-1.4	-1	39	56	52	42	57	53	45	54	54
Roman Catholic	-1.7	-3.1	-2	46	50	23	50	48	25	54	45	27
Jewish	0.9	5.8	1	71	23	3	69	30	2	78	21	2
None	2.2	-0.1	3	67	25	15	70	26	12	75	23	12
Family Income												
Under $50,000	-4.8	-4.8	-5	53	41	36	60	38	41	60	38	38
$50,000–99,999	0.0	1.5	-1	46	49	30	46	52	31	49	49	36
$100,000 and over	4.4	5.1	6	47	47	34	44	54	28	49	49	26

Note: Some numbers do not total to 100 due to rounding.

Note: All data presented in the first two columns of Table 1 refer to the two-party presidential vote. In other words, the percentages exclude third-party candidates. The data presented in the right-side columns of Table 1 are raw percentages. The reader should note that the figures for 2016 generally do not come close to totaling to 100 because of the atypically large number of votes cast for third-party candidates in 2016.

Sources: All figures are taken from the National Exit Poll conducted by Edison Media Research and Mitofsky International for the National Election Pool (a consortium of ABC News, The Associated Press, CBS News, CNN, Fox News, and NBC News. 2008 data as reported by Fox News (available at http://www.foxnews.com/politics/elections/2008-exit-poll. 2012 data as reported by Fox News (available at http://www.foxnews.com/politics/elections/2012-exit-poll. 2016 data as reported by *The New York Times*, (available at https://www.nytimes.com/interactive/2016/11/08/us/politics/election-exit-polls).

Hispanics

In particular, Hispanics have been regarded as an increasingly critical group in American electoral politics due to their continued growth as a segment of the electorate, particularly in a number of critical swing states such as Colorado, Florida, Nevada, and Virginia.

Although Hispanic voters sided overwhelmingly with Barack Obama in 2008 (67%) and 2012 (71%), Republicans have continued to make overtures to this group because they are not viewed as a monolithic voting bloc to the same degree as other racial and ethnic groups. In 2000, George W. Bush won 45 percent of the Hispanic vote in his race against Vice President Al Gore. Republicans have long believed that their message has potential appeal to Hispanic voters, many of whom hold conservative social views rooted in their relatively high level of religiosity.

Despite the fact that Mitt Romney's campaign made numerous efforts to appeal to Hispanic voters in 2012, the Democrats won historically high support from this group. As a result, the official post-mortem produced by the Republican National Committee following the 2012 election highlighted the importance of making inroads with Hispanics. In particular, the report stressed the need for the party to soften and downplay its stands on immigration, which remained an important gateway issue for many Hispanic voters. Moreover, many of the early frontrunners for the Republican nomination seemed poised to appeal to Hispanic voters, especially Senators Marco Rubio (FL) and Ted Cruz (TX), who came from Cuban-American families, and former Florida governor Jeb Bush, who speaks fluent Spanish and whose spouse, Columba, was born in Mexico.

The carefully arranged plans of Republicans to improve their standing with Hispanics was quickly derailed once the nomination campaign began, due to the unexpected emergence of Donald Trump as a leading candidate for the nomination. Kicking off his campaign for president on June 16, 2015, Trump immediately focused on illegal immigration as his major campaign theme, saying, "When Mexico sends its people, they're not sending their best. They're not sending you. They're not sending you. They're sending people that have lots of problems, and they're bringing those problems with us. They're bringing drugs. They're bringing crime. They're rapists. And some, I assume, are good people (*Washington Post* Staff Writers 2015)." These comments were just the opening salvo for Trump in what seemed like a tailor-made effort to repel Hispanic voters. Without a doubt, Trump's signature issue in the 2016 presidential campaign was his repeated promise to build a wall along the United States' border with Mexico and to make the Mexicans pay for it. And, during the general election campaign, Trump used the phrase "bad hombres" to characterize some Mexican immigrants.

For her part, Hilary Clinton recognized the importance of Hispanic voters from the outset of her campaign, and worked to carefully court this segment of the electorate by capitalizing on Trump's inflammatory rhetoric and through the use of sophisticated micro-targeting of Hispanic voters. For example, during the fall campaign Clinton spent $3 million on Spanish-language ads in the key swing states of Florida and Nevada (Hellman 2016). The campaign also ran a Spanish-language ad campaign in Florida targeting conservative Hispanic voters that featured Carlos Gutierrez, a former Secretary of Commerce under President George W. Bush, saying he could not vote for Trump because he regarded him as dangerous for the country (Halper 2016).

The Clinton campaign also developed a highly differentiated view of Hispanic voters that attempted to tap into important sub-group identities. For example, Clinton used extensive micro-targeting to attract Puerto Rican voters in Florida, a group that had grown significantly since 2012 as Puerto Ricans fled the economic troubles of their island territory (Frizell 2016). She also invested a considerable amount of resources in mobilization efforts to "low-propensity" Hispanic voters in Florida, using door-to-door canvassing (Hohman 2016).

The vice-presidential candidates also became part of the campaign dynamic as it related to Hispanic voters. Clinton's selection of Senator Tim Kaine (VA) as her running mate was particularly well received among Hispanics. Kaine was used extensively in ads and events targeting Hispanic voters since he spoke fluent Spanish from his time working with Jesuit missionaries in Honduras (Horowitz 2016; Wagner 2016). On the other side, Mike Pence, the governor of Indiana, received a great deal of criticism for his response in the vice-presidential debate when Kaine asked him to defend Trump's earlier reference to Mexicans as rapists and murderers. In reply, Pence said, "Senator, you've whipped out that Mexican thing again (Rogers 2016)." The comment became a rallying cry for Democrats and "#thatmexicanthing" went viral as an anti-Pence hashtag on Twitter with numerous Mexican-Americans tweeting about the pride they felt regarding their ancestry.

In the end, the voting results were somewhat surprising given the expectations of conventional wisdom. Undoubtedly, Clinton performed well among Hispanics, just as Democrats have done in all recent presidential elections. However, in winning 66 percent of the Hispanic vote, Clinton actually underperformed with Hispanics relative to Obama in 2012 (71%). This was especially surprising given Trump's heated rhetoric on issues of central concern to Hispanic voters. Given the anti-immigrant themes of Trump's campaign it was shocking that he actually outperformed Romney in 2012 in terms of the Hispanic vote—and Romney had made Hispanics a key constituency for outreach based on shared values and small business-friendly proposals.

Blacks

Blacks have made up a central part of the Democratic coalition for generations in American politics. As such, this is not considered to be a swing group within the electorate, but outreach to black voters is still critical because differences in voter turnout can have important implications in the outcome of the vote in key swing states. The 2016 campaign kicked off against the backdrop of the 2008 and 2012 races in which black voters were highly energized by the candidacies of Barack Obama. Obama won historic victories among this group, with 95 and 93 percent of the black vote in 2008 and 2012, respectively. Sustained high levels of black support for Democrats was a key linchpin of Clinton's strategy in 2016.

As with other key swing groups, conventional wisdom held that Clinton's task was made easier by the missteps of the Trump campaign. Certainly, Clinton's ability to attract the same levels of support as Obama among black voters was in question from the start. Although Bill Clinton had been overwhelmingly popular with black Americans during his presidency, some aspects of the Clinton legacy had come to be reinterpreted over time, especially in relation to tough anti-crime legislation passed during his presidency which many had come to believe imposed an unjust burden on blacks. For her part, Hillary Clinton had been criticized for her nearly two-decade-old reference to "super-predators," a phrase many felt was racially charged. Clinton also drew criticism from black religious leaders for her support of progressive social policies, such as abortion and LGBTQ rights, they found problematic (Richardson 2016). Nevertheless, the contrast with Trump, and the historic support of Democrats among blacks, gave Clinton a substantial advantage.

Just as he did with reference to Hispanics, Trump ran a campaign that risked alienating black voters on a number of fronts. Of course, the most notable aspect this regard were Trump's dominant themes of white nationalism, advocated by his key campaign adviser, Stephen Bannon, the former head of Breitbart News. Trump's original rise to political prominence, during and after the 2012 campaign, was due to his repeated questioning of President Barack Obama's birthplace and eligibility to be president, something that most political observers felt carried racist overtones. Moreover, during the 2016 campaign Trump's candidacy attracted extensive support from the KKK and other white supremacist groups. When asked, Trump was slow and tepid in his disavowal of such groups. During the campaign, a number of unflattering news stories arose that focused on Trump properties that had been investigated for housing discrimination (Caldwell 2016).

Throughout the campaign, Trump became repeatedly embroiled in controversies regarding black Americans. For example, his speeches routinely conflated black with inner-city urban poverty. He also expressed support of an anti-crime policy unpopular with blacks, saying "One of the things I'd do, is I would do stop-and-frisk. I think you have to. We did it in New York, it worked incredibly well and you have to be proactive (Barbaro, Haberman, and Alcindor 2016)."

Trump did make some attempts to court black voters. In a speech to one black group, he said "You're living in poverty, your schools are no good, you have no jobs, 58% of your youth is unemployed–what the hell do you have to lose (Henderson 2016)?" This was generally consistent with his efforts to attract black support with appeals to economic development. In early September he highlighted those themes in a visit to the Great Faith International Ministries church in Detroit to highlight those themes, a group that had complained about Clinton's support for progressive social policies (Fox News 2016).

The Clinton campaign aggressively countered Trump's appeals to black voters, in addition to making overtures to black voters a central feature of its campaign strategy. For example, the campaign dispatched Bill Clinton to Detroit to refute Trump's comments at Great Faith International Ministries where he appeared in a parade in Detroit that attempted to highlight Republican shortcomings in response to Flint, MI water crisis (Dalbey 2016). The Clinton campaign also used a number of high-profile black surrogates, such as congressman and civil rights leader John Lewis, the mother of Trayvon Martin and DeRay Mckesson, the civil rights leader who had risen to prominence in Ferguson, Missouri before running for mayor of Baltimore (Griffiths 2016). Without a doubt though, the most effective surrogates for Clinton effort in its appeals to black voters were Barack and Michelle Obama who appeared in numerous campaign events on behalf of Clinton. On multiple occasions, President Obama told mostly black audiences that he would regard it as a personal insult if blacks did not turn out to vote for Clinton (Chozik and Davis 2016). These appearances were buttressed by targeted campaign expenditures, such as a $3 million ad buy in September targeted to black voters in the key swing states Florida, North Carolina, and Ohio (Hellman 2016). Clinton made numerous visits to speak with black audiences, especially in Philadelphia where black voters were considered to be an important part of the "blue wall"—states that seemed to be securely in the Democratic column throughout the campaign.

On Election Day, it was no surprise that Hillary Clinton performed well among blacks, although her support lagged behind that of Obama in 2008 and 2012. While Clinton received 89 percent of the black vote, that bloc comprised a slightly lower proportion of the electorate in 2016 (12%) than in 2012 (13%). Among blacks, the drop off in the Democratic vote cost Clinton a net of 1.2 percent of the national popular vote as compared to Obama in 2012.

SEX

More than any presidential election in U.S. history, sex was front and center in the 2016 race. On the Democratic side was the first woman nominee of a major presidential party, with a chance to become the first female president in history. On the Republican side was Donald Trump, a notorious womanizer on his third marriage who had a well-publicized history of saying controversial things about women.

In recent years, political observers have noted the growth in the "gender gap" in American elections—the fact that men and women have developed increasingly divergent voting patterns and viewpoints about a wide range of political issues. In terms of voting patterns, this trend has been most evident in women supporting Democratic presidential candidates, while men have supported Republicans. The gender gap in 2008 in support of the Democratic nominee, Barack Obama, was 7 percentage points, with Obama winning 56 percent of women and only 49 of men. By 2012 this grew to 10 percentage points. This divergence grew to 13 percentage points with the 2016 election, with Clinton winning 54 percent of women but only 41 percent of men.

Delving more deeply into the data, we see that women voted for Clinton at about the same rate (54%) as they did for Obama in 2012 (55%) and 2008 (56%). For Obama, black voters had turned out in droves to elect the nation's first black president. Unfortunately for Clinton, women did not rush to her side to the same extent in an attempt to elect the first woman. Throughout the campaign, Clinton faced a number of "double-binds" common to women candidates running for executive office, including questions about her ability to display openness and personal warmth. She had long wrestled with such issues in her public life.

In most any other election, Clinton's status as the first female nominee would have been the dominant story, especially in discussions of sex. However, the coverage of issues surrounding sex tended to be focused on various controversies surrounding Donald Trump. Of course, the most dramatic of those stories was the surfacing of an *Access Hollywood* tape in early October that had been recorded in 2005, in which Trump seemed to suggest to Billy Bush that he sexually assaulted women by groping their genitals, saying that "when you're a star, they let you do it (Fahrenthold 2016)." Although Trump and his campaign dismissed the comments as "locker room banter," the tape continued to receive prominent attention throughout the fall campaign.

By itself the *Access Hollywood* tape would have doomed virtually any presidential candidate, especially with women voters. However, the tape was just one of many controversies in which Trump became embroiled. Starting with comments he made in the first presidential debate on September 26, Trump became embroiled in a lengthy dispute with former Miss Universe, Alicia Machado, in addition to renewing a long-simmering public dispute with comedian Rosie O'Donnell. Trump also had a high-profile and long-running feud with then-Fox media personality Megyn Kelly that had substantial gendered elements to it (Hampson 2016; Rutenberg 2016).

Trump's controversies with women tended to overshadow the more traditional policy-based appeals that his campaign made to women voters. In fact, on some specific issues Trump championed proposals aimed at female voters that were quite progressive for a Republicans and that might have received more favorable attention had the campaign not been on the defensive with women throughout much of the fall. Most notably, Trump campaigned for policies to increase government subsidies for child care, as well as paid parental leave, issues that had long been advocated by his high-profile daughter, Ivanka (Hook 2016). For example, he stated at a rally in Pennsylvania aimed at suburban women, "We need working mothers to be fairly compensated for their work, and to have access to affordable, quality child care for their kids (Slattery 2016)."

In reaching out to women voters, Clinton combined her meta-message of shattering the "highest glass ceiling" by being the first woman to win the presidency with a wide range of more specific appeals on traditional issues of importance to female voters. Throughout the campaign, she described her support of progressive policies in the areas such as reproductive rights, education reform, guns, and bullying (Karni 2016). Still, the bulk of Clinton's gender-based appeals focused on her assertions that Trump had a history of poor personal treatment of women in her advertising, public speeches, and in the debates (Krieg 2016). Most notably, Democrats ran an ad that featured women and girls reciting offensive remarks that Trump had said about females.

Although Trump became embroiled in numerous controversies that damaged his potential appeal to women, he was almost single-mindedly devoted to his core constituency of white, working-class men. Ultimately, it was his careful cultivation of this demographic group that made the most significant difference for him on Election Day. Trump matched Mitt Romney's performance in 2012 among all men and white men. However, most post-election analysis failed to notice that he also won a larger share of the vote among black men than other recent Republican candidates. When taking into account the results of the election and the share of the electorate men and women comprised, Trump actually improved upon Romney's performance from 2012. Although he performed much worse among women, this was more than offset by his appeal to male voters.

AGE

Although much analysis has focused on the gender gap in American elections, age has also become a significant dividing line among American voters in recent presidential elections. For example, in 2008 Barack Obama won 66 percent of the vote among those aged 18–29, but only 45 percent from those aged 65 or older. This has been indicative of recent elections in which young voters have overwhelmingly supported Democrats while older Americans have supported Republicans. The 2016 presidential election provided some interesting new twists. In particular, Senator Bernie Sanders attracted considerable support from younger voters in the Democratic primary. This proved to present a persistent problem for Hillary Clinton throughout the fall campaign, as she struggled to incorporate those voters into her coalition. Few younger voters had much memory of the Bill Clinton presidency. And, much of what they did know was unfavorable, since many younger voters looked with disfavor on President Clinton's well-publicized marital infidelity. As a result, many of the Sanders supporters from the primary campaign found the Green Party candidate, Jill Steyn, to be a more appealing choice. Similarly, many Republican and independent-minded young voters were drawn to the Libertarian Party candidacy of Gary Johnson (Peters and Alcindor 2016).

From the earliest stages of the campaign, the Clinton campaign understood the importance of the youth vote and made numerous appeals to them. Most notably, Clinton campaigned on a plan to make college education debt free at in-state public institutions (Winberg 2016). She also focused extensively on climate change, a hot button issue for this voting demographic. On a more symbolic note, she attended a tailgate party at a Penn State football game, publicized her campaign through Snapchat, and hosted a wide range of pop culture stars at her rallies, including Katy Perry (Figueroa 2016) and Beyonce and Jay-Z the week before the election (Megerian 2016). Similarly, Miley Cyrus campaigned door-to-door from Clinton on the campus of George Mason University (Shapira 2016). Clinton also appeared on "Between Two Ferns" a show hosted by Zach Galifianakis that was popular with younger voters (Griffiths 2016).

As with outreach efforts to other demographic groups, the use of surrogates was a notable strategy that Clinton used to target younger voters. In particular, the Clinton campaign relied very heavily on Senators Bernie Sanders and Elizabeth Warren in their campaign for the youth vote (Karni 2016). Additionally, Chelsea Clinton was dispatched to a number of college campuses to rally students. A racial gap also developed among traditionally Democratic youth voters. That Clinton would win among black millennials by a wide margin was never in question. However, her campaign understood that mobilizing this group to turn out to vote was key to their electoral strategy in a number of key battleground states. Throughout much of the campaign, young black voters, many of whom felt left behind in the campaign, seemed unenthused by Clinton's candidacy. To counter this problem, Clinton relied very heavily on Barack and Michelle Obama to hold high-profile events in key states (Martin 2016; Williams 2016). She also held a series of rallies at historically black colleges (Caputo and Ducassi 2016).

In terms of outreach to older voters, Clinton relied on a two-prong strategy. One part consisted of attempting to remind this group of the relatively peaceful and prosperous presidency of her husband. The second part relied on traditional Democratic appeals based on programs that were popular with older Americans, especially Social Security and Medicare. For at least a generation in American politics, Democrats had been successful at portraying Republicans as a threat to government funding for those popular programs. The Democratic candidate approached 2016 in much the same way.

As we noted earlier, in contrast to most modern presidential campaigns, Donald Trump did not tend to rely on a nuanced campaign strategy of making specific appeals to differentiated demographic groups. In general, he made very few targeted appeals to voters of different age groups. The one significant exception to this was in the policy areas of Social Security and Medicare. In contrast to typical Republican candidates, Trump explicitly denounced any efforts to cut spending for those programs. Instead, he positioned himself as a champion of senior citizens. In a more general sense, his promise to "Make America Great Again," held the potential for nostalgic appeal for older Americans who might wish to return to a time that they perceived as simpler and more in keeping with their values.

Looking at the exit polls, for all of the reasons we discussed above, the age gap persisted in 2016, but to a lessened degree. Older voters cast their ballots for Trump at very close to the same rate as they had Romney and McCain. Younger voters did support Clinton, but to a lesser degree than they had Obama. Clinton won 55 percent of the vote for those in the 18–29 age bracket, a group from which Obama had won 60 percent of the vote in 2012 and 66 percent in 2008. In short, younger voters did not so much move to Trump as they did abandon Clinton. Among voters 65 and older, only 3 percent cast their ballots for a candidate other than Clinton or Trump. However, 9 percent of voters in the 18–29 age category cast their votes for a third-party candidate, as did 8 percent of those in the 30–44 age group. These defections were just enough to deprive Clinton of enough votes to prevail on Election Day.

RELIGION

For an issue accustomed to playing a large role in American presidential elections in recent years it certainly seemed as though religion was keeping an extremely low profile during the 2016 presidential campaign, especially in the general election phase. Neither Hillary Clinton nor Donald Trump projected an overtly religious identity. While Clinton is a long-standing and apparently active member of the United Methodist Church who claims to take its social gospel message seriously (Moorthy 2016), she did not regularly tout any of this on the campaign trail nor did she make this central to the identity she presented to voters. Trump, who in his lengthy time in the public spotlight has never claimed to be overly religious, was raised Presbyterian but in recent years has extolled the virtues of Florida megachurch pastor and prosperity gospel proponent Paula White. Trump stated that his busy schedule prevents him from attending church services very often, but that he did sometimes attend on important religious holidays (Burke 2016). Similarly, neither candidate made a habit of using religiously tinged language. Clinton seemed to only speak about religion when explicitly asked about the topic and while Trump did come around to raising the matter of religion more frequently, doing so often resulted in gaffes (e.g., "2 Corinthians," eating the "little crackers") or in otherwise awkward situations. The main issues that each campaign was attempting to focus on—immigration and trade for Trump and Trump's unfitness for the White House (along with a somewhat smaller message of four more years of the policies of President Barack Obama) for Clinton—did not include prominent religious elements on their face, although clearly one can see at least some religions elements in them if one chooses. Perhaps the one area where religion did rise to prominence in the 2016 presidential campaign was focused much more beyond—rather than within—American borders. This of course refers to Trump's discourse surrounding Islam and Muslims. Whether it was calling for a ban on Muslim immigration, promising to attack and eradicate "radical Islamic terrorism," or telling CNN's Anderson Cooper "I think Islam hates us" (Newsday 2016), Trump clearly, loudly, and frequently signaled to voters that he possessed a very negative view of the world's second largest religious faith. But Trump's derisive and combative rhetoric around Islam was the exception to the rule in the 2016 presidential campaign—Religion simply did not seem to play a very large role. Until it did.

As a shocked nation awoke on November 9, 2016 (if they had ever gone to sleep) and tried to make sense of Donald Trump as president-elect, many turned to the exit polls. As they scrolled down the results, electoral cleavages surrounding religion presented themselves as they have for the most part since 1980—large and significant. Not only were the religious divisions big and important, they looked about the same as they have looked since George

W. Bush won his first term in the White House in 2000 if not since Ronald Reagan's first presidential victory in 1980 (Smith 2016). Perhaps the most eye-catching result was that of white born-again or evangelical Christians, the largest single religious tradition in the United States. This group was large—26 percent of the electorate—and went heavily for Trump, giving him 80 percent of their vote versus only 16 percent for Clinton. This figure was higher than white evangelical support for Mitt Romney in 2012 (78%) and John McCain in 2008 (74%). One could argue that Trump's 80 percent support from white born-again Christians is both the most unsurprising and surprising figure in the exit poll results at the same time. It is unsurprising because white evangelicals have become a large and staunch part of the Republican coalition, routinely supporting GOP presidential candidates at very high levels even when the candidate in question has not exactly had the best evangelical bona fides (see both Romney and McCain). This being said, the GOP has never nominated a candidate like Donald Trump. Thrice-married (with children with all three wives) and twice-divorced, Trump has long embraced a playboy lifestyle that runs counter to much of the evangelical Protestant worldview. In his numerous appearances with radio personality Howard Stern over the years, his taped *Access Hollywood* comments, and in numerous other venues Trump has routinely made comments and endorsed behaviors that would make many evangelicals (and, of course, others as well) cringe in embarrassment, disagreement, and/or disgust. Heading into Election Day many wondered whether some evangelicals would abandon Trump over concerns about his personal life and/or past statements but in the end white evangelical Protestants stayed loyal to their team and voted heavily for Trump. Post-election analysis indicated that many evangelicals looked past Trump the person and focused on Trump's professed policy positions on abortion, LGBTQ issues, and religious freedom (Bailey 2016; Goodstein 2016). Early on the decision calculus of these evangelicals seems to be paying dividends as Trump nominated reliable social conservative Neil Gorsuch for the Supreme Court, reinstated the Mexico City Policy, rescinded the Obama administration's policy on transgender student bathroom usage, and promised (at the National Prayer Breakfast) to eliminate the Johnson Amendment. Vice President Mike Pence also appeared at the annual antiabortion March for Life event, becoming the highest ranking official ever to appear in person at the event (Bruinius 2017; Feldmann 2017; Peters et al. 2017). While not one to regularly exhibit such behavior, Trump himself has seemed almost sheepish at time regarding his strong support by evangelicals, even going so far as to state in his GOP presidential nomination acceptance speech that he was "not totally sure I deserve" his high levels of evangelical support. But deserving or not, white born-again Christians did strongly support Trump, and one could make the case that he would not be president without them.

Another important religious cleavage involves Roman Catholics. After many years as a key part of the Democratic Party coalition (Brewer 2003) Catholics have become a critical swing bloc in recent elections. They also represent a substantial portion of the electorate (23%). Obama won Catholics in 2008 (54-45) and 2012 (50-48), and for a time in 2016 it seemed that Clinton was poised to do even better among Catholics. Trump engaged in a highly publicized spat with very popular Pope Francis[3] (Healy 2016) and many speculated that this combined with portions of Trump's personal life and his policy stands on immigration could hurt him among Catholics. Indeed, a *Washington Post-ABC News* poll conducted in August 2016 showed Clinton leading Trump among Catholics by a 61-34 margin (Blake 2016). Clearly this division did not endure as Trump bested Clinton among Catholics 50-46, becoming the first Republican presidential nominee to win outright among Catholics since George W. Bush in 2004. Trump fared particularly well among white Catholics, winning this group 60-37. While American Catholics are generally not single issue area voters, it is certainly possible that Trump's pro-manufacturing and fair trade massages appealed to some working-class Catholics (see more on class, below) and also that Trump's positions on social issues appealed to socially conservative Catholics who follow the church's teachings and direction on these issues (USCCB 2015). It will be interesting to see how Catholics respond to President Trump as strong differences continue to exist between Trump and Pope Francis (Carroll 2017; Ivereigh 2017), and many (but certainly not all) of Trump's main policy goals go against central tenets of Catholic teaching and social thought.

The final religious cleavage to break in favor of Trump involves religious salience, often defined as how important religion is to an individual. While the ideal indicator of religious salience will include measures of religious belief, belonging, and behavior (Guth and Green 1993), exit poll data include only church attendance as an indicator of religious salience. Here Trump beat Clinton handily among those who attended church weekly or more—55-41, in line with the results from 2012 and 2008. What was different in 2016 was that Trump was able to run virtually even with Clinton among those who attended monthly (49-47) or a few times a year (46-48). Obama won these groups by large margins in both 2012 and 2008. In 2016 Clinton's only large win in terms of church attendance came with those who never attend worship services, 62-30. This is roughly the same as Obama's performances in his two elections, and matches patterns in place since the 1980s.

Keeping for a moment with the positive for Clinton theme, we close the religious cleavage section by briefly noting two religious groups who maintained their long histories of Democratic support and went heavily for Clinton 2016. American Jews preferred Clinton over Trump 71-23, continuing a long history of Jewish support for Democratic presidential candidates. While Trump did try to appeal to Jews for their support (as have many Republican presidential candidates before him), concerns regarding anti-Semitism likely hampered these efforts at least somewhat (Kampeas 2016). Clinton also won easily among those without a religious affiliation, generally referred to (inaccurately, in our view) as the "nones," besting Trump with this group 67-25. While this was down slightly from Obama's showing with this group (70-26 in 2012 and 75-23 in 2008) it is also important to note that this group increased in size to 15 percent of the electorate in 2016, up from 12 percent in both 2012 and 2008.

SOCIAL CLASS

While there is a long-standing belief held by many that U.S. politics is often bereft of social class divisions, those who study how class plays out in Americans' electoral behavior recognize that such views are little more than myth (Bartels 2008; Stonecash 2000). Class conflict has almost always been present in American politics and in some elections the degree of class conflict reaches relatively high levels. At least in the eyes of some observers, 2016 was such an election. In the aftermath of the election headlines across the country described Trump's presidential victory as the revenge of the working class, or at least the white portion of the working class.

The 2016 exit poll data provide at least some support for such claims. But before we get to this evidence it is worth taking a moment to discuss what social class means in American society and how it can/should be measured. On these questions there is far less scholarly agreement than on the importance of class conflict noted above. While there would certainly be some objection to what is about to come and there would even more certainly be disagreement as to the proper proportion of these attributes, most would grant that social class entails levels of wealth and other tangible resources, access to opportunities, societal status (both self and other perceived), and the nature of the work one does. How class should be measured has seen even greater scholarly dispute. First, many would agree that aggregate wealth would be the most desirable measure of social class, but unfortunately this measure is never available in public survey election data and indeed is rarely available in any data at all. Given this, some, including one of us (Brewer 2009), have argued that income is the best measure of social class as it provides an indicator of the amount of financial resources available to an individual or family and also some insight into the opportunities available. Others would argue that educational achievement is the best available measure of social class as it too provides insight into the availability of opportunity, while also tapping into the issues of status and prestige. Still others prefer occupation as a proxy for class for many of these same reasons. Finally, a number of researchers see it as preferable to simply ask individuals what class they belong to and use this self-identification as the best measure of class. After all, who knows better what class a person is in than the person her or himself?

There are strengths and weaknesses for each of these perspectives, and sorting through them all would take far more space than we have here (For a lengthy discussion of these discussions surrounding social class see Bartels 2008; Stonecash 2000; Stonecash et al. 2000). Fortunately we do not have to do so. The exit polls provide us with two possible measures of social class—family income level and educational achievement level—and both provide support to the view that social class was an important factor in the 2016 presidential election. Looking first at family income levels, one sees that Clinton continued the long-standing trend of Democratic candidates winning lower income voters, besting Trump among voters with yearly family income of less than $50,000 by a margin of 53-41. While this margin is nothing to sneeze at, it is important to note that this percentage is down significantly from Obama's 60 percent of the vote in this group in both 2012 and 2008. It is also important to point out that under-$50,000 voters made up 36 percent of the electorate in 2016, down from 41 percent in 2012 and 38 percent in 2008. Trump beat Clinton among voters with family incomes between $50,000 and $99,999 49-46, a margin that was worse than Romney achieved in 2012 but an improvement over McCain's performance in 2008. Trump and Clinton tied among voters with family incomes of $100,000 or more with 47 percent of the vote each. Romney beat Obama here 54-44 in 2012 while Obama and McCain tied 49-49 in 2008. So on the family income measure of social class, Clinton won with lower-class voters but at a significantly lower degree than Obama in his two races while Clinton and Trump ran relatively even among middle- and upper-class voters.

It is when one turns to educational achievement however that one begins to see the real impact of social class in the 2016 presidential election, and some meaningful differences between 2016 and the two presidential elections that came immediately prior. Among those with no college degree (18% of the electorate) Trump beat Clinton 51-44, a significant difference from Obama's wins among this group by 4 points in 2012 and 7 points in 2008. Trump also bested Clinton among those with some college 51-43. Obama won this group in both 2012 and 2008 as well, by 1 and 4 points, respectively. Clinton carried the day with voters having a college by a 49-44 margin, besting Obama's performance in both 2012 (lost 47-51) and 2008 (won 50-48). The results among those with postgraduate degrees were very similar in all three elections with Clinton winning 58-37 in 2016 and Obama winning 55-42 and 59-40 in 2012 and 2008, respectively.

When looking at vote choice by education level one can see evidence of the class inversion of American politics predicted by Ladd and Hadley (1976) in the 1970s. Democrats were now winning higher-class voters—at least as measured by education level—while Republicans were seeing more success among less-educated—and thus lower-class—voters, especially in 2016. This interpretation gains more strength when one looks at whites only. Trump beat Clinton among whites with less than a college education by a resounding margin of 66-29. This edge of 39 points—up from Romney's win by 25 points in 2012—is truly a remarkable development. It is this figure that led two of the nation's leading newspaper to run articles with the headlines of "How Trump Won: The Revenge of Working Class Whites" (*Washington Post*, Tankersley 2016) and "Why Trump Won: Working Class Whites" (*New York Times*, Cohn 2016) the day after Election Day. Trump's margin of victory among non-college degree whites was the largest since 1980, as was the difference between college grads (Clinton 52-43) and non-college grads (Trump 52-44) (Tyson 2016). Any way one slices it, education level was a large cleavage in the 2016 presidential election. This makes sense when one considers how much energy and attention Trump and his surrogates devoted to appealing to the working class. Trump routinely extolled the virtues of factory workers and those employed in the construction trades. He regularly promised to return manufacturing jobs to the United States, and make America once again a place that makes things. One of Trump's two main campaign issues—better trade deals—was targeted explicitly at working-class Americans, providing them with both an explanation for their recent economic woes and hope for an improved economic future. Indeed, according to survey data collected by the Pew Research Center from October 25 to November 8, 2016, 71 percent of Trump voters believed the economy had gotten worse since 2008, and 69 percent said the job situation had gotten worse as well. On the other hand, 67 percent of Clinton supporters believed the economy had improved since 2008, and 60 percent felt similarly about the job situation (Pew 2016). Economists tell us that the recovery from the Great Recession has been incredibly bifurcated, with educated professionals doing quite well while others with less education are being left behind. Trump appealed to those being left behind, and they responded.

RURAL-URBAN DIVIDE

All of the cleavages we have discussed in this chapter—with the exception of voting differences by sex—likely contribute to the last electoral division we wish to highlight as important in understanding the 2016 presidential election. This divide is the increasing gap between urban Americans and their rural counterparts. This cleavage is certainly not unprecedented—the rural/urban divide was a significant source of American political conflict in the late nineteenth and early twentieth centuries (Wiebe 1967)—and its current manifestation did not appear out of nowhere in the 2016 election. With the exception of 2008 when Obama beat McCain among rural voters 53-45, the Republican presidential candidate has defeated his Democratic opponent by large margins among rural voters. George W. Bush beat John Kerry among this demographic 59-40 in 2004, while Romney bested Obama here 59-39 in 2012. Trump outdid them all in 2016, defeating Clinton 61-34 among rural voters. So while Trump's dominance in rural areas is not a new development for Republican presidential candidates (save for McCain), the magnitude of Trump's support among rural voters points to possibility that this division is accelerating (Badger 2016; Badger et al. 2016; Gamio 2016; Zitner and Overberg 2016). Some attribute growing Republican support in rural areas to the economic divisions discussed earlier in this chapter, noting that rural Americans are being left behind in America's post-industrial economy (Muro and Liu 2016; Porter 2016). Others point to the vast cultural differences that exist between rural America and the nation's big metropolitan areas (Brownstein 2016). Intriguing recent research by University of Wisconsin political scientist Katherine Cramer posits resentment on the part of rural voters as the primary source for the current rural/urban split (Cramer 2016a; 2016b). Minnesota congressman Collin Peterson (MN-7), one of the few rural Democrats left in Congress, lent credence to all of these explanations in a post-election interview with the *Washington Post* (Ingraham 2016). In our view Peterson is likely correct. But regardless, it is now abundantly clear that rural Americans are behaving very differently from urban Americans when it comes to voting and party identification. Scholars need to turn their attention here.

CONCLUSION

As will be discussed at length in this book, the 2016 presidential campaign in many ways defined conventional wisdom. But as we detailed in this chapter, the recent patterns of partisan polarization and demographic cleavages were not among the elements disrupted. Overwhelmingly partisans voted for the candidate of their party, and for the most part the significant demographic cleavages of the past 30–40 years held firm. We did, however, see substantial increases in recent electoral cleavages around education and a rural/urban divide. These two divisions in particular merit close attention moving forward.

NOTES

1. We would like to thank Eric Authelet for his assistance in helping gather data for this project.

2. All exit poll/voting data presented in this chapter can be referenced in Table 1.1, unless otherwise noted.

3. According to Pew as of January 2017, 70 percent of American adults and 87 percent of American Catholic adults viewed Pope Francis favorably (Gecewicz 2017).

REFERENCES

Badger, Emily. 2016. "As American as Apple Pie? The Rural Vote's Disproportionate Slice of Power." *New York Times*. November 20.

Badger, Emily, Quoctrung Bui, and Adam Pearce. 2016. "The Election Highlighted a Growing Rural–Urban Split." *New York Times*. November 11.

Bailey, Sarah Pulliam. 2016. "White Evangelicals Voted Overwhelmingly for Donald Trump, Exit Polls Show." *Washington Post*. November 9.

Barbaro, Michael; Haberman, Maggie; and Alcindor, Yamiche. 2016. "Donald Trump Embraces Wider Use of Stop–and–Frisk by Police" *New York Times*. September 21. Accessed September 22, 2016.

Bartels, Larry M. 2008. *Unequal Democracy: The Political Economy of the New Gilded Age*. Princeton, NJ: Princeton University Press, New York: Russell Sage Foundation.

Blake, Aaron. 2016. "Donald Trump Has a Massive Catholic Problem." *Washington Post*. August 30.

Brewer, Mark D. 2009. *Party Images in the American Electorate*. New York: Routledge.

Brownstein, Ronald. 2016. "How the Election Revealed the Divide Between City and Country." *Atlantic Monthly*. November 17.

Bruinius, Henry. 2017. "Trump's Evangelical Support is Wide. But How Deep?" *Christian Science Monitor*. February 3.

Bump, Philip. 2016. "Asian–American voters continue to shift to the political left" *The Washington Post*. October 06. Accessed October 06, 2016.

Burke, Daniel. 2016. "The Guilt–Free Gospel of Donald Trump." *CNN*. October 24.

Caldwell, Leigh Ann. 2016. "Trump, Clinton Present Vastly Different Visions on Race." *NBC News*. September 27. Accessed September 27, 2016.

Caputo, Mark, and Ducassi, Daniel. 2016. "Clinton campaign in 'panic mode' over Florida black voters" *Politico*. September 28. Accessed September 28, 2016.

Carroll, James. 2017. "Pope Francis is the Anti–Trump." *New Yorker*. February 1.

Carswell, Simon. 2016. "Blue–collar whites still honking for Donald Trump in Ohio" *The Irish Times*. October 12. Accessed October 12, 2016.

Chozick, Amy, and Davis, Julie Hirschfeld. 2016. "Obama Sees 'Personal Insult' if Black Don't Rally for Hillary Clinton" *New York Times*. September 18. Accessed September 20, 2016

Cohn, Nate. 2016. "Why Trump Won: Working–Class Whites." *New York Times*. November 9.

Cramer, Katherine. 2016. *The Politics of Resentment*. Chicago: University of Chicago Press. 2016.

———. 2016. "How Rural Resentment Helps Explain the Surprising Victory of Donald Trump." *Washington Post*. November 13.

Dalbey, Beth. 2016 "Bill Clinton Promises Prosperity, Scoffs at Trump's Outreach to Black Voters" *Patch.com*. September 06, 2016. Accessed September 06, 2016.

Decker, Cathleen. 2016. "Asian American voters are spurning Trump—and threatening to spurn the Republican Party" *Los Angeles Times*. October 05. Accessed October 06, 2016.

Fahrenthold, David A. 2016. "Trump recorded having extremely lewd conversation about women in 2005." *Washington Post*, October 8.

Feldman, Linda. 2017. "Prayer Breakfast: Why Christian Conservatives are Happy with Trump." *Christian Science Monitor*. February 2.

Figueroa, Laura. 2016. "Katy Perry Takes to Stage for Hillary Clinton." *Newsday*. November 5.

Fox News. 2016. "Trump makes first stop in black community, tells Detroit church congregation 'here to listen'" *Fox News*. September 03, 2016. Accessed September 06, 2016.

Frizell, Sam. 2016. "The Puerto Rican Wave That Could Boost Hillary Clinton in Florida." *TIME*. September 15. September 16.

Gamio, Lazaro. 2016. "Urban and Rural America Are Becoming Increasingly Polarized." *Washington Post*. November 17.

Gecewicz, Claire. 2017. "U.S. Catholics, Non–Catholics, Continue to View Pope Francis Favorably." Washington, DC: Pew Research Center. January 18.

Goodstein, Laurie. 2016. "Religious Right Believes Donald Trump Will Deliver on His Promises." *New York Times*. November 11.

Griffiths, Brent. 2016. "John Lewis blasts Trump's 'worst shape ever' comments" *Politico*. September 21. Accessed September 21, 2016.

Guth, James L., and John C. Green. 1993. "Salience: The Core Concept?" In David C. Leege and Lyman A. Kellstedt, eds., *Rediscovering the Religious Factor in American Politics*. Armonk, N.Y.: M.E. Sharpe. 157–174.

Halper, Evan. 2016. "Clinton makes pitch to conservative Latinos." *Los Angeles Times*. September 07. Accessed September 08, 2016.

Hampson, Rick. 2016. "Exclusive: Fox Anchor Megyn Kelly Describes Scary, Bullying Year of Trump." *USA Today*. November 15.

Healy, Patrick. 2016. "Donald Trump Fires Back at Sharp Rebuke by Pope Francis." *New York Times*. February 18.

Hellman, Jessie. 2016. "Clinton PAC buys $6M in ads targeting Latino and black voters" *thehill.com*. August 31. Accessed September 1, 2016.

Henderson, Nia Malika. 2016. "Race and Racism in the 2016 Campaign" *CNN*. August 31. Accessed September 1, 2016.

Hohmann, James. 2016. "The Daily 202: If these Latinos vote, Hillary Clinton will probably win Florida" *The Washington Post*. November 01. Accessed November 01, 2016.

Hook, Janet. 2016. "Donald Trump Unveils Child Care Subsidy Aimed at Women, Suburban Swing Voters" *Wall Street Journal*. September 13. Accessed September 13, 2016.

Horowitz, Jason. 2016. "In Honduras, a Spiritual and Political Awakening for Tim Kaine." *New York Times*. September 2.

Ingraham, Christopher. 2016. "Why Rural Voters Don't Vote Democratic Anymore." *Washington Post*. November 23.

Ivereigh, Austen. 2017. "Is the Pope the Anti–Trump?" *New York Times*. March 4.

Kampeas, Ron. 2016. "Anti–Semitism Unleashed by Trump Followers Chills Jewish Voters." *Jewish Telegraphic Agency*. November 7.

Karni, Annie. 2016. "Clinton tries to extend lead among Pennsylvania women" *Politico*. October 04. Accessed October 04, 2016.

Krieg, Gregory. 2016. "Donald Trump's trouble with women — an incomplete list." *CNN*. September 28. Accessed September 28, 2016.

Martin, Jonathan. 2016. "Young Black Voice Skepticism on Hillary Clinton, Worrying Democrats" *New York Times*. September 04. Accessed September 06, 2016.

Megerian, Chris. 2016. "Hillary Clinton has millennials' support, and now she's trying to make sure they vote" *Los Angeles Times*. September 13. Accessed September 14, 2016.

Moorthy, Neelesh. 2016. "What Do We Know About Hillary Clinton's Religion? A Lot, Actually." *Politifact*. June 24. http://www.politifact.com/truth–o–meter/statements/2016/jun/24/donald–trump/what–do–we–know–about–hillary–clintons–religion–lo/.

Muro, Mark, and Sifan Liu. 2016. "Another Clinton–Trump Divide: High–Output America vs. Low–Output America" Washington, DC: Brookings. November 29.

Peters, Jeremy W.; Alcindor, Yamiche. 2016. "Hillary Clinton Struggles to Win Back Young Voters From Third Parties" *New York Times*. September 28. Accessed September 28, 2016.

Peters, Jeremy W., Jo Becker, and Julia Hirschfeld Davis. 2017. "Trump Rescinds Rules on Bathrooms for Transgender Students." *New York Times*. February 22.

Pew Research Center. 2016. "A Divided and Pessimistic Electorate." Washington, DC. November 10.

Porter, Eduardo. 2016. "Where Were Trump's Votes? Where the Jobs Weren't." *New York Times*. December 13.

Richardson, Bradford. 2016. "Black faith leaders reproach Hillary Clinton on religious freedom as enthusiasm chills" *The Washington Times*. October 31. Accessed November 01, 2016.

Rogers, Katie. 2016. "'That Mexican Thing' Takes On Life After the Debate" *New York Times*. October 05. Accessed October 05, 2016.

Rutenberg, Jim. 2016. "Megyn Kelly's Cautionary Tale of Crossing Donald Trump." *New York Times*. November 15.

Shapira, Ian. 2016. "Here's What Happens When Miley Cyrus Door Knocks for Hillary Clinton at a College Dorm." *Washington Post*. October 22.

Slattery, Denis. 2016. "Donald Trump tries to make appeal to working women at Pa. rally" *New York Daily News*. September 14. Accessed September 15, 2016.

Smith, Gregory A. 2016. "How the Faithful Voted: A Preliminary Analysis." Washington, DC: Pew Research Center. November 9.

Stonecash, Jeffrey M. 2000. *Class and Party in American Politics*. Boulder, CO: Westview Press.

Stonecash, Jeffrey M., Mark D. Brewer, Mary P. McGuire, R. Eric Petersen, and Lori Beth Way. 2000. "Class and Party: Secular Realignment and the Survival of Democrats Outside the South." *Political Research Quarterly* 53 (4): 731–752.

Tankersley, Jim. 2016. "How Trump Won: The Revenge of Working Class Whites." *Washington Post.* November 9.

Tyson, Alec. 2016. "Behind Trump's Victory: Divisions by Race, Gender, Education." Washington, DC: Pew Research Center. November 9.

United States Conference of Catholic Bishops (USCCB). 2015. "Forming Consciences for Faithful Citizenship." Washington, DC.

Washington Post Staff Writers. 2015. "Full Text: Donald Trump Announces a Presidential Bid." *Washington Post.* June 16.

Wagner, John. 2016. "Spanish–speaking Tim Kaine debuts in Democratic radio ad" *The Washington Post.* September 13. Accessed September 13, 2016.

Wiebe, Robert H. 1967. *The Search for Order.* New York: Hill and Wang.

Williams, Vanessa. 2016. "For young black activists, an urgent task: Persuading peers to vote" *The Washington Post.* October 18. Accessed October 18, 2016.

Winberg, Michaela. 2016. "Clinton campaigns on Maine Campus" *The Temple News.* September 20. Accessed September 20, 2016.

Zitner, Aaron, and Paul Overberg. 2016. "Rural Vote Fuels Trump; Clinton Loses Urban Grip." *Wall Street Journal.* November 9.

Chapter 2

And the Wall Came Tumbling Down

The Political Geography of the 2016 Presidential Election

Chad Kinsella

The 2016 Presidential Election was arguably the most surprising presidential election in modern American history. Donald Trump, a real estate tycoon and reality star, defied all expectations to win the Republican Primary and then the presidential election against Hillary Clinton. For many, the general election win seemed highly improbable. Many experts, relying on polling data and history, concluded that Trump could not bring down the "Blue Wall" of states that Democrats could rely on to ensure Clinton could win the presidency, even if Trump could win several battleground states. Incredibly, Trump was able to win several battleground states and pick off several states in the Midwest and Pennsylvania, all considered part of the wall, that had voted reliably Democratic for several presidential election cycles.

This chapter will examine the "where" of the 2016 presidential election by examining state and county election results. Given that the Electoral College is the method for choosing the U.S. executive, it is inherently geographic given that states make up the key building blocks of successful coalition needed to obtain 270 electoral votes. In addition, counties are administrative units of the state and a key unit of analysis to examine for a post mortem of what happened within states. Using states and counties along with results from the 2008 presidential election, this chapter will find out where changes occurred, where they did not, what the current state of geographic polarization is, and what it all means for future elections including the midterms in the 2018.

THE ELECTORAL COLLEGE AND THE FALL OF
THE BLUE WALL: STATE RESULTS IN 2016

Regardless, if you were an expert or casual political observer, if you looked at a political map in 2016 and had to speculate on the any Republicans, chances of winning the presidency, you saw an almost impossible situation. In 2008, the last time both parties did not have an incumbent running for office, Democrats, with Obama as their standard-bearer, delivered a massive electoral blow to Republicans. Saddled with a deeply unpopular president, Republicans also had to face off against a charismatic, youthful challenger in Obama whose popularity and funds allowed him to settle on a fifty-state campaign. The result was a crushing win for Democrats. Traditionally, Republicans relied on the Big Sky, upper Midwestern, Rocky Mountain, and the southern states to carry them close enough to the 270 electoral votes needed to win the presidency that all they needed was to win one Midwestern battleground state (usually Ohio) to complete their electoral victory. This coalition of states was smashed in 2008 with the Obama victory. Republicans lost Nevada, Colorado, and New Mexico in the West and North Carolina, Florida, and Virginia in the South. A key feature of the South was that the southern states are only valuable as a regional voting bloc. Democrats had long sought to break the Republican lock on the South (Schaller, 2006) and, by picking off three southern states, had done so. Even with the addition of North Carolina back to the Republican fold in 2012, it seemed unlikely that Republicans would be able to unite the region under its banner again. Given that Obama won 365 electoral votes in 2008 and only shed a handful of those in 2012, evidence seemed to suggest that Democrats had a new hold on the Electoral College that seemed unbreakable.

Looking at the possibilities for a presidential win for a Republican seemed like an impossible task in 2016 regardless of who won the primary. After Trump won a bruising Republican primary, the task seemed even more impossible given his several controversial statements, tweets, and overall brash demeanor. As the campaign season got into full swing in the summer and fall, the race for electoral votes seemed like Clinton's to lose. Based on the 2008 and 2012 elections, it was assumed that Clinton could count on the West Coast states, New England (except New Hampshire), Mid-Atlantic states including Pennsylvania, and New Mexico. The electoral votes from these "safe" states accounted for 247 of the necessary 270 electoral votes. Republicans could count only 191 "safe" electoral votes. Conservatively, there were 100 electoral votes up for grabs among battleground states such as Nevada, Colorado, New Hampshire, Florida, Ohio, Iowa, North Carolina, and Virginia. From this perspective, Republicans needed to win almost every battleground state including the perennial battleground of Florida, which had voted for Obama twice, albeit by the slimmest of margins. Furthermore, many political observers and arguably the Clinton campaign itself considered states like Wisconsin, Michigan, Pennsylvania, and Minnesota as safely Democratic. Pennsylvania, with a prize of 20 electoral votes, has long been a target of Republican presidential contenders as recently as 2012 where Mitt Romney campaigned vigorously in the Philadelphia suburbs. Pennsylvania was considered "fools gold" since no Republican presidential candidates had won there since 1988 despite several attempts. Given these electoral prospects, the fact that Trump had never run for office and never run a campaign, and the fact that the Republican Party had not healed from a bruising primary with several GOP politicians and operatives outright refusing to endorse or support Trump, the prospects of a Republican presidential victory seemed almost impossible.

For all but a few, election night in 2016 was a shock. Early on, several reliable Republican and Democratic states were called for either candidate with most waiting to hear about the key battleground states of Florida and Ohio. Florida was the first key victory for Trump delivering its critical 29 electoral votes. Essentially, had Florida not been won by Trump it was assumed that there would be no path to victory for the Republican presidential candidate. The biggest surprises of the night came out of the Midwest and Pennsylvania. Trump was able to claim two more key battleground states, Ohio and Iowa, but states like Wisconsin, Michigan, and Minnesota were unexpectedly close. Shockingly, before the night was out, Wisconsin and Pennsylvania had, by narrow margins, voted for Trump, turning the tables completely on Clinton and making the electoral map unwinnable, even had she won Michigan and picked up some upsets in the western states such as Arizona. By the early morning on Wednesday, Hillary Clinton had conceded to then president elect Donald Trump, capping off one of the most stunning electoral upsets since Truman in 1948.

The final tally was Trump had won 304 electoral votes to Clinton's 232 electoral votes. Figure 2.1 shows the similarity and change that occurred in states between 2008 and 2016. Overall, the biggest shift came in the Midwest. In 2008, Obama had won all of the Midwestern states east of the Mississippi River save Missouri. In 2012, those states largely remained in the Democratic coalition except Indiana. The swing in 2016 was substantial given that Trump was able to win traditional battleground states of Ohio and Iowa but also win "reliably" blue states such as Wisconsin and Michigan and even come within one and half points of winning in Minnesota (the only state to not vote Republican in Reagan's 1984 landslide victory). Outside of the Midwest, the other key win came from Pennsylvania. Despite many good efforts by Republican candidates, none had been able to win in Pennsylvania and many considered it a waste of campaign time and resources for Republican presidential contenders to campaign in that state. Trump's to win there in 2016 was an improbable key win. Finally, Trump was able to win in two key southern states, including the key battleground states of

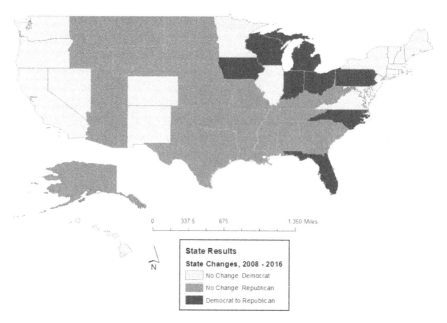

Figure 2.1   How the States Voted, 2008–2016.

Florida and North Carolina, which voted for Obama in 2008 but was one of only two states from the 2008 election to not support Obama again in 2012.

Controversy with the Electoral College

Despite that fact that Donald Trump was elected president, controversy about his election and the Electoral College ensued after the 2016 election. The Electoral College allows presidential candidates to win electoral votes by winning a plurality of votes in each state, with the exceptions of Nebraska and Maine who use a proportional system that allows candidates to win individual electoral votes with each congressional district and a bonus of two electoral votes for winning the most votes in the state. In spite of receiving a clear majority of electoral votes, Trump did not win a plurality of the popular vote or the total number of votes cast in the entire country. Controversy regarding the electoral vote is not new given public opinion polls as recent as 2013 showing that over 60 percent of Americans would prefer if it we abolished (Saad, 2013). Defenders of the Electoral College argue that it worked as intended by not allowing California, a state that voted overwhelmingly for Hillary Clinton and turned a popular vote plurality win for Trump to one for Clinton, to choose who the next president will be (Campbell, 2016). The controversy of the popular vote and the general frustration in both parties spilled over into the formal electoral vote with faithless electors or electors who do not vote the way their state voted. There are no federal laws requiring electors to vote as the state pledged and 29 states and the District of Columbia require electors to vote for winner of the state popular vote (Alexander, Brown, and Kaseman, 2004). Since 1948, only eight electors have broken their pledge; however, after the 2016 election, seven electors voted against the wishes of their state. Two electors from Texas did not vote for Trump and five electors for Clinton, one from Hawaii and four from Washington State, did not vote the way their state voted.

THE COUNTY VOTE, 2016

States are the building blocks of the Electoral College and are key for understanding what happened in a presidential election; however, it is critical to look within the states to understand what and where change and continuity occurred; hence, counties are an excellent way to understand what happened in and across states. County-level voting results "are prime ingredients in the U.S. presidential election system, and an ecological analysis is therefore fully justified" (Lesthaeghe and Neidert 2009, 392). Counties are administrative units of a state and unit of voting aggregation with relatively stable borders that allow comparisons over elections. Like the state analysis above, the county results compare the 2008 and 2016 presidential elections in terms of percentage of the vote received by President Obama and Hillary Clinton eight years later. It is important to note that because Alaska keeps its election results by state house districts and not boroughs (county equivalents), each analysis of Alaska is of its state house districts, otherwise all results are of counties, county equivalents, or independent cities that are found mostly in Virginia.

Figure 2.2 shows the county changes that occurred in the percent that voted for Obama in 2008 compared to the percent of the vote Clinton received in 2016. The map and national numbers show a significant shift as the overall trend was for a decrease in the percent of the vote Clinton received compared to Obama in 2008. The county map and numbers show some important findings that deserve greater discussion. The counties with the largest drop in Democratic presidential voting between 2008 and 2016 occurred in many rural counties especially in states like Kentucky, West Virginia, and across the Midwest. The shift in Kentucky was so strong that Trump's coattails were able to give Republicans control of the State House of Representatives for the first time in almost 100 years. Although Kentucky's electoral votes were not in play in 2016, the massive shift that occurred in some counties there shows how staggering of a shift that occurred in several border and Midwestern rural counties toward Republicans in the 2016 presidential election. Trump was

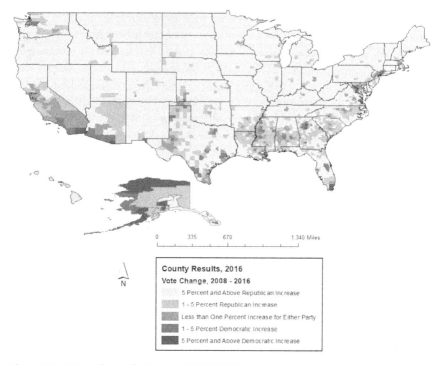

Figure 2.2   Vote Change by County, 2008–2016.

able to win over rural, small town, and outer suburban voters in many key states in 2016 and the shift was dramatic enough in enough counties to turn states like Wisconsin, Michigan, and Pennsylvania "red" and bring states like Ohio and Iowa, typically closely fought battleground states, overwhelmingly into the Republican fold.

The county map is not all good news for Trump and Republicans. Trump underperformed or performed worse in several key Republican areas. First, Trump did not do well in many southern states that had been a core electoral constituency for Republican presidential candidates. Trump underperformed in states like Georgia, Texas, Mississippi, and South Carolina. Two examples of how much Trump underperformed in the South are in Cobb County in Georgia and in Houston, TX. Cobb County, a suburb of Atlanta, had given Mitt Romney an over 12 percent win in 2012. In 2016, Clinton won Cobb County by 2 percent, which is a dramatic shift compared to rest of the country. Houston, in Harris County, Texas, also increased its vote percent for Clinton between 2008 and 2016. A trend that occurred in the South also happened nationally on less dramatic scale. In several southern cities and suburbs, Clinton outperformed President Obama's 2008 vote tallies. To varying degrees, this also happened across the country, including the Midwest. Hamilton County,

Ohio, location of the City of Cincinnati, a perennial Republican bastion in Ohio that has been drifting more Democratic for decades, moved decisively Democratic in 2016. Other suburban counties across the country either saw small decreases in Democratic voting between 2008 and 2016 or increasingly voted Democratic. Considering that suburban and southern voters have been a core constituency for Republicans for decades, this must be an area of concern for Republicans and a bright spot for Democrats moving forward.

When examining county results, where Republican and Democratic candidates performed the best in terms of percentage of the vote and where they received the most votes explains a lot in terms of the coalitions that each party relies on to win states. Tables 2.1 Tables 2.2 show the top 20 counties where both candidates received the most votes and did the best in terms of a percentage of the vote. Table 2.1 shows the results for Hillary Clinton. Clinton received the largest number of votes from counties with major cities in them including Los Angeles County, Cook County (home of Chicago), and several others. Each delivered millions or hundreds of thousands of votes. These counties were not only key to Clinton but are key to Democrats in general. These major urban areas deliver enough votes in some states to allow Democrats to be competitive or win entire states with just a handful of votes from other counties. In a state like Nevada, winning Clarke County, Nevada, is key to winning the entire state. Given that a bulk of the voters in Nevada live in Las Vegas, while other counties are more sparsely populated and have fewer voters, meaning that even if Republicans win heavily in the rest of state, including Reno, they cannot overcome a large loss in Clark County. Clinton and Democrats depend on "running up the score" in many urban areas of a state and then winning enough votes in the surrounding suburbs, small towns, and rural areas to push them over the top. This is evidenced by looking at where Clinton performed the best by percentage. Clinton was able to claim over 90 percent of the vote in the District of Columbia and did well in several other major urban areas. In addition, Clinton did well in several rural counties in the South that traditionally have large African-American populations.

Table 2.2 depicts where Trump performed best as far as total vote and percent of the vote. What is interesting and counterintuitive for many people is that Trump and Republicans typically perform poorly in urban areas but receive a crucial infusion of votes from these places. Again, the best example is the county where Trump received the highest number of votes: Los Angeles County. Typically, Republicans including Trump are only able to receive about 20–30 percent of the vote from Los Angeles County, but in terms of the sheer number of votes received, it typically ranks as the highest amount of votes received by Republican presidential candidates despite the fact they lose the county badly. Trump received almost one million votes out of Los Angeles County and among his top 20 counties in votes received are counties

Table 2.1   Counties Where Clinton Performed Best by Total Votes and Percent, 2016

Rank	County	State	Votes	Percent	Rank	County	State	Votes	Percent
1	Los Angeles	California	2464364	71.76	1	District of Columbia	District of Columbia	282830	90.86
2	Cook	Illinois	1611946	74.31	2	Bronx	New York	353646	88.52
3	San Diego	California	735476	56.30	3	Prince George's	Maryland	344049	88.13
4	King	Washington	718322	71.94	4	Petersburg	Virginia	12021	87.20
5	Harris	Texas	707914	53.95	5	Claiborne	Mississippi	3708	86.80
6	Maricopa	Arizona	702907	44.83	6	New York	New York	579013	86.56
7	Kings	New York	640553	79.51	7	Jefferson	Mississippi	3337	86.45
8	Miami-Dade	Florida	624146	63.68	8	Shannon	South Dakota	2510	86.40
9	Orange	California	609961	50.94	9	San Francisco	California	345084	85.04
10	Philadelphia	Pennsylvania	584025	82.30	10	Baltimore City	Maryland	202673	84.66
11	New York	New York	579013	86.56	11	Clayton	Georgia	78220	84.55
12	Broward	Florida	553320	66.51	12	Holmes	Mississippi	6689	82.83
13	Middlesex	Massachusetts	520360	64.35	13	Macon	Alabama	7566	82.78
14	Wayne	Michigan	519444	66.78	14	Philadelphia	Pennsylvania	584025	82.30
15	Queens	New York	517220	75.35	15	Greene	Alabama	4013	82.23
16	Alameda	California	514842	78.69	16	Orleans	Louisiana	133996	80.81
17	Santa Clara	California	511684	72.71	17	DeKalb	Georgia	251370	80.44
18	Dallas	Texas	461080	60.75	18	Charlottesville	Virginia	17901	79.66
19	Hennepin	Minnesota	429288	63.13	19	Kings	New York	640553	79.51
20	Clark	Nevada	402227	52.43	20	Starr	Texas	9289	79.12

Table 2.2 Counties Where Trump Performed Best by Total Votes and Percent, 2016

Rank	County	State	Votes	Percent	Rank	County	State	Votes	Percent
1	Los Angeles	California	769743	22.41	1	Roberts	Texas	524	94.58
2	Maricopa	Arizona	747361	47.67	2	King	Texas	149	93.71
3	Harris	Texas	545955	41.61	3	Motley	Texas	566	92.03
4	Orange	California	507148	42.35	4	Hayes	Nebraska	472	91.83
5	San Diego	California	477766	36.57	5	Shackelford	Texas	1378	91.62
6	Cook	Illinois	453287	20.90	6	Glasscock	Texas	553	91.56
7	Suffolk	New York	350570	51.46	7	Wallace	Kansas	711	91.27
8	Tarrant	Texas	345921	51.74	8	Garfield	Montana	653	91.20
9	Miami-Dade	Florida	333999	34.07	9	McMullen	Gen 5	454	90.98
10	Riverside	California	333243	44.35	10	Grant	Nebraska	367	90.62
11	Clark	Nevada	320057	41.72	11	Wheeler	Texas	2087	90.50
12	Oakland	Michigan	289203	43.51	12	Armstrong	Texas	924	90.50
13	Nassau	New York	288313	45.26	13	Borden	Texas	330	90.41
14	Palm Beach	Florida	272402	41.13	14	Harding	South Dakota	695	90.26
15	San Bernardino	California	271240	41.48	15	Oldham	Texas	850	89.66
16	Hillsborough	Florida	266870	44.65	16	Haakon	South Dakota	936	89.66
17	Dallas	Texas	262945	34.64	17	McPherson	Nebraska	257	89.55
18	Broward	Florida	260951	31.37	18	Winston	Alabama	9228	89.48
19	Allegheny	Pennsylvania	259480	39.48	19	Leslie	Kentucky	4015	89.38
20	Bexar	Texas	240333	40.76	20	Arthur	Nebraska	244	89.38

with large urban areas that he lost, some by large margins, but still delivered a large infusion of votes. Republican presidential candidates, especially Trump, must rely on a large number of votes from urban areas, despite losing them, and win handily in suburban and rural areas to piece together a winning coalition in a state. Trump did extremely well in rural areas in terms of the percent of the total votes, winning over 90 percent of the votes in small counties across the South and Midwest, most with a small number of total voters. Ultimately, Democrats have concentrated voting bloc in and around densely populate urban areas. Also, in some states, Democrats perform well in rural areas with large number of minorities. Republicans, on the other hand, typically must look far and wide to obtain votes, usually in the suburban areas around urban centers and in rural areas (Gimpel and Schuknecht, 2002).

The "Big Sort" Continues: Geographic Polarization in the 2016 Presidential Election

The topic of polarization has received a lot attention in American politics. Polarization suggests that the electorate has polarized political opinions, or that ideologically extreme members of the electorate increasingly leave a wide, partisan divide on many issues (Abramowitz 2012). Polarization has geographic underpinnings and there are several phenomena in the political geography of the U.S. electorate associated with political polarization. Geographic political sorting, an idea put forth by Bishop (2008), argues that Americans are moving to communities with politically like-minded individuals, or sorting themselves. Bishop argues that this sorting has increased dramatically since 1976 and he uses county-level data to demonstrate the political divisions within the United States. These findings are based on Bishop's analysis of the percent of voters who live in a landslide county during presidential elections since 1948. Bishop uses presidential elections as the measurement of geographic political sorting because it is the one common election among all counties, which avoids the effects of having different candidates and changing voting districts. According to Bishop's methodology, a landslide county is one in which there is a difference of 20 percentage points or more between the presidential candidate of the two major parties. Bishop excludes third parties to even out the comparison over time (Bishop, 2008). Using this same methodology, a map was created (see Figure 2.3) that shows landslide counties, both Democrat and Republican, and non-landslide counties.

In 2016, there were nearly 2500 landslide counties in the United States, meaning that the majority of counties voted overwhelmingly for either Trump or Clinton. The landslide counties largely follow a pattern described above in the discussion on county voting. Clinton landslide counties include urban areas, counties with colleges and universities, and rural areas with large minority populations such as African-Americans in the South and Native Americans in the West and Midwest. Clinton had far fewer landslide counties

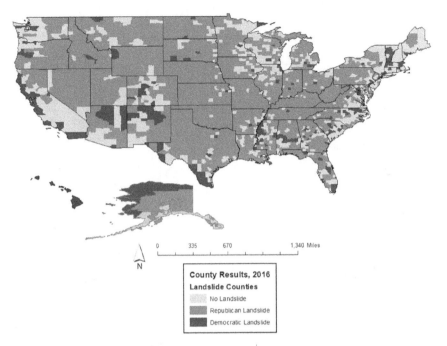

Figure 2.3   Landslide Counties, 2016.

but many were in high population areas. Trump landslide counties include many rural counties across the country, counties with small towns, and suburban areas. Despite having far more landslide counties, many of them are sparsely populated.

The number of landslide counties in the 2016 presidential election was the highest since 1976. Figure 2.4 shows the number of Republican and Democrat landslide counties since 1976. Since Bill Clinton's elections in the 1990s, the number of landslide counties has grown for the last two decades reaching its current high in 2016. There were over 2000 Republican landslide counties and over 200 Democrat landslide counties in the 2016 presidential election. The divide between policy differences among Democrats and Republicans in government and among rank and file party members in the general public continue to widen. It is clear part of the reason for this is that people of certain ideological and partisan viewpoints do not live near others with opposing viewpoints and they elect people with the same, divergent political ideas. The level of geographic polarization indicates that lifestyle and where people choose to live is key piece to understanding partisan affiliation. One of the key factors that may be driving polarization is the geographic divide between partisans. To make the stakes even higher, there is research that suggests the geographic divide even within counties show a deep divide when examining precincts.

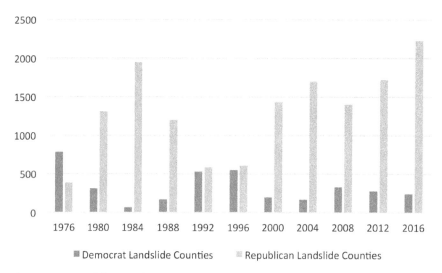

Figure 2.4   Republican and Democrat Landslide Counties, 1976–2016.

CONCLUSION

After the 2008 presidential election, reporters asked the Minority Leader Mitch McConnell if he thought the Republican Party was becoming a regional party, one that could only compete in the Deep South, Mountain West, and Upper Midwest. McConnell indicated that the GOP would work to have a broader appeal and needed to do so given the significant defeat they suffered in 2008. After the 2012 presidential election, where Mitt Romney had faired only slightly better than McCain in 2008, GOP party leaders, including Trump's former Chief of Staff Reince Priebus, authored a report to have the party appeal to a broader demographic of voters. The Trump campaign ignored this advice and almost all other conventional wisdom regarding presidential elections- and won. Geographically, the GOP seemed to be a party without options. The West Coast and East Coast (from Maryland north to Maine) states were not even a remote possibility. The South, without the guarantee of Virginia and Florida, could not deliver enough electoral votes to win the presidency. This left only the Midwest and Pennsylvania as the only possible solutions to winning, and even winning in those states seemed unthinkable. Yet, the Trump campaign was able to create a winning sales pitch to voters in small towns and rural areas to get enough voters to either switch their vote or turnout to flip states that had not voted Republican in decades.

Although Trump's presidential victory was spectacular, it would be unwise to read too much into the win. Despite the fact that Trump was able to win in Florida, Pennsylvania, Wisconsin, and Michigan the margins were razor thin. If one were to look at a state map, it would suggest a major realignment. However, evidence would suggest that the Republican and Democratic geographic coalitions did not change dramatically. An analysis of how counties voted by percent for Obama in 2008 compared to the percent counties voted for Clinton in 2016 shows a slight shift but not a dramatic change. Using a scatterplot and fit line to compare the counties from both presidential elections, Figure 2.5 illustrates that there was not a dramatic national change as most counties are close to their 2008 percentages. The fact that the dots, representing counties, have a slight shift left of the fit line demonstrates the national shift toward Trump in 2016, otherwise the counties mostly line up closely. A regression analysis shows that 82.6 percent of the variance of how counties voted in 2016 is explained by how they voted in 2008. This statistic indicates that most of the county votes in 2016 are explained by how they voted in 2008, with only 17.4 percent of variance that still needs to be explained. Ultimately, voting coalitions did not shift greatly and the electorate is still divided along the same lines as past presidential elections.

The 2016 presidential election will have several potential effects on future elections. For the foreseeable future, it is likely that the campaign focus in presidential elections will be in the Midwest, especially in states like

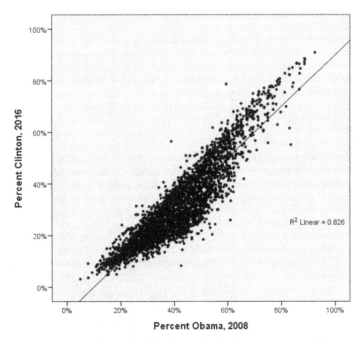

Figure 2.5 **Scatterplot of Counties by Percent Voting Obama 2008 and Percent Voting for Clinton 2016.**

Michigan, Wisconsin, and Minnesota as well as in Pennsylvania and Florida. These states are likely to continue to be the new set of battleground states. On a smaller geographic scale, the suburbs will be a key battleground within states. Despite being the ancestral home of the modern Republican Party, suburbs seem to be the most contentious area for both parties as Republicans appear to have won over rural and small town voters while Democrats continue to maintain a grip on urban voters. Finally, where candidates campaign may be forever changed. Trump frequently campaigned in areas that had many observers scratching their heads. Clinton did not campaign in states that turned out to be "vulnerable" and paid a heavy political price. Ultimately, the 2016 presidential election defied expectations with the election of President Trump and will have long-term consequences for presidential elections in the future. Despite the changes, the 2016 election was also, unexpectedly, a continuation of ongoing trends in American politics.

The analysis presented here is descriptive in nature but still presents key findings through a diverse range of spatial analysis. Ultimately, a geographic study is an essential part of any presidential election study that provides critical details to understand what happened in a parsimonious manner—and a prism through which to gauge the probable fortunes of the two main political parties in future presidential contests.

REFERENCES

Abramowitz, Alan I. 2012. *The Polarized Public? Why Our Government is So Dysfunctional*. New York: Pearson Longman.

Alexander, Robert, David Brown, and Jason Kaseman. 2004. "Pinning a Face on the Electoral College: A Survey of the Class of 2000." *PS: Political Science and Politics* 37 (4): 833–838.

Campbell, James E. 2016. "Hillary Clinton supporters need to quit whining about the Electoral College." *Market Watch* December 19. Accessed January 23, 2017. http://www.marketwatch.com/story/why-hillary-clinton-supporters-need-to-quit-whining-about-the-electoral-college-2016-11-30.

Gimpel, James G. and Jason E. Schuknecht. 2002. "Reconsidering Political Regionalism in the American States." *State Politics and Policy Quarterly* 2(4): 325–352.

Lesthaeghe, Ron, and Lisa Neidert. 2009. "US Presidential Elections and the Spatial Pattern of the American Second Demographic Transition." *Population and Development Review* 35: 391–400.

Saad, Lydia. 2013. "Americans Call for Term Limits, End to Electoral College" *Gallup* January 18. Accessed June 9, 2014. http://www.gallup.com/poll/159881/americans-call-term-limits-end-electoral-college.aspx?g_source=electoral%20college&g_medium=search&g_campaign=tiles, accessed June 9, 2014.

Chapter 3

"The Supreme Court: It's What it's all About"... or Was it?

Analyzing the Court Issue in the 2016 Presidential Election

Kevin J. McMahon

On the morning of February 13, 2016, from the outer stretches of west Texas, word came that the fiery conservative jurist, Justice Antonin Scalia, was dead at the age of 79. The highest court in the land now had eight members, four appointed by Democratic presidents and four by Republican ones. Before the day was out, Senate majority leader Mitch McConnell of Kentucky vowed that he and his fellow Republicans in the upper house of the Congress would resist any and all efforts by the Democrat in the White House, Barack Obama, to fill the vacant seat, even though the president had nearly a year left in his term.

On the presidential campaign trail, one of McConnell's Republican colleagues, Texas senator Ted Cruz, vowed to make the future of the Court *the* issue of the race. For his part, Donald Trump, the leader in the polls for the Republican nomination at the time of Scalia's death, endorsed McConnell's strategy, saying to applause at the beginning of a February 13th GOP debate: "I think it's up to Mitch McConnell and everybody else to stop [President Barack Obama's expected nominee to replace Scalia]. It's called delay, delay, delay" (GOP Debate 2016). On the Democratic side, the Court was less of an issue, with both front-runner Hillary Clinton and insurgent Bernie Sanders sharing their hope for a more progressive Court in the very near future.

Of course, Donald Trump would go on to capture the Republican nomination, ousting Cruz and 15 other contenders for the GOP mantle. And to the surprise of nearly all, including himself, Trump cut an extraordinarily narrow path to the presidency despite losing the popular vote by nearly 3 million votes. In his first press conference after his victory, President-elect Trump spoke of the Supreme Court, confidently proclaiming: "I think it's one of the reasons I got elected." He added somewhat cryptically (and awkwardly): "I think the people of this country did not want to see what was happening with the Supreme Court, so I think it was a very, very big decision as to why I was elected" (Trump Press Conference 2017). Nearly three weeks later, now President Trump announced his choice to replace Antonin Scalia. In naming Neil Gorsuch to the high bench, Trump once again spoke of the importance of the Court issue in the election: "Millions of voters said this was the single most important issue to them when they voted for me for president." And then, he explained how elections matter: "I have always felt that after the defense of our nation, the most important decision a president of the United States can make is the appointment of a Supreme Court justice. Depending on their age, a justice can be active for 50 years and his or her decisions can last a century or more and can often be permanent" (Trump Statement Nominating Gorsuch 2017).[1]

In this chapter, I consider the extent to which the Court played a role in the campaign, analyzing Trump's conclusion about its importance. I begin with a discussion of the Scalia vacancy and how his replacement would potentially alter the overall ideological makeup of the Court. Then, I discuss the five judicial issues that attracted the most attention in the campaign, and consider how Scalia's replacement would potentially shift the Court's treatment of them. Next, I show how the candidates dealt with the question of judicial appointments generally and with these five issues specifically during the race. Finally, I assess the extent to which the Court issue mattered in Trump's victory, focusing not just on the figures nationally but on those in the three "deciding states" of Michigan, Pennsylvania, and Wisconsin.

THE SITUATION: SCALIA'S DEATH AND A 4-4 COURT

It is unlikely any other justice appointed to the Court during the Republican dominance of the presidency from 1969 to 1993 will achieve the legendary status of Antonin Scalia in legal circles, particularly conservatives ones. Of the 10 justices appointed during those 24 years—all by the four Republican presidents who served during that time—Scalia best represented the character of the conservative challenge to the constitutional thinking of the Warren era.[2] Known for his stinging writing style, keen intellect, and laugh-out-loud sense of humor, Scalia helped sharpen and simultaneously soften the conservative criticisms of Warren era decisions in a way that Nixon-appointed and Ronald Reagan-elevated (to chief) William Rehnquist and Senate-rejected Reagan nominee Robert Bork could not do. He could rightfully be defined as one of the intellectual founders of the conservative legal movement, and his death meant the Court would undergo a clear transition from the past. Of course, the Court's future path depended on who would have the opportunity to name Scalia's replacement: Barack Obama, Hillary Clinton, or Donald Trump.

Consider Figure 3.1. Based on ideological scores for the Court's members produced by Andrew D. Martin and Kevin M. Quinn, and focusing on the swing justice—the justice who represents the ideological middle of the Court—it is clear just how much the election mattered to the direction of the Court, especially given the Senate's refusal to consider President Obama's nominee, Merrick Garland (Martin and Quinn 2015; see also, Epstein, Landes, and Posner 2013). A Hillary Clinton victory and a successful confirmation of a liberal nominee would have shifted the swing justice from Anthony Kennedy (sitting between +0.5 and -0.5 on the ideological scale in recent years) to Stephen Breyer (sitting at approximately -1.5 on the scale). The last time such a significant ideological shift occurred was during the late 1960s and early 1970s when Richard Nixon replaced four justices—three of them leading liberals—with three moderate conservatives (Warren Burger, Harry Blackmun, and Lewis Powell) and a conservative ideologue (Rehnquist). Additionally, during the 2016 campaign, many noted the possibility that one or both of the Court's oldest liberals or Kennedy, the swing justice, might retire during the next president's first term. If Ruth Bader Ginsburg (83 years old at the time of the election) and Stephen Breyer (78) did retire following a Clinton victory, liberals would have been virtually assured of Supreme Court majority for a generation, assuming successful Senate confirmation. The last time such a majority existed was in the mid-1960s, and that lasted for only a brief period. Alternatively, a Trump victory followed by the selection of a nominee ideologically similar to Justice Scalia promised to return the Court to its ideological point before his death. Of course, if Donald Trump was elected

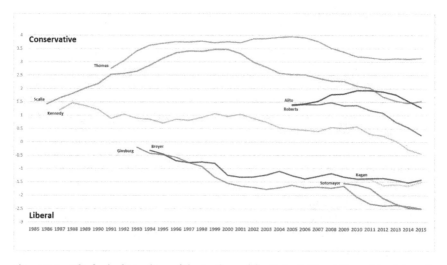

Figure 3.1   Ideological Leanings of the Justices of the Roberts Court Since Appointment.

and Justice Kennedy (aged 80 on Election Day) retired, conservatives would
be able to solidify an ideological majority, likely with someone more committed to their cause than Kennedy. Considering these possibilities, a Clinton
victory—followed by the retirement of both Ginsburg and Breyer—would
have possibly produced a Court with the swing justice at approximately -1.5
(Elena Kagan), and a comparatively youthful five justice majority. Alternatively, a Trump victory—followed by a Kennedy retirement—would have
produced a Court with a swing justice at approximately +0.5 (John Roberts).

Few other elections have offered the possibility of such an ideological shift
of the Court since 1937, when the Martin-Quinn scores begin. The closest
is certainly the 1968 presidential contest between Richard Nixon, Hubert
Humphrey, and George Wallace; a race where the Court was a central component of the campaign (see McMahon, 2011). The election of 2004 also
offered the possibility of a significant ideological shift on the high bench, and
as discussed below, featured Court-centered social issues as a distinguishing
feature in the race between Republican George W. Bush and Democrat John
Kerry. Even with this possibility of a dramatically different Court, its future
did not garner as much attention as expected in the general conversation of
the 2016 presidential campaign. Nevertheless, by examining the specific judicial issues where a change in the Court's makeup had the potential to alter
doctrine, the possibility that the Court issue made a difference in the election
results becomes clearer.

THE JUDICIAL ISSUES

In this section, I discuss the five judicial issues—gun rights, campaign
finance, abortion, same-sex marriage, and the constitutionality of the Affordable Care Act—that attracted the most attention during the 2016 presidential
campaign. Each issue is connected to at least one Supreme Court decision,
all of which were decided with just five justices in the majority. In three of
those cases, Justice Scalia was in the minority. In two of them, he joined the
majority, including the 2008 gun rights case of *District of Columbia v. Heller,*
in which he wrote for the Court. I begin there.

On April 27, 2008, during a piece on *60 Minutes,* CBS reporter Leslie Stahl
read to Justice Scalia a note he had written to Justice Blackmun years earlier,
at the end of the 1995–1996 term. It read in part: "I am more discouraged than
I have been at the end of any of my previous nine terms. ... The Court must
be living in another world. Day by day, case by case it is busy designing a
Constitution for a country I don't recognize." In response to Stahl 12 years
later, Scalia confirmed that he had felt that way back then. But he quickly
added: "It's been less dire in more recent years" (*60 Minutes* 2008). It is easy

to understand Scalia's 2008 optimism. At the time of that airing, he was penning what would become one of his more notable majority opinions for a 5-4 Court in *Heller;* a decision that established for the first time in the nation's history the basis for an individual right to bear arms.

In the seven years between that decision and the beginning of the nomination phase of the presidential race in 2015, the Court had changed little with regard to the presumed lineup of justices on the issue of gun rights. President Barack Obama had named two justices, Sonia Sotomayor and Elena Kagan, but each had replaced a justice (David Souter and John Paul Stevens, respectively) who dissented in *Heller.* And while Obama, as a candidate for the presidency, had announced his support for the *Heller* decision, given their liberal leanings, most did not expect Sotomayor and Kagan to join Scalia's position as articulated in *Heller.*[3] Scalia's death, therefore, allowed Republican candidates to highlight the gun rights issue as an area where a Hillary Clinton-appointed justice would potentially overturn doctrine. And Trump consistently emphasized this issue when discussing the Supreme Court. It was also an issue on which Clinton sought to position herself to the left of Vermont senator Bernie Sanders in the Democratic primary, further complicating her standing among gun owners in the general election.

The other case where Scalia joined the majority in the five issue areas identified above was the 2010 campaign finance decision of *Citizens United v Federal Election Commission.* In addition to joining the majority opinion, written by Justice Kennedy, Scalia authored a concurring opinion. He did so principally to respond to portions of Justice Stevens's dissent that argued the Court's majority opinion was inconsistent with Scalia's long-standing commitment to the ideals of originalism. Taking exception with this charge, Scalia concluded in the following terms:

> The Amendment is written in terms of "speech," not speakers. Its text offers no foothold for excluding any category of speaker, from single individuals to partnerships of individuals, to unincorporated associations of individuals, to incorporated associations of individuals—and the dissent offers no evidence about the original meaning of the text to support any such exclusion. ... A documentary film critical of a potential Presidential candidate is core political speech, and its nature as such does not change simply because it was funded by a corporation. ... We should celebrate rather than condemn the addition of this speech to the public debate (Scalia, *Citizens United v Federal Election Commission* 2010).

Given that Republicans generally celebrated the *Citizens United* decision while Democrats lamented it, it is not surprising that much of the criticism of the ruling came from Senator Sanders or Secretary Clinton during the nomination phase of the election. To be sure, Donald Trump did critique

the campaign finance system in more general terms, especially during the
Republican primaries. However, as discussed below, Clinton consistently and
specifically emphasized her desire to overturn *Citizens United* when discussing the Supreme Court.

Justice Scalia was well known for his biting dissents, including his opinion
in the 1992 abortion case of *Planned Parenthood of Southeastern Pennsylvania v. Casey*; a dissent that took on a plurality opinion co-written by
Republican-appointed justices Sandra Day O'Connor, Kennedy, and Souter.
Scalia began his *Casey* dissent by restating his well-known views: "The
States may, if they wish, permit abortion on demand, but the Constitution
does not *require* them to do so. The permissibility of abortion, and the limitations upon it, are to be resolved like most important questions in our democracy: by citizens trying to persuade one another and then voting." Before
long, however, his scorn set in. After quoting the first line of the plurality
opinion—"Liberty finds no refuge in a jurisprudence of doubt"—he added:
"One might have feared to encounter this august and sonorous phrase in an
opinion defending the real *Roe* v. *Wade*, rather than the revised version fabri-
cated today by the authors of the joint opinion" (Scalia, *Planned Parenthood
of Southeastern Pennsylvania v. Casey* 1992). To be sure, with *Casey* and a
series of other decisions, the Court has slowly restricted the right of a woman
to terminate an unwanted pregnancy since the 1973 *Roe v. Wade* decision.
But Scalia and his fellow conservatives were never able to cobble together a
majority to overturn essence of *Roe*, despite Republican presidents appointing 8 of the 12 new additions to the Court since 1973 (see Keck and McMahon,
2016). In 2016, just months after Scalia's death, in *Whole Women's Health
v. Hellerstedt,* a five justice majority once again affirmed the *Roe* and *Casey*
decisions by striking down a Texas law that sought to restrict access to
abortion in the name of furthering the state's interest in protecting women's
health. Given his past opinions, it is almost certain that Scalia would have
joined the three conservatives in dissent.

As discussed below, the abortion issue received the most attention during the third and final debate, with Hillary Clinton articulating a stridently
liberal position and Donald Trump providing full-throated pro-life defense.
Assuming she was able to successfully appoint justices to match her rhetoric,
a Clinton victory would have made one of the fundamental goals of social
conservatives—overturning *Roe*—even further out of reach. Alternatively,
with a Trump's victory and the appointment of the Scalia-like replacement,
the possibility would be closer to reality, especially if one of the three aging
justices in the *Whole Women's Health v. Hellerstedt* majority (i.e., Breyer,
Ginsburg, or Kennedy) left the Court during his presidency.

Same-sex marriage was yet another area where Justice Scalia held strong
views. And in the 2015 *Obergefell v. Hodges* case, where a 5-4 Court held

that the right to marry was a fundamental liberty and applied to both opposite and same-sex unions, he authored yet another cutting dissent. After joining Chief Justice John Roberts's dissent in full, Scalia authored his own opinion (joined by Clarence Thomas) to, as he put it in his opening sentence, "call attention to this Court's threat to American democracy." In particular, Scalia took exception to the likelihood that the decision would stifle democratic debate. "Until the courts put a stop to it, public debate over same-sex marriage displayed American democracy at its best. Individuals on both sides of the issue passionately, but respectfully, attempted to persuade their fellow citizens to accept their views. Americans considered the arguments and put the question to a vote." In Scalia's view, the *Obergefell* Court was employing "super-legislative power," and its opinion was "lacking even a thin veneer of law." He continued: "Buried beneath the mummeries and straining-to-be-memorable passages of the opinion is a candid and startling assertion: No matter *what* it was the People ratified, the Fourteenth Amendment protects those rights that the Judiciary, in its 'reasoned judgment,' thinks the Fourteenth Amendment ought to protect" (Scalia, *Obergefell v. Hodges* 2015). Whether it was due to *Obergefell* or other reasons, during the 2016 race the same-sex marriage issue was not as much of a defining issue as it had been in past presidential contests. While Hillary Clinton defended the right and suggested Donald Trump wouldn't, Trump in fact consistently sought to avoid taking a direct position on whether he would push the Court to overturn *Obergefell* (although he certainly made statements that supported Clinton's charge, Gillin 2016). Additionally, at times, the issue of how the Court might resolve questions about religious-based refusals of services to same-sex couples was raised, but that was very much a marginal issue in the overall conversation of the campaign.[4]

The final judicial issue that attracted notable attention during the campaign dealt with the constitutionality of the Affordable Care Act (i.e., Obamacare). While this issue was seemingly settled after the cases of *National Federation of Independent Businesses v. Sebelius* (2012) and *King v. Burwell* (2015), it nevertheless reappeared in the Republican primary campaign. In each of the cases (decided 5-4 and 6-3, respectively) Justice Scalia dissented. In *King v. Burwell,* he wrote separately in a "searing snarky" opinion that attracted significant attention for its string of conservative zingers (Barnes 2015). For example, Scalia accused the Court's majority of performing "somersaults of statutory interpretation," "interpretive jiggery-pokery," and making an argument that was "pure applesauce." Because the Court had done so much to save Obamacare, he also suggested: "We should start calling the law SCO-TUScare" (Scalia, *King v. Burwell* 2015). After these cases, most assumed that if conservatives were going to end Obamacare as they promised, they would need to do so via the legislative route. In other words, these two decisions had closed off the judicial course. Therefore, the fact that they were raised at all during the campaign was a bit of a surprise. Nevertheless, as discussed below, criticism of Chief Justice John Roberts's majority opinions in both cases allowed Donald Trump to fend off attacks from his challengers about liberal positions he had once held on social issues, and to instead put them on the defensive for their support of Roberts. As with the issue of same-sex marriage, at times questions of Obamacare's reach into the realm of "religious liberty"—similar to the issues raised in the Court's 5-4 decision in *Burwell v Hobby Lobby Stores* (in which Scalia joined the conservative majority)—were raised during the campaign. But not very often.

In the following section, I further highlight how these five judicial issues helped to define the presidential campaign of 2016.

THE COURT ISSUE AND THE CONVERSATION OF THE CAMPAIGN

Fate shaped the Republican debate on February 13, 2016, for it began mere hours after the world learned of Justice Scalia's death. After a moment of silence, moderator John Dickerson of CBS News began the questioning with one focused on the future of the Court. Most of the GOP candidates assembled in Greenville, South Carolina spoke kindly about Justice Scalia, specifically about the politics of the appointment process, and in vague generalities about the desire for less divisiveness and the need for a more conservative Court. But Ted Cruz set a different course, hoping to assume the mantle of the social conservative warrior most committed to installing jurists on the Court who thought similarly to him on these issues. And once given the opportunity, he unleashed rhetoric designed to do just that:

> We are one justice away from a Supreme Court that will strike down every restriction on abortion adopted by the states. We are one justice away from a Supreme Court that will reverse the Heller decision, one of Justice Scalia's seminal decisions, that upheld the Second Amendment right to keep and to bear arms. We are one justice away from a Supreme Court that would undermine the religious liberty of millions of Americans —and the stakes of this election, for this year, for the Senate, the Senate needs to stand strong and say, "We're not going to give up the U.S. Supreme Court for a generation by allowing Barack Obama to make one more liberal appointee (sic)" (GOP Debate 2016).

While Republicans largely agreed on the Court's direction, that didn't prevent Cruz from going on the attack. With Donald Trump leading in the polls and the runaway winner of the recent New Hampshire primary, Cruz set his telescopic sight on the Manhattan billionaire's previously held liberal positions on social issues like abortion and his continuing support for funding some aspects of Planned Parenthood.

But Trump seemed prepared for the charge and responded by criticizing Cruz for daring to offer kind words for the Republican-appointed Chief Justice of the United States, John G. Roberts. Specifically, Trump denounced Cruz for penning an op-ed praising Roberts. Writing in the *National Review* soon after President George W. Bush nominated the future chief justice in 2005, the then solicitor general of Texas had called Roberts "brilliant," adding he "is undoubtedly a principled conservative, as is the president who appointed him" (Cruz 2005). In the February 13th debate, shortly after calling Cruz a "liar" and "a nasty guy," Trump criticized his support of Roberts and included an attack on former Florida governor Jeb Bush too: "Ted Cruz told your brother that he wanted John Roberts to be on the United States Supreme Court. They both pushed him, he twice approved Obamacare." After a few exchanges between Bush and the moderator, Cruz and Trump continued:

Cruz: I did not nominate John Roberts. I would not have nominated John Roberts.
Trump: You pushed him. You pushed him.
Cruz: I supported...
Trump: You worked with him and you pushed him. Why do you lie? (GOP Debate 2016).

This was not the first time Trump had used this form of attack. On repeated occasions, Trump was willing to directly challenge—even mock—judges who disagreed with him, most notably Indiana-born U.S. district court judge Gonzalo Curiel, whom he dismissed as biased because, according to Trump, "he's a Mexican" (Trump quoted in Rappeport 2016). And very early in the race, when Jeb Bush was clear and away the front-runner for the Republican nomination, Trump criticized Bush for his support of Roberts. He did so by using his favorite vehicle for getting his message out, Twitter. Soon after the second Obamacare decision, *King v. Burwell*, he tweeted: "Once again the Bush appointed Supreme Court Justice John Roberts has let us down. Jeb pushed him hard! Remember!" (Gillin 2016).[5] With Jeb Bush's candidacy—following Trump's predictions—running low on fuel, Trump repeated the attack on the seemingly less venerable Cruz; the candidate who, like Scalia, had graduated from Harvard Law School, and who had served as a one of Chief Justice William Rehnquist's law clerks in 1996.

If Cruz had thought his conservative legal credentials and his social conservative positions would push him to victory in the more culturally conservative southern states rich with evangelical voters in their upcoming primaries, he was mistaken. In the first contest in the South, in South Carolina, and in the so-called SEC primary—named after the southern-based collegiate athletic conference—Trump outperformed expectations. Specifically, the Manhattanite easily won South Carolina, and then, ten days later, captured five of the six southern contests, losing only Cruz's home state of Texas.[6] In doing so, Trump severely undercut Cruz's campaign strategy, which focused on winning the front-loaded southern primaries. With the race moving into more unfriendly territory, the possibility that Cruz would emerge as the GOP nominee lessened dramatically after losing so many southern states. Moreover, on the judicial front, Trump took a decisive step to reassure his conservative doubters of his commitment to their cause. He had promised to release a list of conservative jurists he considered leading contenders for a nomination to the high bench if he had the opportunity to choose Scalia's replacement. And on May 19, 2016, he released that list. It included Neil Gorsuch.

As mentioned earlier on the Democratic side, the Court was less of an issue. Front-runner Hillary Clinton denounced the Republican strategy of delaying Senate consideration of Obama nominee Merrick Garland, suggesting that in doing so those senators "dishonor our Constitution." In the first debate after Scalia's death, she added: "we must all support President Obama's right to nominate a successor to Justice Scalia and demand that the Senate hold hearings and a vote on that successor because there are so many issues at stake." She then vowed "to reverse *Citizens United*," promising: "if we can't get it done through the court, I will lead a constitutional amendment effort to reverse it that way" (Democratic Debate 2016). Her Democratic opponent, Senator Bernie Sanders, supported her call for the end of *Citizens United*. Their agreement on the issue and their shared hope for a progressive Court meant that they would mainly focus on other concerns to distinguish themselves. Nevertheless, they did differ on gun control. While Sanders was willing to endorse litmus tests for upholding *Roe* and overturning *Citizens United* for his Supreme Court choices, he was not willing to say he would search for jurists willing to overturn the *Heller* decision. Neither was Secretary Clinton. But, as was highlighted in a question in the final debate of the general election, she had said the following in reference to *Heller*: "The Supreme Court is wrong on the Second Amendment" (Third Presidential Debate 2016). Coupled with her consistent critique of Sanders's voting record on gun control, voters could have certainly been left with a perception that she thought the Court should reverse its *Heller* ruling (Christopher 2016).

As the campaign moved from the primary stage to the general election, the Court issue, despite expectations, did not command a great deal of attention. Consider, for example, the acceptance speeches of the two candidates at their respective party conventions. This is all Trump said about the Court in accepting the GOP nomination: "We are also going to appoint justices to the United States Supreme Court who will uphold our laws and our Constitution." He added:

> The replacement for Justice Scalia will be a person of similar views and principles. This will be one of the most important issues decided by this election. My opponent wants to essentially abolish the 2nd amendment. I, on the other hand, received the early and strong endorsement of the National Rifle Association and will protect the right of all Americans to keep their families safe (Trump Convention Speech 2016).

Hillary Clinton said even less in her speech to the Democratic Party convention: "That's why we need to appoint Supreme Court justices who will get money out of politics and expand voting rights, not restrict them" (Clinton Convention Speech 2016.) Moreover, each articulated similar lines on the campaign trails, with Trump consistently highlighting his list of potential nominees for the Court and promising to protect second amendment rights and Clinton vowing to upend *Citizens United* and protect the right to franchise.

Unlike past Democratic nominees, Clinton chose not to emphasize this possibility of the end of *Roe v. Wade* with a conservative Court, except for one brief moment following the release of the *Access Hollywood* video, in which Trump was heard bragging about sexually assaulting women. (Immediately after the video's release, some speculated Trump would abandon his run in favor vice-presidential candidate Mike Pence. And the Clinton campaign preemptively sought to highlight Pence's staunchly conservative pro-life positions.) Instead, in both stump speeches and especially on television ads, Clinton focused on the shortcomings of Trump, the "man"; on his personal indiscretions and his lack of qualifications to hold the highest office in the land. Consider, for example, a statement she made during late September speech in New Hampshire when she did briefly address the Court issue: "I never thought I'd hear someone running for president, my opponent, who says he wants to appoint Supreme Court justices who would overturn marriage equality and turn the clock back on LGBT Americans, overturn a woman's right to make her own healthcare decisions and reverse that fundamental right and so much more" (Clinton New Hampshire Speech 2016, see also, Gillin 2016). It is striking that in discussing the Court, Clinton defended a women's right to choose to terminate a pregnancy in such tame terms; choosing not to use the word "abortion" or even the phrase "pro-choice." Rather, she seemingly referred to a longtime conservative effort to reverse *Roe* as "overturning a woman's right to make her own health care decisions." In doing so, she was obviously attempting to downplay a divisive issue in the battleground states where she needed to campaign to win the Electoral College.

During the debates, however, Secretary Clinton would use much different, and decidedly more strident, language to defend the right to choose. The Court issue first came up first at the end of the second debate. At that point, both candidates slipped into their routine lines. Clinton began by agreeing with the audience questioner that the Court "was one of the most important issues in this election," before highlighting her call to end *Citizens United,* and protect the right to franchise. She then added:

> I want a Supreme Court that will stick with *Roe v. Wade* and a woman's right to choose, and I want a Supreme Court that will stick with marriage equality. Now, Donald has put forth the names of some people that he would consider. And among the ones that he has suggested are people who would reverse *Roe v. Wade* and reverse marriage equality. I think that would be a terrible mistake and would take us backwards (Second Presidential Debate 2016).

For his part, Trump largely dismissed the question. He began with a short statement about Scalia before moving onto his pledge to protect the second amendment. But most of his answer was a response to Clinton's focus on "dark money" in the campaign. He wanted the audience to know just how much of his own money—he claimed a "$100 million"—he was putting into the campaign (Second Presidential Debate 2016). And then asked why Secretary Clinton wasn't doing the same.

The Court issue received the most extensive and noteworthy attention in the third and final debate. FoxNews's Chris Wallace started things off with a question about the future of the Court:

> [T]he next president will almost certainly have at least one appointment and likely or possibly two or three appointments. Which means that you will, in effect, determine the balance of the court for what could be the next quarter century, First of all, where do you want to see the court take the country? And secondly, what's your view on how the Constitution should be interpreted? Do the founders' words mean what they say or is it a living document to be applied flexibly according to changing circumstances? (Third Presidential Debate 2016)

Clinton began by giving an expanded version of her answer in the previous debate. Trump responded with a dig at Justice Ruth Bader Ginsburg before highlighting his list of 20 possible nominees for the Scalia seat. The exchange then shifted to the issue of gun control with both candidates emphasizing their differences. Trump reasserted his strong support for *Heller,* and stressed that Clinton was "extremely upset, extremely angry" with that decision. Clinton responded by noting she was upset because "dozens of toddlers injure themselves, even kill people with guns, because, unfortunately, not everyone who has loaded guns in their homes takes appropriate precautions." She then reassured voters that she "respect[ed] the Second Amendment" and believed "in an individual right to bear arms," but thought that "sensible, common-sense regulations"—like the one the Court struck down in *Heller*—should be allowed in the interests of safety (Third Presidential Debate 2016).

Next, Wallace sought to "drill down" on issue of abortion, inquiring about how far "the right to abortion goes." He then added in a question for Clinton: "You have been quoted as saying that the fetus has no constitutional rights. You also voted against a ban on late-term partial birth abortions. Why?" After earlier expressing her strong support for *Roe v. Wade* and criticizing Trump's backing of the effort to defund Planned Parenthood—even if it meant shutting down the federal government—Secretary Clinton reiterated her belief that "the United States government should [not] be stepping in and making those most personal of decisions," like those to end a late-term pregnancy. This led Mr. Trump to respond: "Well I think it is terrible. If you go with what Hillary is saying, in the ninth month you can take the baby and rip the baby out of the womb of the mother just prior to the birth of the baby." But Clinton held firm, denouncing Trump for using "scare rhetoric," and restating her position: "This is one of the worst possible choices that any woman and her family has to make. And I do not believe the government should be making it" (Third Presidential Debate 2016). In contrast to her husband's call for abortion that was "safe, legal, and rare," and Barack Obama's successful avoidance of the issue (largely because of the importance of the economy in 2008), Hillary Clinton's answer was strikingly liberal; likely driven by a confidence in her position in the polls; a confidence that would prove fatal to her chances for victory on Election Day (on Clinton and Obama, see Keck and McMahon 2016 and McMahon 2009).

ASSESSING THE IMPORTANCE OF THE COURT ISSUE IN TRUMP'S VICTORY

While the Court issue was not as distinctive a feature of the campaign's conversation during the general election phase as many expected, Donald Trump does have reason to believe the Supreme Court played a significant role in his victory. Consider, for example, the response to one of the questions posed in the Election Day exit poll. As Table 3.1 shows, in answering the question about the importance of Supreme Court appointments in their vote, 21 percent of exit poll respondents said the appointments were *the* most important factor. And 56 percent of those voters supported Donald Trump's candidacy.

Given this result, I suggest it is quite useful to compare the 2016 race to a recent election—namely, 2004—where there was the possibility of a significant shift in the Court and where judicially centered social issues played a

Table 3.1   2016 Exit Poll Responses to: "In Your Vote, were Supreme Court
Appointments"

Answer	Percent of Total	Trump	Clinton	Other/No Answer
The most important factor	21	56	41	3
An important factor	48	46	49	5
A minor factor	14	40	49	11
Not a factor at all	14	37	55	8

central role. Recall, the 2004 presidential election earned the label the "moral
values" election based on exit poll results. More specifically, when asked
what issue was most important in determining their vote, more respondents
chose "moral values" (22%) than any other of the seven choices (see McMahon
2005). And of those 22%, 80% voted for Republican George W. Bush. Recall
also, in hopes of boosting conservative turnout from 2000, the Bush campaign had successfully added "values-based" referenda to the ballot in several
states, including the battleground state of Ohio. As Table 3.2 shows, there
was a close correlation between the number of "values voters" and their support for Bush and the number of Born-Again or Christian Evangelicals and
their support for him, particularly at the national level. There, the figures were
nearly identical. As mentioned above, 22 percent of respondents identified
themselves as "values voters" and 80 percent of those voters supported President
Bush. Similarly, 23 percent of voters identified as Born-Again or Christian
Evangelical and 78 percent of that group voted to reelect the incumbent.

Notably, Bush identified himself as a Born-Again Christian and had
worked closely with evangelical groups for many years, beginning with
his father's 1988 presidential campaign. So his success with those voters
was not all that surprising. Donald Trump's ability to perform so well with

Table 3.2   2004 "Values Voters" Compared to White Born-Again/Evangelicals, 2004
and 2016

State	% Values 2004	% Bush 2004	% BA/EC 2004	% Bush 2004	% BA/EC 2016	% Trump 2016
National	22	80	23	78	26	80
Georgia	24	88	35	84	34	92
Iowa	22	87	33	66	34	70
Kentucky	26	93	45	71	53	79
Michigan	19	82	24	71	27	81
Missouri	24	86	35	75	35	73
N. Carolina	24	89	36	84	38	81
Ohio	23	85	25	76	33	77
S. Carolina	23	88	30	88	44	85

evangelical voters in 2016 was more striking, particularly given his difficulty naming books of the Bible and his celebrity lifestyle. Most notably, the exit polls show that nationally and in all of the states where the evangelical question was asked in both elections, the number of evangelical Christians was about the same or greater in 2016 than in 2004. And with the exception of the Carolinas, Trump outperformed Bush from 12 years earlier, sometimes substantially (Table 3.2). While pollsters did not ask a moral values question in 2016 and there is no state-level data on the importance of Supreme Court appointments question, these figures clearly show that evangelical Christians were not turned off by Trump's personal indiscretions or his one-time advocacy of liberal positions on social issues like abortion.

Of course, most of these states were not expected to be close. Trump won five of the eight listed in Table 3.2 easily, and ultimately won all of them. However, given the importance of the "deciding states" of Michigan, Pennsylvania, and Wisconsin, it is enlightening to take a closer look at them. Notably, as Table 3.3 shows, George W. Bush outperformed Donald Trump in all of these three states in terms of the percentage of the vote. However, Bush lost all three states to John Kerry while Trump won them, all by less than one percent. Significantly, if Hillary Clinton had won all three, she would have won the presidency. While exit poll data on evangelicals is only available from Michigan for both 2004 and 2016 (Table 3.3), it shows that more voters in this group went to the polls on Election Day in 2016 than in 2004 (by 3%), and substantially more of them supported Trump than Bush 12 years earlier (by 10%).

Catholics, particularly white Catholics, were another group of voters where Donald Trump's positioning with regard to the Supreme Court might have made a difference. Nationally, Trump significantly improved his vote among white Catholics compared to the three previous Republican nominees: Bush, John McCain, and Mitt Romney. And in Michigan, the only of the three deciding states where exit pollsters identified voters by religion, Trump won 57 percent of the Catholic vote, who were 24 percent of all voters. In 2004 and 2008 (when Catholics made of 29 and 26 percent of all Michigan voters, respectively, Bush and McCain won just 49 and 46 percent of that group, respectively). In 2012, Mitt Romney turned things around for Republicans in

Table 3.3   Results in the Deciding States, 2004 and 2016

Deciding State	Bush—2004	Margin/ Result	Trump—2016	Margin/ Result
Michigan	47.81%	.38% loss	47.25%	.77 win
Pennsylvania	48.42%	3.42% loss	48.17%	.22 win
Wisconsin	49.32%	2.5% loss	47.22%	.71 win

his native state as he won 55 percent of Catholics (25 percent of all voters). The exit polls from 2012 also provide more clarifying information about Romney's strength with white Catholics. Romney won 58 percent of white Catholics. According to the same exit poll, 23 percent of all voters were white Catholics, meaning that the vast majority of Catholics in Michigan that year were white. (Pew's Religious Landscape Study supports this figure, finding in 2014 that 85% of Catholics in Michigan were white). While that more specific data isn't available for 2016, it is unlikely that the numbers changed dramatically in the space of four years. And again, Trump improved upon Romney's vote among all Michigan Catholic voters by 2 percent.

Still, it is not clear if the Court issue was as significant a factor as Trump concluded after his victory. Consider another representation of the same exit poll responses about the importance of Supreme Court appointments (Table 3.1). This time the four possible responses are combined into two: those respondents who said the appointments were "important" in their Election Day decision and those who said they weren't. Here, the data suggest not much difference as only 2 percent more of the 70 percent answering "important" favored Donald Trump over Hillary Clinton (49 to 47%).

Moreover, similar to 2004, some social conservative groups have highlighted the importance of the Court in the election because it potentially advances their agenda. Consider, for example, National Rifle Association head Wayne LaPierre's video statement to NRA members and other gun owners shortly after the election. Looking straight at the camera, LaPierre boldly proclaimed: "the 5 million men and women of the National Rifle Association of America, along with the tens of millions of gun owners all over this country who followed your lead—achieved a truly extraordinary, historic, even heroic, accomplishment … you were the special forces that swung this election and sent Donald Trump and Mike Pence to the White House." He then explained the significance of the victory: "Soon, President Trump will nominate a constitutionally sound justice to replace Antonin Scalia on the Supreme Court. Make no mistake: that will be a generational victory for Second Amendment freedom—and you made it happen" (LaPierre, 2016). LaPierre may have a point. Donald Trump's razor-thin victories in Michigan, Pennsylvania, and Wisconsin—states with deep traditions of hunting and gun ownership—may have been aided by his stance on gun rights, especially given the possibility that *Heller* might be overturned with a Clinton appointee to the Court. But of course, many factors can be attributed to races decided by so few votes.

Nevertheless, there is some evidence from one of the deciding states— namely Wisconsin—to suggest the gun issue was a factor in Trump's success there. Consider, for example, the Wisconsin Senate race, which featured a rematch between Republican incumbent Ron Johnson and the former senator he beat six years earlier, Russ Feingold. For much of the campaign season,

Feingold held a comfortable lead. However, as the campaign heated up, Johnson closed the gap. And one of the commercials that helped distinguish him from his Democratic opponent focused on the issue of gun rights. Strikingly, in the August-released ad, Johnson does not challenge Feingold's record on gun rights by highlighting the former senator's votes on specific pieces of legislation while in the Senate. Rather, he notes that during his "eighteen year Senate career he supported judges who voted to deny your individual right" (Johnson 2016). Presumably, Johnson is referring to the *Heller* decision and Feingold's votes to confirm dissenting justices Ginsburg and Breyer because he adds: "one more liberal justice will flip the Court" (see also, Anderson).[7]

On the other hand, in Pennsylvania, the issue of gun rights played a different role. There, incumbent Republican Pat Toomey attracted significant attention for his decision to support gun control legislation requiring background checks following the late 2012 massacre at the Sandy Hook school in Newtown, Connecticut. That decision cost him the NRA's endorsement, and threatened to cost him votes with his Republican base. As one report concluded, from the standpoint of gun rights advocates, the choice was between "the lesser of two evils" in the Senate race. "Gun rights groups in Pennsylvania are now forced to choose between Toomey, whom they see as a threat to the Second Amendment, and Democrat Katie McGinty, whom they see as a bigger threat." None other than Mike Bloomberg, the former New York City mayor and a staunch advocate of stricter gun control regulations, endorsed Toomey, which no doubt aided in his appeal to independents and more moderate voters (Garcia 2016). If it hurt him with his base, it didn't prove to be decisive at the polls. Despite many predictions to the contrary, Toomey narrowly defeated McGinty by 1.3 percent.

CONCLUSIONS

In the third and final debate, Donald Trump began his answer to the Supreme Court question in the following terms: "The Supreme Court: It's What It's All About." And after the election results were in, Trump consistently pointed to his promise to appoint conservative justices as one of the principle reasons for his victory. To be sure, according to exit polls, Trump is correct in concluding that millions of voters did cast their vote for him based on his determination to select conservative nominees for the federal judiciary, especially the Supreme Court. However, millions did the same for Hillary Clinton based on her promise to choose more progressive jurists for the high bench. Given the importance of the deciding states in Trump's victory, at the very least his positioning on the most salient judicial issues convinced enough social conservatives who may have been disturbed by his personal shortcomings.

True to his promise, Trump appointed one of the names on his list of potential nominees, Neil Gorsuch. The Senate confirmed Gorsuch after changing the terms of votes on Supreme Court nominees. For the first time in its history, the Senate employed the so-called nuclear option in the Gorsuch confirmation vote. This allowed the Republican majority to overcome a Democratic filibuster. Under the new rules, the Senate could confirm Gorsuch with only a bare majority of votes. In the end, he was confirmed by a vote of 54-45. While the sample size is small, Justice Gorsuch's short time on the high bench has shown he's a worthy ideological replacement for Scalia, voting "a 100 percent of the time with the Court's most conservative member, Clarence Thomas" (Totenberg 2017). Whether he will reach Scalia's legendary status in conservative legal circles is an entirely different question.

NOTES

1. If history holds, serving on the Court for 50 years would be unlikely. William O. Douglas has the record for the longest service on the Court. He was a justice was 36 years and 7 months.
2. Jimmy Carter was the only Democrat to serve as president during this time period, and there was no Supreme Court vacancy during his four years in the White House.
3. Notably, Sotomayor joined Ginsburg and Breyer in dissent in the 2010 gun rights case of *McDonald V. City of Chicago.* Kagan did join the Court in 2010, but after that case had already been decided.
4. This issue attracted some attention after Trump's selection of Indiana Governor Mike Pence as his vice-presidential nominee given his state's passage of the Religious Freedom Restoration Act in 2015. After widespread protests, the law was amended.
5. Gillin misidentifies this tweet as in response to the *Obergefell* decision, announced the day after *King v. Burwell.* Roberts dissented in *Obergefell,* and Trump tweeted a few hours before the announcement of *Obergefell.*
6. This does not include Oklahoma, which is traditionally considered a border state. Trump lost that state to Cruz as well.
7. Feingold also voted against the confirmation of Samuel Alito and supported John Roberts. Both justices joined Scalia's majority opinion in *Heller.*

REFERENCES

2016 Exit polls. 2016. *CNN.* Accessed March 17, 2017. www.cnn.com/election/results/exit-polls.
Anderson, Jonathan. 2016. "Testing Ron Johnson claim on Russ Feingold, Judges and Second Amendment." *PolitiFact,* October 19. Accessed March

17, 2017. www.politifact.com/wisconsin/statements/2016/oct/19/ron-johnson/testing-ron-johnson-claim-russ-feingold-judges-and/.

Barnes, Robert. 2015. "Affordable Care Act Survives Supreme Court Challenge." *Washington Post*, June 25. Accessed March 17, 2017. www.washingtonpost.com/politics/courts_law/obamacare-survives-supreme-court-challenge/2015/06/25/af87608e-188a-11e5-93b7 5eddc056ad8a_story.html?utm_term=.37bd399128c4.

Christopher, Tommy. 2016. "Bernie Sanders Won't Make Gun Control a Litmus Test for Supreme Court Nominees," *Mediaite*, March 24. Accessed March 17, 2017. www.mediaite.com/tv/bernie-sanders-wont-make-gun-control-a-litmus-test-for-supreme-court-nominees/.

Citizens United v Federal Election Commission 558 U.S. 310. 2010.

Clinton, Hillary R. 2017. "Address Accepting the Presidential Nomination at the Democratic National Convention in Philadelphia, Pennsylvania." July 28. Accessed March 17, 2017.Transcript. www.presidency.ucsb.edu/ws/index.php?pid=118051.

Clinton, Hillary R. 2016. "Remarks at the University of New Hampshire in Durham," September 28. Accessed March 17, 2017. Transcript. www.presidency.ucsb.edu/ws/index.php?pid=119164.

Cruz, Ted. 2005. "The Right Stuff," *National Review*, July 20. Accessed March 17, 2017. www.nationalreview.com/article/214989/right-stuff-ted-cruz.

Democratic Candidates Debate. 2016. Flint, Michigan, March 6. Accessed March 17, 2017. Transcript. www.presidency.ucsb.edu/ws/index.php?pid=112718.

Epstein, Lee, William M. Landes, and Richard A. Posner. 2013. *The Behavior of Federal Judges: A Theoretical and Empirical Study of Rational Choice.* Cambridge: Harvard University Press.

Garcia, Eric. 2016. "Pennsylvania Senate Race Could Come Down to Guns," *Roll Call,* August 29. Accessed March 17, 2017. www.rollcall.com/news/politics/toomey-might-be-lesser-of-two-evils-for-gun-owners.

Gillin, Joshua. 2016. "Hillary Clinton Says Donald Trump 'Wants to Undo Marriage Equality." *PolitiFact*, November 3. Accessed March 17, 2017. www.politifact.com/truth-o-meter/statements/2016/nov/03/hillary-clinton/hillary-clinton-says-donald-trump-wants-undo-marri/.

Johnson, Ron. 2016. "Protecting the 2nd Amendment." August. Accessed March 17, 2017. www.youtube.com/watch?v=oka8exyPph4.

Keck, Thomas M., and Kevin J. McMahon. 2016. "Why *Roe* Still Stands: Abortion Law, the Supreme Court, and the Republican Regime." *Studies in Law, Politics, and Society* 70: 33-83.

King v. Burwell, 576 U.S. ___ (2015).

LaPierre, Wayne. 2016. "Our Time is Now." November. Transcript. Accessed March 17, 2017. www.nratv.com/series/wayne-lapierre/episode/wayne-lapierre-season-1-episode-11-our-time-is-now.

Martin Andrew D., and Kevin M. Quinn. 2015. "Martin-Quinn Scores," Database. Accessed March 17, 2017. mqscores.berkeley.edu.

McMahon, Kevin J. 2005. "A 'Moral Values Election?: The Culture War, the Supreme Court, and a Divided America," In *Winning the White House, 2004: Region by Region, Vote by Vote,* edited by Kevin J. McMahon, David M. Rankin, Donald W. Beachler, and John Kenneth White, 23-46. New York: Palgrave Macmillan.

_____. 2009. "Searching for the Social Issue," In *Winning the White House, 2008,* edited by Kevin J. McMahon, David M. Rankin, Donald W. Beachler, and John Kenneth White, 59-78. New York: Palgrave Macmillan.

_____. 2011. *Nixon's Court: His Challenge to Judicial Liberalism and Its Political Consequences,* Chicago: University of Chicago Press.

Obergefell v. Hodges 576 U.S. ___ (2015).

Pew's Religious Landscape Study. 2014. Accessed March 17, 2017. www.pewforum. org/religious-landscape-study/.

Planned Parenthood of Southeastern Pennsylvania v. Casey 505 U.S. 833 (1992).

Presidential Debate. 2016. Washington University in Saint Louis, Missouri, October 9. Transcript. Accessed March 17, 2017. www.presidency.ucsb.edu/ws/index. php?pid=119038.

Presidential Debate. 2016. University of Nevada in Las Vegas, October 19. Transcript. Accessed March 17, 2017. www.presidency.ucsb.edu/ws/index.php?pid=119039.

Rappeport, Alan. 2016. "That Judge Attacked by Donald Trump? He's Faced a Lot Worse," *New York Times,* June 3. Accessed March 17, 2017. https://www.nytimes. com/2016/06/04/us/politics/donald-trump-university-judge-gonzalo-curiel.html.

Republican Candidates Debate. 2016. Greenville, South Carolina. February 13. Transcript. Accessed March 17, 2017. www.presidency.ucsb.edu/ws/index. php?pid=111500.

Stahl, Lesley. 2008. "Justice Scalia on the Record," *60 Minutes,* April 27. Accessed March 17, 2017. Transcript. www.cbsnews.com/news/justice-scalia-on-the-record/2/.

Totenberg, Nina. 2017. "Justice Neil Gorsuch Votes 100 Percent of the Time with Most Conservative Colleague," *NPR.org*; July 1. Accessed March 27, 2017. www.npr. org/2017/07/01/535085491/justice-neil-gorsuch-votes-100-percent-of-the-time-with-most-conservative-collea.

Trump, Donald J. 2017. "Donald Trump's News Conference: Full Transcript and Video." *New York Times*, January 11. Accessed March 17, 2017. Transcript. www. nytimes.com/2017/01/11/us/politics/trump-press-conference-transcript.html.

Trump, Donald J. 2017. "Full Transcript and Video: Trump Picks Neil Gorsuch for Supreme Court" *New York Times,* January 31. Accessed March 17, 2017. www. nytimes.com/2017/01/31/us/politics/full-transcript-video-trump-neil-gorsuch-supreme-court.html.

Trump, Donald J. 2016. "Address Accepting the Presidential Nomination at the Republican National Convention in Cleveland, Ohio." July 21. Transcript. Accessed March 17, 2017. www.presidency.ucsb.edu/ws/index.php?pid=117935.

Chapter 4

The Latino Vote in the 2016 Election—Myths and Realities about the "Trump Effect"

Atiya Stokes-Brown

According to U.S. Census projections, Latinos are one of the fastest-growing racial/ethnic groups in the country. Since 1970s, the Latino population has grown by 592 percent and by 2060 is expected to reach 28.6 percent by 2060 (Pew Hispanic Center 2016). In light of this growth, Latinos have long been referred to a sleeping giant in American politics—a growing minority group primed to have cultural, economic, social, and political power in the United States. Latinos (with the exception of Latinos of Cuban heritage) have historically been Democratic voters and since 2008, have been key members of the Democratic coalition. Conventional wisdom suggested that Latino voters, mobilized by Republican nominee Donald Trump's campaign rhetoric and proposed immigration policies, would serve as a firewall for Democratic nominee Hillary Clinton, essentially guaranteeing a Democratic victory in the 2016 presidential election. This chapter assesses the role of Latino voters, positing that the general convention about Latinos and their support for Democratic presidential candidates largely held. Latinos were overwhelming supportive of the Democratic presidential nominee, helped seal Democratic victories in several down ballot elections in Colorado, New Mexico, Virginia and California, and helped elect several new members of Congress, including the first Latina in the U.S. Senate, Catherine Cortez Masto, from Nevada. Latinos also provided Democrats with unprecedented support in states with large Latino populations including Arizona and Texas.

Yet, the question remains: Why weren't Latino voters the demographic firewall so many expected them to be (see for example Suro 2016; Taylor 2016; Decker 2016)? Why weren't they able to push Clinton to the presidency? Here I explore how various factors influenced the Latino vote in the 2016 election. Despite their growing political power, I argue that four key factors limited Latinos' ability to secure a Clinton victory: 1) the demographic location of Latinos in the United States; 2) the level and type of engagement in Latino communities by the Clinton campaign compared to that of the Obama campaigns; 3) the impact of state voter identification laws on Latino voting; and 4) the heterogeneity of the Latino population and how differences in religion and group consciousness may have impacted Latino political participation and behavior.

CONVENTIONAL WISDOM IN THE 2016 ELECTION— LATINOS, TRUMP, AND THE MINORITY BLUE FIREWALL

As the fastest-growing ethnic group among eligible voters in the United States, Latinos have been recognized as an influential and key voting constituency. The share of the Latino vote has rapidly increased, moving from 9 percent in 2008, to 10 percent in 2012, and 11 percent in 2016 (Krogstad and Lopez 2016). One need only consider this rapid growth and the election results of the 2008 and 2012 presidential elections to see how the groundwork for the firewall narrative began.

National exit poll data shows that in 2008, Latinos voted for Democratic nominee Barack Obama over Republican nominee John McCain by approximately a two-to-one margin, 67 percent versus 32 percent (Lopez 2008). While McCain's share of the Latino vote in 2008 was slightly lower but comparable to that of the Republican candidate George W. Bush in 2004 (39%), what was noticeable was the amount of support Obama received compared to the 2004 Democratic nominee, John Kerry, and the amount of support Obama received from all Latino demographic subgroups. Within four years, Latino support for the Democratic nominee increased by 14 points, from 53 percent to 67 percent. In addition to winning 64 percent of Latino men, 68 percent of Latinas, and 76 percent of young Latinos, Obama also won a sizable percentage of the Latino vote (ranging from 73 to 79%) in states with significant Latino populations, and won the Latino vote in states like Florida (57%) where Latinos had historically supported Republican presidential candidates (Lopez 2008).

From this historic level of Latino support eventually grew the narrative that Latinos would be a formative Democratic voting bloc in presidential elections (e.g., Preston 2008). Speaking to the press about the election, Efrain Escobedo, then director of civic engagement at the National Association of Latino Elected and Appointed Officials, noted that having "delivered" the election, the Latino electorate "now understands the importance of voting, and they made a significant shift in the political landscape" (Preston 2008). Similarly, former New Mexico Democratic governor, Bill Richardson, who is Latino, noted that "[Latinos] turned out, erasing the fame of Latino voters as a sleeping giant and making them an actual giant" (Preston 2008).

The outcome of the 2012 presidential election only helped to solidify this narrative. Latinos voted for President Barack Obama over Republican Mitt Romney, 71 percent to 27 percent, making Obama's percentage to the Latino vote the highest won by a Democratic candidate since the 1996 president election when Bill Clinton won 72 percent of the Latino vote (Lopez and Taylor 2012). In addition, the Latino percentage of electorate increased by 1 percent while the African-American percentage of the electorate remained stable (13%) and the white percentage dropped from 74 percent to 72 percent (Pew Research Center 2012).

While most scholars and media pundits focused exclusively on Latinos as key to Obama's successful election, a full assessment of the 2008 and 2012 elections clearly shows that the Democratic nominee's support from Latinos and other racial and ethnic minorities, as well as women and young people enabled the candidate to offset record low levels of support among white voters, who are still an overwhelming majority of the electorate. Thus while the strength and influence of the Latino vote became the primary narrative from these elections, the ability of Latinos alone to determine the outcome in a presidential election had yet to be proved.[1]

In many ways, the 2016 presidential election ultimately became the perfect environment to test out the strength and influence of the Latino vote. In light of changing demographics, presidential election campaigns have long crafted campaigns that target the Latino vote (Abrajano 2010, 31-32). Democratic and Republican presidential nominees in 2008 and 2012 actively targeted Latino voters via campaign advertisements and appearances (e.g., Barretto et al 2010, 915). Anti-immigrant rhetoric can also influence Latino voting. Recognizing the importance of Latino support, Obama in a 2012 interview stated "Should I win a second term, a big reason I will win a second term is because the Republican nominee and the Republican Party have so alienated the fastest-growing demographic group in the country, the Latino community" (Rodriguez 2012). Obama was commenting on Mitt Romney's position on policies and proposals regarding immigration. Throughout the campaign, Romney expressed opposition to the DREAM Act, which would allow some undocumented youth to stay in the United States; advocated for "self-deportation" and sanctions for employers who hire undocumented workers; and reversed his support of 2007 immigration reform act that created path to citizenship for undocumented immigrants (Halloran 2012). Yet, in an effort to moderate his stance, Romney also stated that he supported family reunification programs for immigrants, temporary work permits, and permanent resident cards for immigrants who obtain advanced degrees (Wallace 2012, 1367).

Whereas Romney attempted to moderate his hard-line position on immigration policy, Trump wasted little time making clear his position on immigration as he announced his candidacy on June 16, 2015, making disparaging remarks about Mexican immigrants, calling most of them "rapists"

and "criminals."[2] Trump would go on to discuss a series of immigration policies including building a wall across the U.S.-Mexico border to secure the
U.S. border, ending "catch and release" policies, enacting a "zero tolerance"
policy on undocumented immigrants who have committed crimes, blocking
funding for sanctuary cities, revoking President Obama's executive orders on
immigration and use a biometric entry-exit system for tracking visa holders
(Schultheis 2016). Upon winning the Republican nomination and thereby
driving the Republican Party further right on immigration issues, it was
widely believed that both his inflammatory rhetoric and proposed immigration policies would energize the Latino population, mobilizing them to turnout in record numbers and vote, largely in opposition to Trump.

2016 AND THE DEATH OF CONVENTIONAL WISDOM—THE REALITIES ABOUT LATINO POLITICAL INFLUENCE AND POWER

On Election Day 2016, Trump's victory shattered the conventional wisdom
that Latinos would be a demographic firewall for the Clinton campaign.
According to updated National Election Pool exit poll data, Latinos voted
for Clinton over Trump by 66 percent to 28 percent.[3] While comparable to
the percentage of Latino votes won by Obama in 2008, Clinton's share of
the Latino vote was lower than that received by Obama just four years earlier (Pew Hispanic Center 2016). Census Bureau data also shows that while
number of Latino voters grew to a record 12.7 million in 2016, up from 11.2
million in 2012, Latino turnout in 2016 fell almost two percentage points, to
47.6 percent, after hitting 49.9 percent in 2008 and 48 percent in 2012 (Krogstad
and Lopez 2017; see Figure 4.1). In an effort to understand why the Latino
wall cracked, scholars and political pundits have explored numerous reasons
to explain Clinton was not able to build a Latino firewall that could secure the
election. Despite their growing political power, it is clear that several factors
influenced the impact of the Latino vote. This chapter discusses in depth four
key factors: 1) the demographic location of Latinos in the United States; 2) the
level and type of engagement in Latino communities by the Clinton campaign
compared to that of the Obama campaigns; 3) the impact of state voter identification laws on Latino voting; and 4) the heterogeneity of the Latino population
and how differences in religion and group consciousness may have impacted
Latino political participation and behavior.

The Electoral College and the Reality of Political Demography

Central to American presidential elections is the Electoral College process—
a system in which electors (usually comprised of state party officials and

Figure 4.1   Presidential Election Turnout Rates by Race and Ethnicity

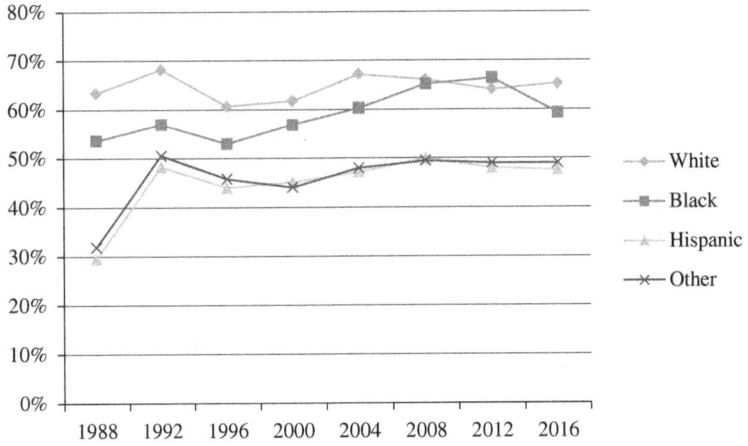

Note: Voter turnout rates calculated from the Census Bureau's Current Population Survey, November Supplements for 1998–2016. *Source*: United States Election Project, http://www.electproject.org/home/voter-turnout/demographics.

generally chosen at the party's state conventions) cast ballots awarding states' votes to candidates based on the number of representatives and senators a state sends to Congress. All but two states (Maine and Nebraska) award all of their electoral votes to the presidential candidate that wins the popular vote in the state. Thus, while the individual-level popular vote is meaningful, presidential victories are also greatly informed by group-level voting—specifically how the groups which a particular state are likely to vote.

As previously noted, Latinos have long been noted as a potentially powerful voting bloc in U.S. political because of their growth relative to other racial/ethnic groups in the United States. In the 52 years since the 1965 Immigration and Nationality Act was passed, the Latino population has grown to 56.9 million people—18 percent of the total U.S. population in 2015 (Pew Hispanic Center 2015; see Table 4.1). Not only has the Latino population grown in size but it is no longer geographically concentrated in a few states in the West and Southwest, having migrated to new regions of the country since the 1990s (Durand et al 2006, 69). Latinos now have a sizable presence in several important battleground states including Nevada, Florida, Colorado, and New Mexico. They comprise a significant percentage of the population in these states, including 26.5 percent in Nevada, 22.5 percent in Florida, 20.7 percent in Colorado, and 46.3 percent in New Mexico (Ennis et al 2011). Thus, recent settlement patterns to nontraditional gateway metropolitan areas in United States have resulted in a diverse Latino population that is increasingly dispersed across the United States (de la Garza et al. 2008, 97).

Table 4.1 Estimated U.S. Population by Race and Hispanic Origin, 1965–2015, With and Without Immigrants Entering 1965–2015

	Estimate					Estimate with no 1965–2015 immigration				
	Total	White	Black	Hispanic	Asian	Total	White	Black	Hispanic	Asian
	Population (in thousands)									
1965	193,419	161,750	20,504	8,092	1,326	193,419	161,750	20,504	8,092	1,326
1975	214,042	173,061	23,876	12,229	2,531	208,697	171,300	23,486	10,196	1,440
1985	238,211	183,167	27,767	18,944	5,111	223,477	179,784	26,567	12,593	1,525
1995	267,487	192,062	32,177	29,887	9,015	237,156	186,446	29,905	15,238	1,617
2005	297,532	197,297	36,265	44,560	13,600	244,838	188,330	32,369	17,531	1,643
2015	323,517	200,060	40,271	55,975	18,232	251,548	189,027	34,580	19,928	1,611
	Percent of total									
1965	100%	84%	11%	4%	1%	100%	84%	11%	4%	1%
1975	100%	81%	11%	6%	1%	100%	82%	11%	5%	1%
1985	100%	77%	12%	8%	2%	100%	80%	12%	6%	1%
1995	100%	72%	12%	11%	3%	100%	79%	13%	6%	1%
2005	100%	66%	12%	15%	5%	100%	77%	13%	7%	1%
2015	100%	62%	12%	18%	6%	100%	75%	14%	8%	1%

Note: Whites, Blacks, and Asians, include only single-race non-Hispanics. Asians include Pacific Islanders. Hispanics are of any race. Other races not shown but included in total.

Source: "Modern Immigration Wave Brings 59 Million to U.S. Driving Population Growth and Change Through 2065" Pew Research Center, Washington, D.C. (September 2015) http:...www.pewhispanic.org/2015/09/28/modern-immigration-wave-brings-59-million-to-u-s-driving-population-growth-and-change-through-2065/".

Yet, the growth and dispersion of this group has not yet been enough to impact voting outcomes through the Electoral College. More than half of the Latino population still lives in just three states: California, Texas, and Florida (Brown and Lopez 2013). Seventy-five percent of Latinos live in just eight states: California, Texas, Florida, New York, Illinois, Arizona, New Jersey, and Colorado (U.S. Census Bureau 2011; Stepler and Lopez 2016). Latinos exceed their national share of the population in just nine states, only three (Colorado, Florida, and Nevada) of which are swing states (Trende 2015). This means that non-Hispanic whites are disproportionately represented in states like Michigan, Pennsylvania, and Wisconsin where ultimately unusually high support among whites without a college degree for the 2016 Republican nominee helped pushed Trump to 270, making him the first Republican presidential nominee since 1988 to carry Michigan and Pennsylvania and the first since 1984 to win Wisconsin (Tyson and Maniam 2016).

Despite the narrative, Latinos alone were never influential enough to deliver a presidential victory in 2016 or any other presidential election. Only as members of coalition with African-Americans (who like Latinos are geographically concentrated in a few states) and moderate whites have Democratic presidential victories been possible. Even if, as many presumed, Trump's anti-Mexican and anti-immigrant rhetoric had served as a rallying cry mobilizing a surge in Latino voter turnout, the geographic distribution of Latinos suggests that their ability to be a firewall would still have been greatly limited.

The growing magnitude of the Latino population means these voters will one day exercise an increasingly powerful effect on the U.S. political landscape. By 2040, the U.S. Census Bureau projects that Latinos will be 28.6 percent of the total U.S. population, an increase of approximately 115 percent from the current total of 18 percent and in some states, the Latino population will grow at an even higher rate (Colby and Ortman 2015). Yet with the Electoral College in place and with unevenly dispersed demographic change, we are not likely to experience anytime soon the point at which electoral support from the sleeping giant alone will foreshadow electoral destiny.

The Importance of Latino Outreach and Mobilization—Did Clinton Get It Right?

Numerous studies in political science have explored how Latinos are mobilized and what impact various forms of mobilization can have on their voting behavior (e.g., Michelson 2003, 249; Michelson 2005, 92; Shaw et al. 2000, 342). While Latino voter turnout is shaped by many of the same factors that influence white voting behavior (e.g., Jackson 2003, 350; Shaw et al. 2000, 345), research shows that efforts by candidates and political parties, utilizing a variety of voter outreach strategies to reach out to Latinos, are effective in mobilizing the Latino electorate, increasing turnout and support for candidates (e.g., Shaw et al. 2000, 346; DeFrancesco Soto and Merolla 2008, 120).

By several accounts, there was some concern expressed by Latino-elected officials and others during the general election campaign that Clinton's campaign outreach to Latinos was unfocused, at best, and phoned-in, at worst (Phillip and O'Keefe 2016). Thus, Latinos weren't fully mobilized to serve as a demographic firewall for the Clinton campaign. To be clear, polls consistently showed that Clinton held a significant lead over Trump, but there was real doubt, as result of the campaign's outreach strategy, that Latinos would turn out in numbers that Clinton needed to win. This criticism is largely framed by the academic research focused on how best to effectively engage Latino voters. For example, much of the research highlights the value of Spanish-language ads (e.g., Panagopoulos and Green 2011, 651; Abrajano 2010, 42). A significant portion of the Latino population in the United States is foreign born, thus Spanish-language ads help foreign-born naturalized citizens better understand how to vote and for whom they should vote. Yet by several accounts, the Clinton team did not launch a significant and sustained campaign of traditional, Spanish-language ads in key Latino markets, including Florida, until September, choosing instead to center the campaign's Latino strategy on reaching millennials through new media such as Facebook and YouTube social media (Phillip and O'Keefe 2016). Most of Clinton's television outreach was produced primarily in English in an effort to reach bilingual households. Both scholars and practitioners agree that delivery matters with regard to mobilization. For example, Frederico de Jesus, who served as Obama's Hispanic communications director during the 2008 campaign, noted that the campaign received overwhelming positive feedback in 2008 when Obama's Spanish ads included him approving the ad in Spanish: *Soy Barack Obama y yo apruebo este mensaje*. In comparison, Clinton's Spanish ads only have her saying, "Soy Hillary Clinton and I approve this message." This example, however small, shows how Clinton may have missed important opportunities to target the Latino electorate.

Research shows that in 2008 and 2012, Obama aggressively courted the Latino vote translating his campaign materials into Spanish, hired several staff as communications experts on Latino and immigration politics, and spent millions on Spanish-language advertisements and other outreach programs (e.g., Collingwood et al. 2014, 639). Clinton also hired Latino staff to focus on Latino communications and spend millions on advertisements but has been criticized for not establishing a long-term presence in Latino communities. Whereas Obama team spent time creating Latino organizing teams in battleground states, the Clinton campaign relied heavily on the opportunity to use Trump's ugly rhetoric as a rallying cry to mobilize Latinos. When the campaign did put Latino organizing teams on the ground (not until May by most accounts), these efforts emphasized Trump and his threats about immigration and failed to significantly address topics beyond immigration such as the economy and job creation, education, particularly issues raised by Bernie Sander's campaign including free college and the minimum wage, and health care—issues that are important to most voters, including Latinos (Phillip and O'Keefe 2016). Referencing this campaign, Janet Murguia, president of the National Council of La Raza, suggested that the Democratic Party, and by extension, Clinton's campaign was not taking "advantage of this moment in time, really looking to leverage more engagement in a more strategic way with our [Latino] community" (Phillip and O'Keefe 2016).

Conversely, Obama's team is credited for targeting the intricacies of the Latino community in 2008 and 2012. According to Freddy Balsera, a Miami-based political consultant who crafted much of Obama's Spanish-language advertising campaign in 2008, "When we were talking to a Latino voter in Colorado, we were discussing issues that mattered to them there. We did the same thing in Florida and took it a step further by talking to South Florida Hispanics with an announcer who was more Cuban-sounding. It was a more Puerto Rican-sounding voice in Orlando …. The campaign took care to localize the message and understood there's not a pan-Hispanic community. And as such, there's no universal pan-Latino messages" (Phillip and O'Keefe 2016). Thus, it is argued that Clinton's campaign failed to hire consultants who fully understand the cultural nuances of the Latino community and lacked culturally relevant and sensitive outreach toward the Latino community.

Lastly, Clinton's selection of Tim Kaine as her vice president can also be viewed as a missed opportunity to appeal to Latinos and mobilize the electorate. The presence of a co-ethnic candidate has been found to be a mobilizing force for Latinos (e.g., Barreto and Masuoka 2004, 9; Barreto et al. 2005, 76; Barreto 2007, 440).There was much speculation prior to her selection that Mexican-American Julian Castro, the former San Antonio mayor and Secretary of Housing and Urban Development under Obama, was being seriously considered as a vice-presidential running mate for Clinton (Debenedetti and Karni 2016). Often referred to as the "Latino Obama" because of their similar personal backgrounds and start in politics as grassroots community organizers, Castro offered the Clinton campaign an important substantive and symbolic gesture that may have helped turn out minority voters—especially Latinos—in anticipation of a drop off in support among white voters.

State Voter Identification Laws and Their Impact on Voting

The right to vote has long been a controversial and contested issue in American politics. Essentially denied the right and access to vote until the passage of the Voting Rights Act in 1965, racial and ethnic minorities in the United States have resisted and protested against systematic efforts to deny them the vote. In recent years, states have increasingly and aggressively adopted voter identification requirements. Before 2006, no state required photo identification to vote. As of 2016, 33 states had enacted some type of voter identification requirement. In the strictest of requirements, voters who do not possess the required form of identification are permitted to cast a provisional ballot, whereby the ballot is only counted after election officials verify the voter's eligibility. Less strict voter identification requirements allow individuals without identification to vote cast a ballot. While the enactment of these requirements has often been framed around issues of voter fraud and the quality of elections, the enactment of these laws has a disparate impact on racial and ethnic minorities and young people—both of whom tend to support Democratic candidates.

The 1965 Voting Rights Act, passed to end state disenfranchisement and voter suppression, had long been interpreted by the Court in such a way as to require states with a history of racial discrimination in voting to obtain federal approval to make changes in voting procedures and policies, with the specific intent of assuring that any change in the law did not have a discriminatory purpose or have a discriminatory effect. Several of these voter identification laws have been challenged in court and in many cases the Court has struck down or weakened these laws (e.g., Lee 2016). However, in 2013, the Supreme Court in a 5-4 vote struck down anti-discrimination protections in the Voting Rights Act, freeing nine states—Alabama, Alaska, Arizona, Georgia, Louisiana, Mississippi, South Carolina, Texas, and Virginia—and scores of counties and municipalities in other states from the preapproval process known as pre-clearance thereby allowing them to change their election laws without advance federal authorization.

Dropping this provision in the law has essentially eased the process by which states can enact voter identification laws whose purpose may not be to discriminate but do just that in its impact. 2016 was first presidential election held since the Supreme Court decision and 14 states had new voting restrictions in place for the first time in a presidential election. Several of those states including were states with large and/or rapidly growing African-American populations (e.g., Mississippi, Alabama, South Carolina, Virginia, Tennessee) and Latino populations (Arizona, Texas, Tennessee, South Carolina) (Brennan Center 2016).

Several studies examining the impact of voter identification laws on turnout show that when implemented, these laws making voting more difficult for eligible voters. For example, a report issued by the National Association of Latino Elected Officials concluded that laws implemented since Election Day 2012 would make voting in 2016 more difficult for at least 875,000 eligible

Latino voters (Gamboa 2016). Those laws include placing restrictions on registration, requiring specific IDs to vote, restrictions on absentee voting by mail, proof of citizenship requirements, and shortening registration and early voting periods. Using data from elections ranging from 2006 to 2014 to compare voter turnout rates between states with voter identification laws and those without, scholars Zoltan Hajnal, Nazita Lajevardi, and Lindsay Nielson (2017, 373) found that strict identification laws have a disproportionate impact on racial and ethnic minorities, affecting Latinos the most as turnout decreases by seven percentage points in general elections and five percentage points in primaries.

While a record of 137.5 million Americans voted in the 2016 presidential election, exit poll data suggests that minority turnout dropped (e.g., African-Americans) or held steady (e.g., Latinos). While there are a multitude of reasons why voter turnout may decline in an election year, the research on voter identification laws suggests that despite efforts by candidates and parties to mobilize Latino voters, systemic barriers put in place at the state level may hinder their ability to participate in and influence the electoral process.

NOT ALL LATINOS VOTE THE SAME—THE ROLE OF RELIGION AND GROUP CONSCIOUSNESS IN 2016

Latinos in the United States are not a monolithic group but rather a diverse group comprising people whose heritage reaches out to all corners of Latin America. Currently, the nation's Latino population is composed of people who trace their heritage to Mexico (63.4%), Puerto Rico (9.5%), El Salvador (3.8%), Cuba (3.7%), the Dominican Republic (3.3%), and Guatemala (2.4%). The remaining Latinos in the United States are of some other Central American, South American, or other Latino origin (U.S. Census Bureau 2015). Recognizing the heterogeneity of the Latino population, empirical evidence demonstrates that socioeconomic and demographic variables are consistently related to various forms of participation and shapes political behavior (e.g., Verba and Nie 1972, 95). National origin is highly important in the Latino community, as it is tied to differences in history and experience (DeSipio 1996, 78). Latinos of Mexican and Puerto Rican origin typically support the Democratic Party (DeSipio 1996, 103; Alvarez and Bedolla 2003, 43) while Cubans typically support the Republican Party. While the Democratic Party has historically done well with Latinos, winning a majority of Latino votes in presidential elections since 1960, the Latino vote in the 2016 election suggests that religion and group consciousness (specifically the low level of group consciousness among Latinos) may have had strong political consequences, negatively impacting Latinos' ability to collectively serve as a firewall for Clinton.

Religion

Religious affiliation has long been shown to influence political participation (e.g., Kellstedt and Green) and is a significant part of the Latino community. Catholicism has long been a core component Latino cultures and has been a point of cultural similarity. Yet, Latinos are becoming less Catholic over time. According to the Pew Research Center's 2013 National Survey of Latinos and Religion, a majority (55%) of the nation's Latino adults identify as Catholic today, as compared to the 22 percent who identify as Protestant (including 16% who describe themselves as born-again or evangelical) and the 18 percent of Latino who say they are religiously unaffiliated. This current percentage indicates a significant decline in the share of Hispanics who self-identify as Catholic, as more than two-thirds of Latinos in 2010 (67%) were Catholic (Pew Research Center 2014). Projections suggest that by 2030 at least 50 percent of all Latinos in the United States will be Protestant (Pew Research Center 2014).

In the 2016 election, Protestants favored Trump over Clinton, 58 percent to 39 percent. Latino Catholics supported Clinton 67 percent to 26 percent but Clinton's share of the Latino Catholic vote was down from percentage of Catholics who supported Obama in 2008 (72 %) and 2012 (75%) (see Table 4.2). This 8 percent drop in support from Latino Catholics might be explained by the emails released from the hack of Clinton campaign chairman John Podesta's private account less than a month before Election Day. In the emails, comments from staff were widely viewed as antagonistic to Catholics and their beliefs (Bailey 2016; Wolfgang 2016). According to Raymond Arroyo, lead anchor and managing editor of EWTN, the global Catholic network, the emails had the potential to tip the balance for undecided Catholic voters (Bailey 2016). Immediately after being released, Trump's campaign capitalized on leak, decrying the emails in remarks at Liberty University and the media (Bailey 2016). The Trump campaign also made a concerted effort to reach out to Latino conservative Christians, creating a Hispanic advisory council and meeting with ministers and visiting Latino congregations on the final Sunday before the election (Khalid 2016).

Group Consciousness

Empirical studies on Latino voting behavior suggest that ethnicity is a significant determinant of voting behavior (e.g., Calvo and Rosenstone 1989; de la Garza and DeSipio, 1992; 21). Latinos, when stimulated by sense of

Table 4.2   Presidential Vote by Religious Affiliation and Race

	2000		2004		2008		2012		2016		Dem change
	Gore	Bush	Kerry	Bush	Obama	McCain	Obama	Romney	Clinton	Trump	'12–'16
	%	%	%	%	%	%	%	%	%	%	%
Protestant/other Christian	42	56	40	59	45	54	42	57	39	58	–3
Catholic	50	47	47	52	54	45	50	48	45	52	–5
White Catholic	45	52	43	56	47	52	40	59	37	60	–3
Hispanic Catholic	65	33	65	33	72	26	75	21	67	26	–8
Jewish	79	19	74	25	78	21	69	30	71	24	+2
Other faiths	62	28	74	23	73	22	74	23	62	29	–12
Religiously unaffiliated	61	30	67	31	75	23	70	26	68	26	–2
White, born-again/ evangelical Christian	n/a	n/a	21	78	24	74	21	78	16	81	–5
Mormon	n/a	n/a	19	80	n/a	n/a	21	78	25	61	+4

Note: "Protestant" refers to people who describe themselves as "Protestant," "Mormon," or "other Christian" in exit polls; this categorization most closely approximates the exit poll data reported immediately after the election by media sources. The "white, born-again/evangelical Christian" row includes both Protestants and non-Protestants (e.g., Catholics, Mormons, etc.) who self-identify as born-again or evangelical Christians.
Source: Gregory A. Smith and Jessica Martinez, "How the Faithful Voters: A Preliminary 2016 Analysis." Pew Hispanic Center, November 9, 2016. Washington, D.C. (November 2016) http://www.pewresearch.org/fact-tank/2016/11/09/how-the-faithful-voted-a-preliminary-2016-analysis/.

commonality and ethnic group consciousness, are more likely to participate in a wide range of political activities, including voting (Stokes 2003). Despite being an extremely heterogeneous population, it is often presumed that there is a high level of group consciousness among Latinos. Research also shows that Latino group consciousness can also activate collective action members of a group feel threatened (Garcia, 2003). This in part may explain why it was widely believed that Trump's anti-Mexican and anti-immigrant comments throughout the campaign season would have the same energizing effect on Latinos, motivating them en masse to cast their vote against Trump.

Immediately following the 2016 election, scholars questioned the accuracy of national exits polls showing Trump with 28 percent of the Latino vote. Arguing that the National Election Poll systematically misrepresent voters of color, an election eve poll of 5600 Latino voters conducted by Latino Decisions shows Trump winning only 18 percent of the Latino vote (Sanchez and Barreto 2016). This 10 percent point difference between the polls has sparked some methodological debate about degree to which polls focus on the geographic and language diversity within the Latino community. Yet, regardless of which poll is most accurate, one might still argue that a substantial number of Latinos voted for Trump. Why? Preliminary qualitative research in the form of interviews suggests that some Latinos, well aware of Trump's remarks and policy positions, still were not mobilized to vote against him because they did not feel personally attacked. As one Latino noted, "Me, as a Puerto Rican, I did not really think he was addressing the entire Hispanic community…. I didn't feel that, me, as a Puerto Rican, that I was part of that group he was talking about." (Khalid 2016). This comment highlights the reality that Latinos can opt for many different forms of ethnic group identity, ranging from that based on national origin to that based on a racialized non-White status (Stokes-Brown 2012; 36). The development of group consciousness among Latinos requires a feeling of commonality and affinity among a large and diverse number of national-origin subgroups. When given the choice to self-identify, most Latinos prefer their family's country of origin over pan-ethnic terms like Latino or Hispanic. Furthermore, Latinos do not typically feel a strong sense of commonality or affinity with other Latino nationality groups, particularly Mexicans (Kauffman 2003, 205). Thus, to suggest that a sizable portion of the Latino electorate would indeed support Trump, despite kicking off his presidential campaign with anti-Mexican, anti-immigrant rhetoric and arguing that a Mexican-American judge was not capable of being impartial because of his ethnic heritage, is not unimaginable. This also suggests that despite its powerful impact on Latino political behavior in the 2012 election (e.g., Barreto and Collingwood 2015, 494; Wallace 2012, 1382), immigration, particularly when explicitly framed as Mexican immigration, was a weaker mobilizing issue in 2016. Thus when

Trump discussed tightening borders, increasing deportations, and building a wall, some Latinos, ambivalent or strongly opposed to undocumented immigration, were supportive of his proposed policies.

Trump famously campaigned on the slogan "Make America Great Again"—a phrase where "great" was interpreted as "white" by many Americans and many were mobilized, particularly working-class whites and white women, giving Trump victories in traditionally Democratic states like Michigan, Wisconsin, and Pennsylvania. But that same slogan and campaign rhetoric did not appear to incite a common enmity among Latinos so great that they alone could be a firewall to ensure a Clinton victory. Extant research suggests that in the future as Latino group consciousness grows, the Democratic Party may be able to rely solidly on the Latino vote given that group consciousness significantly increases the probability of Democratic identification (Urbano 2011, 12). But until the number of group conscious Latinos in the United States grows, it is presumptuous to suggest that Latinos will inherently serve as a Democratic firewall.

CONCLUSION

Latinos have long been discussed as potential game changers and difference makers in American politics. Yet, the narrative of the 2016 presidential election was somehow different. Given the tone and climate expressed by Republican Party candidates during the primaries, and ascension of Trump as the eventual nominee, Latinos were not only predicted to turnout in record numbers but overwhelmingly give their support to the Democratic nominee Clinton to openly repudiate Trump.

What we do know is that part of this narrative is true. A record number of Latinos—27.3 million—were eligible to vote in 2016, up 4 million from four years ago, representing the largest increases of any racial or ethnic group (Krogstad and Lopez 2016). The number of Latino voters grew to a record 12.7 million in 2016, up from 11.2 million in 2012 and the Latino electorate also grew in many states including Arizona, Florida, and Nevada (Krogstad and Lopez 2017; 2016). Yet, Latino voter turnout dropped slightly from 48 percent in 2012 to 47.6 percent in 2016, despite predictions of a historic surge.

What we do know is that Also, while most Latinos voted Democratic as in past elections, we did not see Latinos move in droves away from the Republican Party and Trump.

Examining the myths and realities of the Trump Effect in the 2016 election, this chapter suggests that four factors, among others, contributed the outcome of the election. While there is still much to learn about the role and impact of the Latino electorate, it is clear that while Latino participation benefited the

Democratic Party (due to the higher levels of Democratic partisanship among most Latinos in the United States) and Clinton won handily among Latinos, neither Trump nor Clinton campaigns spurred Latinos to the polls and Latinos did not serve as Clinton's blue firewall.

Yet, the political importance of Latinos has in no way diminished. As one of the fastest-growing portion of the electorate, Latinos constitutes a significant presence in the United States and, through coalition-building with other key constituencies, are poised to play an ever growing role in shaping national as well as state and local policy. Where the Latino influence may have been limited in the 2016 presidential race, it is likely to be more dramatic and impactful in 2020 and beyond. Therefore, scholars and pundits alike will continue to hold on to expectations of Latino influence and intensely watch and wait for the "sleeping giant" in American politics to awake.

NOTES

1. To be clear Latinos in some states like Nevada, Colorado, and New Mexico did provide Obama with the margin of victory (St George and Dennis 2012).

2. "When Mexico sends its people, they're not sending their best. They're not sending you. They're sending people that have lots of problems, and they're bringing those problems with us. They're bringing drugs. They're bringing crime. They're rapists. And some, I assume, are good people." Donald Trump, announcement speech, June 2015.

3. Several scholars have questioned the accuracy of national exit polls, arguing the polls systematically misrepresent all voters of color. An election eve poll of 5600 Latino voters conducted by Latino Decisions shows Clinton winning Latinos by 79 percent with 18 percent supporting Trump (Sanchez and Barreto 2016). For the sake of consistency, I reference the national exit polls throughout the paper. I also discuss the Latino Decisions poll in greater depth in the section of the paper addressing group consciousness.

REFERENCES

Abrajano, Marisa A. 2010. *Campaigning to the New Electorate*. Palo Alto, CA: Stanford University Press.

Abrajano, Marisa and Costas Panagopoulos. 2011. "Does Language Matter? The Impact of Spanish Versus English-Language GOTV Efforts on Latino Turnout." *American Politics Research* 39: 643–663.

Alvarez, R. Michael, and Lisa Garcia Bedolla. 2003. "The Foundations of Latino Voter Partisanship: Evidence from the 2000 Election." *Journal of Politics* 65: 31–49.

Bailey, Sarah Pulliam. 2016. "WikiLeaks Emails Appear to Show Clinton Spokeswoman Joking About Catholics and Evangelicals." *Washington Post*, October 13. Accessed December 1, 2016. https://www.washingtonpost.com/news/acts-of-faith/

wp/2016/10/12/wikileaks-emails-show-clinton-spokeswoman-joking-about-catho-lics-and-evangelicals/?utm_term=.93aad8ef4b3b.

Barreto, Matt A. and Loren Collingwood. 2015. "Group –Based Appeals and the Latino Vote in 2012: How Immigration Became a Mobilizing Issue." *Electoral Studies* 40: 490–499.

Barreto, Matt A. 2007. "¡Sí Se Puede! Latino Candidates and the Mobilization of Latino Voters." *American Political Science Review* 101: 425–441.

Barreto, Matt A., Mario Villarreal and Nathan D. Woods. 2005. "Metropolitan Latino Political Behavior: Voter Turnout and Candidate Preference in Los Angeles." *Journal of Urban Affairs* 27: 71–91.

Barreto, Matt A., and Natalie Masuoka. 2004. "Do Co-ethnic Candidates Change the Stakes for Latino and Asian American voters? Voter turnout in 2002." Paper presented at the annual meeting of the American Political Science Association, Chicago.

Barreto, Matt A., Loren Collingwood, and Sylvia Manzano. 2010. "A New Measure of Group Influence in Presidential Elections: Assessing Latino Influence in 2008." *Political Research Quarterly* 63: 908–21.

Brown, Anna and Mark Hugo Lopez. 2013. "Mapping the Latino Population, By State, County and City: Ranking Latino Populations in the States" *Pew Hispanic Center*, August 29. Accessed December 2, 2016. http://www.pewhispanic.org/2013/08/29/ii-ranking-latino-populations-in-the-states/.

Calvo, Maria Antonia, and Steven J. Rosenstone. *Hispanic Political Participation.* Southwest Voter Research Institute, San Antonio: Southwest Voter Research Institute, 1989.

Colby, Sandra L. and Jennifer M. Ortman. 2015. "Projections of the Size and Composition of the U.S. Population: 2014 to 2060 Population Estimates and Projections Current Population Reports," U.S. Census Bureau, March. Accessed on December 2, 2016. https://www.census.gov/content/dam/Census/library/publications/2015/demo/p25-1143.pdf.

Collins, Eliza. 2015. "Why Hispanics are Thanking Donald Trump." *Politico*, September 19. http://www.politico.com/story/2015/09/donald-trump-hispanics-213831 (accessed November 28, 2016).

Collingwood, Loren, Matt A. Barreto, and Sergio I. Garica-Rios. 2014. "Revisiting Latino Voting Cross-Racial Mobilization in the 2012 Election." *Political Research Quarterly* 67: 632–45.

de la Garza, Rodolfo O., and Louis DeSipio, ed. 1992. From Rhetoric to Reality: Latino Politics in the 1988 elections." *Boulder, CO: Westview.*

de la Garza, Rodolfo O., Marissa Abrajano, and Jeronima Cortina. 2008. "Get Me to the Polls on Time: Co- ethnic Mobilization and Latino Turnout." In *New Race Politics in America: Understanding Minority and Immigrant Politics*, edited by Jane Junn and Kerry Haynie, 95–113. New York, NY: Cambridge University Press.

Debenedetti, Gabriel and Annie Karni. 2015. "The Campaign to Put 2016 Juliam Castro on Hillary's VP Short List" *Politico*, June 4. Accessed December 4, 2016. http://www.politico.com/story/2015/06/clinton-campaign-julian-castro-hillary-vp-hispanic-118619.

Decker, Cathleen. 2016. "Pennsylvania Was Once Merely Important in Presidential Elections. Now, it's Hillary Clinton's Firewall." *Los Angeles Times*, October 3. Accessed December 2, 2016. http://www.latimes.com/politics/la-na-pol-pennsyl-vania-firewall-20161003-snap-story.html.

DeFrancesco Soto, Victoria M. and Jennifer L. Merolla. 2008. "Se Habla Espanol: Ethnic Campaign Strategies and Latino Voting Behavior." In *New Race Politics in America: Understanding Minority and Immigrant Politics*, edited by Jane Junn and Kerry Haynie, 114-129. New York, NY: Cambridge University Press.

DeSipio, Louis. 1996. *Counting on the Latino Vote: Latinos as a New Electorate.* Charlottesville, VA: University of Virginia Press.

Durand, Jorge, Edward Telles, and Jennifer Flashman. 2006. "The Demographic Foundations of the Latino Population." In *Hispanics and the Future of America*, edited by Marta Tienda and Faith Mitchell, 66-99. National Academies Press: Washington, D.C.

Ennis Sharon R., Merarys Rios-Vargas, and Nora G. Albert. 2011. *The Hispanic population, 2010 (Census brief C2010BR-4).* Washington, DC: U.S. Census Bureau.

Gamboa, Suzanne. 2016. "Tougher Voting Laws Will Heavily Impact Latinos in 2016: Report " NBC News, May 11. Accessed December 9, 2016. http://www.nbcnews.com/news/latino/tougher-voting-laws-will-heavily-impact-latinos-2016-report-n571396.

Garcia, John. 2003. *Latino Politics in America: Community, Culture, and Interests.* New York, NY: Rowman & Littlefield Publishers, Inc.

Hajnal, Zoltan, Nazita Lajevardi, and Lindsay Nielson. 2017. "Voter Identification Laws and the Suppression of Minority Votes," *The Journal of Politics* 79: 363–379.

Halloran, Liz. 2012. "Where They Stand: Obama, Romney On Immigration." *NPR* July 11. Accessed December 22, 2016. http://www.npr.org/2012/07/06/156381703/where-they-stand-obama-romney-on-immigration.

Jackson, Melinda S. 2011. "Priming the Sleeping Giant: The Dynamics of Latino Political Identity and Vote Choice." *Political Psychology* 32: 691–716.

Jackson, Robert A. 2003. "Differential Influences on Latino Electoral Participation." *Political Behavior* 25: 339—366.

Kaufmann, Karen M. 2003. "Cracks in the Rainbow: Group Commonality as a Basis for Latino and African-American Political Coalitions." *Political Research Quarterly* 56: 199–210.

Khalid, Asma. 2016. "Latinos Will Never Vote For A Republican, And Other Myths About Hispanics From 2016." *NPR,* December 22. Accessed December 4, 2016. http://www.npr.org/2016/12/22/506347254/latinos-will-never-vote-for-a-republican-and-other-myths-about-hispanics-from-20.

Krogstad, Jens Manuel and Mark Hugo Lopez. 2017. "Black Voter Turnout Fell in 2016, Even as a Record Number of Americans Cast Ballots." *Pew Research Center*, May 12. Accessed May 20, 2017. http://www.pewresearch.org/fact-tank/2017/05/12/black-voter-turnout-fell-in-2016-even-as-a-record-number-of-americans-cast-ballots/.

Kellstedt, Lyman, and John Green. 1993. "Knowing God's Many People: Denominational Preference and Political Behavior." In *Rediscovering the Religious Factor in*

American Politics, edited by David Leege and Lyman Kellstedt, 53–71. Armonk, NY: M.E. Sharpe.

Leal, David L., Jerod Patterson, and Joe R. Tafoya. 2016. "Religion and the Political Engagement of Latino Immigrants: Bridging Capital or Segmented Religious Assimilation?" *RSF: The Russell Sage Foundation Journal of the Social Sciences* 2: 125–146.

Lee, Jasmine C. 2016. "How States Moved Toward Stricter Voter ID Laws" *New York Times*, November 3. Accessed December 20, 2016. https://www.nytimes. com/interactive/2016/11/03/us/elections/how-states-moved-toward-stricter-voter-id-laws.html.

Lopez, Mark Hugo. 2008. "The Hispanic Vote in the 2008 Election." *Pew Research Center*, November 5. Accessed December 2, 2016. http://www.pewhispanic. org/2008/11/05/the-hispanic-vote-in-the-2008-election/.

Lopez, Mark Hugo and Paul Taylor. 2012. "Latino Voters in the 2012 Election." *Pew Research Center*, November 7. Accessed December 1, 2016. http://www.pewhispanic.org/2012/11/07/latino-voters-in-the-2012-election/.

Michelson, Melissa R. 2005. "Meeting the Challenge of Latino Voter Mobilization." *The Annals of the American Academy of Political and Social Science* 601: 85–101.

Michelson Melissa. 2003. "Getting out the Latino Vote: How Door-to-Door Canvassing Influences Voter Turnout in Rural Central California." *Political Behavior* 25: 247–63.

Panagopoulous, Costas and Donald P. Green. 2010. "Spanish-Language Radio Advertisements and Latino Voter Turnout in the 2006 Congressional Elections: Field Experimental Evidence." *Political Research Quarterly* 64: 588–599.

Pew Research Center. 2014. "The Shifting Religious Identity of Latinos in the United States." May 7. Accessed December 1, 2016. http://www.pewforum. org/2014/05/07/the-shifting-religious-identity-of-latinos-in-the-united-states/.

Pew Research Center. 2012. "Changing Face of American Helps Assure Obama Victory." November 7. Accessed December 15, 2016. http://www.people-press. org/2012/11/07/changing-face-of-america-helps-assure-obama-victory/.

Phillip, Abby and Ed O'Keefe. 2016. "Among Democrats, Deep Concern About Clinton's Hispanic Strategy" *Washington Post*, September 18. Accessed November 5, 2016. (https://www.washingtonpost.com/politics/among-democrats-deep-concern-about-clintons-hispanic-strategy/2016/09/18/38d3b99a-7c54-11e6-bd86-b7bbd53d2b5d_story.html?utm_term=.59dc61936bde).

Preston, Julia. 2008. "In Big Shift, Latino Vote Was Heavily for Obama." *New York Times* November 6. Accessed November 20, 2016. http://www.nytimes. com/2008/11/07/us/politics/07latino.html.

Rodriguez, Cindy Y. 2012. "Latino Vote Key to Obama's Re-election." *CNN* November 11. Accessed December 1, 2016. http://www.cnn.com/2012/11/09/politics/latino-vote-key-election/index.html.

Schulthesis, Emily. 2016. "Donald Trump Doubles Down in Immigration Speech: "Mexico Will Pay for the Wall" *CBS News*. August 31. Accessed December 7, 2016. http://www.cbsnews.com/news/donald-trump-delivers-immigration-speech-in-phoenix/.

Shaw, Daron, Rodolfo O de la Garza, Jongho Lee. 2000. "Examining Latino Turnout in 1996: A Three State, Validated Survey Approach." *American Journal of Political Science* 44: 338–346.

St George, Donna and Brady Dennis. 2012. "Growing Share of Hispanic Voters Helped Push Obama to Victory." *Washington Post* November 7. Accessed December 14, 2016. https://www.washingtonpost.com/politics/decision2012/growing-share-of-hispanic-voters-helped-push-obama-to-victory/2012/11/07/b4087d0a-28ff-11e2-b4e0-346287b7e56c_story.html?utm_term=.ddbdada58f95\.

Stepler, Renee and Mark Hugo Lopez. 2016. "U.S. Latino Population Growth and Dispersion Has Slowed Since Onset of the Great Recession: Ranking the Latino Population in the States." *Pew Hispanic Center* September 8. Accessed November 11, 2016. http://www.pewhispanic.org/2016/09/08/4-ranking-the-latino-population-in-the-states/.

Stokes, Atiya Kai. 2003. "Latino Group Consciousness and Political Participation." *American Politics Research* 31: 361–378.

Stokes-Brown, Atiya Kai. 2012. *The Politics of Race in Latino Communities: Walking the Color Line*. New York, NY: Routledge.

Taylor, Ramon. 2016. "Clinton Campaign Aims to Build Latino Firewall in New York" *VOA News*, April 7. Accessed December 15, 2016. https://www.voanews.com/a/hillary-clinton-presidential-campaign-new-york-latinos/3273368.html\.

Trende, Sean. 2015. "The Path to the Presidency: The Past and Future Look of the Electoral College." *The Surge: 2014's Big GOP Win and What it Means for the Next Presidential Election*, edited by Larry Sabato, Kyle Kondik and Geoffrey Skelly, 195-210. Lanham, MD: Rowman and Littlefield.

Tyson, Alec and Shiva Maniam. 2016. "Behind Trump's Victory: Divisions by Race, Gender, Education," *Pew Research Center*, November 9. Accessed December 1, 2016. http://www.pewresearch.org/fact-tank/2016/11/09/behind-trumps-victory-divisions-by-race-gender-education/.

U.S. Census Bureau. 2011. "2010 Census Shows Nation's Hispanic Population Grew Four Times Faster Than Total U.S. Population," May 26. Accessed November 20, 2016. https://www.census.gov/newsroom/releases/archives/2010_census/cb11-cn146.html.

Urbano, Juan. 2011. "All For One? Latino Group Consciousness and Partisanship." Paper presented at the Western Political Science Association Annual Meeting.

Verba, Sidney, and Norman H. Nie. 1972. *Participation in America*. Harper & Row.

Wallace, Sophia J. 2012. "It's Complicated: Latinos, President Obama, and the 2012 Election." *Social Science Quarterly* 93: 1360–1383.

Wolfgang, Ben. 2016. "Clinton Campaign Mocks Catholics, Southerners, 'needy Latinos' in Emails." *Washington Times* October 12. Accessed December 1, 2016. http://www.washingtontimes.com/news/2016/oct/12/hillary-clinton-campaigns-wikileaks-emails-reveal-/.

Chapter 5

Age and Gender Intersectionality in the 2016 Presidential Election

Elizabeth Hahn Rickenbach and Elizabeth P. Ossoff

The 2016 U.S. presidential election included the two oldest candidates in the country's history and the first female presidential nominee for a major political party. Media coverage of the election often focused on the role of key voter characteristics including younger age (i.e., Millenials), race, and socioeconomic status in terms of candidate preference, party preference, voter enthusiasm, and turnout (e.g., Alcindor 2016, Rucker 2016, Montanaro 2016). However, less attention in the coverage of the election was given to the role of age across the adult lifespan and gender in relation to voting behavior as well as the interaction of age and gender. It is well documented in the experimental and social psychological literature that social norms are predictive of behavior (Asch 1956, Milgram, Bickman, and Berkowitz 1969) such that individuals ascribe to the expected behaviors as well as approvals and disapprovals of the group(s) with which they identify, such as an age or gender group. Research that incorporates psychological and sociological perspectives, and in particular, gender and gerontological frameworks, is therefore needed to better understand the role and relation of age and gender in terms of behavior related to voting and politics. This chapter will 1) review the historical influence of gender, age, and their intersectionality in voting behavior, 2) provide an overview of voting preference and behaviors broken down by age and gender for the 2016 presidential election, and 3) provide scholarly and theoretical explanations drawn from psychological, sociological, gender, and gerontological research for their possible role in the election. The chapter will conclude with considerations for the future role of age and gender for voting behavior and political preference.

Age

A number of factors necessitate the empirical and theoretical examination of the role of age across the lifespan in relation to voting behavior. Over the next few decades, the United States is expected to double in the number of individuals aged 65 years and older from 43.1 million in 2012 to an estimated 83.7 million in 2050 (Ortman, Velkoff, and Hogan 2014). Challenges that may accompany older adulthood include adjustment to a fixed income and an increased risk of chronic health problems. Public programs like Social Security and Medicare have improved the quality of life of older adults by providing greater financial security and access to health care since their enactment in 1935 and 1965, respectively (Schulz and Binstock 2008). Since the early 1960s, Social Security has provided the largest share of income for adults aged 65 and over (Social Security Administration 2014). An aging population, a decline in employer-sponsored pension plans, and the retirement of the Baby Boomer population (born 1946–1964) present challenges to the sustainability of Social Security and Medicare.

Another factor important for the discussion of age and voting is the historical trend for older adults (OA) to have a higher voter turnout rate (Binstock 2012, Plutzer 2002, Binstock 2000) compared to other age groups. In the 2012 presidential election, voter turnout was 71.9 percent among adults 65 and older compared to 41.2 percent among those 18–24 (United States Census Bureau 2012). Political analyses of elections in the past few decades have pointed to the "senior" vote as an increasingly important issue to shape political discussions (Binstock 2012). Since the election of John F. Kennedy in 1960, politicians have dedicated campaign resources to older voters and issues relevant to OA (Riemer and Binstock 1978, Binstock 2012). Conversely, young adults (YA) (i.e., the Millennial generation born 1981–1997) are also a large cohort; in 2016, Millennials for the first time outnumbered Generation X (born 1965–1980) in the workplace and they outnumbered Baby Boomers in total size within the population (Fry, 2016). Thus, YA increasingly make up a significant portion of the electorate and will play a greater role in politics as they are increasingly likely to function as voters, parents, workers, and other roles within society with relevance for political discussions. These changing demographics point to the need for an examination of the behaviors, preferences, and voting characteristics across the adult lifespan.

From a social psychological perspective, an examination of the role of age in voting behavior includes an examination of whether individuals identify with their age (as compared to other factors like gender or race) when they vote. Since the 2004 election of George W. Bush, OAs have leaned Republican and been increasingly conservative compared to other age groups (Binstock 2009, 2012, Norrander and Wilcox 2008). Perceived threats to issues important to older adults, such as Medicare, have been predictive of OAs' recent voting behavior. For example, in the 2010 Midterm elections, concerns of changes to Medicare as part of the Affordable Care Act (ACA) spread throughout town hall meetings across the United States (e.g., fear of *death panels*) and these concerns were identified as a key factor leading to the Republican-leaning results in Congress (for middle-aged men, in particular, and older adults, in general) (Binstock 2012). This *death panel* myth, initiated by former vice-presidential candidate Sarah Palin, was in reference to proposed payment to physicians for voluntary counseling for end-of-life issues among older adult patients. This proposal was eventually taken out of the Patient Protection and Affordable Care Act (ACA, 2010). Overall, the ACA changes largely increased the long-term sustainability of Medicare through increased accessibility to prescription drugs and increased access to preventive care. In the 2016 presidential campaign, both major party candidates stated that they would not make any cuts to Medicaid, Medicare, or Social Security. In addition, Donald Trump campaigned on the promise to repeal and replace the ACA without a detailed plan for replacement, a promise that resonated with some conservatives, including seniors.

Gerontological and developmental psychology research provide a framework for the examination of age and its role in voting behavior. In particular, Heckhausen's (1997) work on primary and secondary control strategies posits that individuals develop tools to regulate decreases in age-related gains and increases in age-related losses. This theory posits that younger adults engage more in primary control strategies, which are "attempts to change the external world so that it fits the needs and desires of the individual" (176) while older adults may recognize potential for loss and therefore engage more in secondary control strategies (Heckhausen 1997). Secondary control strategies refer to efforts by the individual to modify or change the "internal world" so that he or she adapts to their world (Heckhausen 1997). In the context of the 2016 presidential election, younger adults may have been more likely to engage in primary control strategies such as canvassing, phone banking to "change the external world" to more closely fit within their beliefs. On the other hand, older adults may have been more likely to engage in secondary control strategies, including internal processes to more closely align their ideals with their world (e.g., rationalizing that he or she could be worse, goal flexibility, and increased satisfaction with current situation in relation to other possible situations). Similarly, classic psychological research on cognitive dissonance by Festinger (1962) demonstrated that individuals seek to make two seemingly inconsistent beliefs or actions (e.g., loving your spouse but disagreeing with them politically, not liking a candidate but voting for them) consistent through techniques (e.g., changing beliefs, seek alternative information) in order to reduce the tension or discomfort produced by the inconsistency.

Gender

Historically, gender has played a prominent role in the analyses of political behavior. Since the 1970s, women have consistently voted at higher rates for Democratic presidential candidates and identified as more liberal compared to men (Norrander and Wilcox 2008). One explanation for the gender gap in recent decades involves voters' response to the current administrations and policies and their subsequent desire for changes to those policies (Kellstedt, Peterson, and Ramirez 2010). Specifically, Kellstedt and colleagues (2010) identified that when policies are more liberal, (e.g., the past eight years of the Obama administration) voters in general move toward a conservative direction. Kellstedt also documented that men are less stable in their views over time and change their views at a faster rate than women. Thus, over time this gender-related trend in voting behavior can increase the gender gap and especially during times of liberal policy. In the 2016 presidential election, women may have also been motivated by a first-time female candidate for a major political party. In an analyses of 35 different countries, Karp & Banducci (2008) documented that women are more likely to engage in the political process when fellow women are elected to national legislatures. In the current election, it is also relevant to note the Republican candidate's questionable record with respect to women and issues important to women.

Additionally, although men historically favor Republican candidates, this year's Republican presidential nominee had no prior political experience and this election was also unique in that it included a female candidate for the first time for a major political party. Experimental research has demonstrated that men may tolerate less experience from male candidates than female candidates, supporting a "competence-based stereotype" (Huddy and Terkildsen 1993). Research by Ditonto and colleagues showed that the gender of the candidate influenced the information that voters seek out and attend to (Ditonto, Hamilton, and Redlawsk 2014). Voters, especially Republican women sought out more "competence-related" information for female candidates as compared to male candidates (Ditonto, Hamilton, and Redlawsk 2014). Other information available to the participants in the study was information regarding candidate traits and candidate stance on issues. The finding of Republican women, in particular, as driving the search for competence information was explained by the authors in part by the 2008 vice-presidential candidate, Sarah Palin.

Social psychological research also frames the analyses of gender and political behavior in the 2016 presidential election. In particular, role congruity theory (RCT) (Eagly and Karau 2002) posits that women seeking leadership roles encounter at least two specific challenges: 1) to be deemed competent and confident for the role and 2) to overcome the "backlash" for the incongruity between their agentic traits and accepted gender norms for female behavior such as nurturance and interpersonal sensitivity. According to RCT, men do not face similar hurdles given the congruence between agentic traits and gender norms for male behavior. Experimental research has provided support for this theory (Rudman et al. 2012, Joshi 2014). In Rudman and colleagues' (2012) research, participants' showed preference for men to have traits that are status-enhancing (e.g., dominant) whereas women were preferred to have traits that are status neutral or attenuating (e.g., emotional). Their research, using written and phone interview methodologies with trained confederates, showed that when female (but not male) hypothetical job candidates were identified as more agentic, they were simultaneously also judged as less "likable." Similarly, Joshi (2014) examined how male and females rated fellow team members in typically male-dominated fields such as science or engineering. This work showed that highly educated females are rated higher by females than by males; however, highly educated males receive high ratings regardless of the gender of the rater. In addition, male raters evaluated male team members as higher (regardless of their education level) as compared to their ratings for female team members (Joshi 2014).

Religiosity of voters may also be informative for understanding the role of gender. Work by Cassese & Holman (2016) examined the role of gender differences in religiosity, and in particular, beliefs of Biblical literalism (i.e., "that the Bible is the actual word of God and should be taken literally"). Their findings showed that while church attendance is related to greater political participation, Biblical literalism is "demobilizing." Furthermore, for women, Biblical literalism reinforces gender norms associated with inequality toward women (Cassese and Holman 2016). These perspectives may extend to their candidate, voting, and party preferences and may have been relevant for the 2016 presidential election which included a female candidate.

Intersectionality of Age and Gender

While research has long documented a gender gap in politics (Klein 1984, Kaufmann 2002, Norrander and Wilcox 2008), there has been less research focused on whether the gender gap varies across the lifespan (i.e., gender by age effects). Separate examinations of the role of age and gender ignores the possibility and likelihood that patterns among women differ for younger versus older voters, for example, and patterns related to age may differ for men versus women. An examination of the role of age (and age by gender effects) in voting behavior must also consider whether any differences that exist are due to age or cohort. While middle-aged and older women are part of the "second wave of feminism," younger women who came of age during the 1990s are part of the "third wave" of feminism (Snyder 2008) and therefore may approach women in leadership roles differently and feminism more ambiguously (Aronson 2003). They may find it more normative to see women in leadership roles but they may also believe the need for feminism is over and taken care of by their mothers and grandmothers. Among men, there may also be generational differences in terms of acceptance of women in leadership roles and/or Republican-leaning tendencies.

It should be noted that the data examined here do not permit the examination of variations by race, ethnicity, socioeconomic status, or other factors that further differentiate and reflect the diversity and variation within the "older adult vote" or the "gender gap." Binstock's (2012) work identified that the right-leaning "senior bloc" varied substantially by race and ethnicity. While 63 percent of the older adult White voters voted for Republican congressional candidates in the 2010 election, only 40 percent of older adults Hispanic voters and 8 percent of older adult Black voters endorsed Republican congressional candidates. The salience of issues important for older adults may also differ as a function of socioeconomic status; for example, the lowest quintile of older adults rely on Social Security for 80.7 percent of their income, while the highest quintile relies on Social Security, on average, for only 15.4 percent of their income (Social Security Administration 2014). Furthermore, within the gender gap, highly educated women have become more liberal whereas less-educated, religious, and/or non-working women have become more conservative. Norrander and Wilcox (2008) explain that the discussion of a "gender gap" ignores this division of women whereby some have become more conservative and others more liberal-leaning. For further discussion of some of these additional influences of race, ethnicity, and religiosity, we refer to the previous chapter on the Latino vote, in particular, as well as the future directions at the end of this chapter.

Current Study

This chapter will review exit poll data from the 2016 presidential election to better understand the roles of age, gender, and their intersectionality in the 2016 election. Specifically, this study will examine the main and interaction effects of age and gender trends in relation to presidential voting behavior as well as perspectives on the Democratic and Republican parties and their respective candidates.

METHOD

Sample and Procedure

Edison Research Institute exit poll data from voters (n=24,558) across the United States was analyzed for the current study. Demographic information for the entire sample is reported in Table 5.1. Exit polls were conducted with

Table 5.1   Demographic Characteristics of Exit Poll Sample (n=24,558)

Age	18–24	10
	25–29	9
	30–39	17
	40–44	9
	45–49	10
	50–59	21
	60–64	9
	65+	16
Gender (Female)		53
Education	High school or less	18
	Some college/assoc.	32
	College graduate	32
	Postgraduate	18
Race	White	72
	Black	12
	Hispanic/Latino	8
	Asian	4
	American Indian	1
	Other	2
Family income	Under 30,000	17
	30–49,999	19
	50–99,999	30
	100–199,999	24
	200,000+	10
Hispanic or Latino		13
LGBT		5
Married		59
Religion	Protestant	27
	Catholic	23
	Mormon	1
	Other Christian	24
	Jewish	3
	Muslim	1
	Other	7
	None	15
Citizen		91
Party ID	Democrat	36
	Republican	33
	Independent	24
	Something else	7
On most matters, do you consider yourself	Liberal	26
	Moderate	39
	Conservative	35
Veteran		13

Source: Edison Exit Poll (2016).

voters after their votes had been cast at their polling places. Interviews were conducted from poll opening until an hour before closing. Stratified probability sampling from each state was conducted and sample sizes vary from state to state. Participation in the exit polls was voluntary and anonymous. In the current study, polling data included demographic information, questions about the individual's presidential vote, as well as questions about the Democratic Party and Hillary Clinton and the Republican Party and Donald Trump. All questions except the demographic information are presented separately by age (young adults: 18–29 years, middle-aged adults: 30–64, and older voters: 65+) and gender categories.

Measures

Demographic Information

Participants reported their age, gender, education, race, ethnicity, family income, sexual orientation, marital status, veteran status, religion, citizenship, political party identification, as well as their political ideology. Education included four categories: high school or less, some college or associates degree, college graduate, and postgraduate. Participants identified their race as White, Black, Hispanic/Latino, Asian, American Indian, or other. Participants reported whether they identified their sexual orientation as Lesbian, Gay, Bisexual, or Transgender. Participants identified as Protestant, Catholic, Mormon, Other Christian, Jewish, Muslim, other, or none. Participants identified their party affiliation as Democrat, Republican, Independent, or "something else." Finally, participants also identified their political ideology as liberal, moderate, or conservative.

Presidential Vote

Participants self-reported their choice for presidential vote, their choice in a hypothetical two-way race, and their perspective regarding the candidate who would make the best commander in chief. Participants then reported how strongly they favor their candidate (*strongly favor, like my candidate with reservations, or dislike the other candidates*), which qualities matter most in deciding their vote for president, and when they decided their vote for president. These last three items were reported as a function of who they voted for (in addition to age and gender).

Democratic Party and Candidate Preferences

Participants self-reported favorability (or unfavorability) for the Democratic party and Hillary Clinton. They then self-reported whether they thought Hillary Clinton was qualified, had the temperament to serve effectively as president, and was honest and trustworthy. Lastly, they self-reported how they would feel if she were elected president (*excited, optimistic, concerned, or scared*) and the extent to which Hillary Clinton's use of private email while Secretary of State bothered them (*a lot, some, not much,* or *not at all*).

Republican Party and Candidate Preferences

Participants self-reported favorability (or unfavorability) for the Republican party and Donald Trump. They also self-reported whether they thought Donald Trump was qualified, had the temperament to serve effectively as president, and was honest and trustworthy. Participants then self-reported how they would feel if Donald Trump were elected president (*excited, optimistic, concerned,* or *scared*) and to what extent his treatment of women bothered them (*a lot, some, not much,* or *not at all*).

RESULTS

Presidential Vote

Figure 5.1 displays an age by gender breakdown for presidential vote and voter preference for the better commander in chief. As Figure 5.1 shows, the gender gap was qualified by age. While middle-aged and older men were more likely to vote for Trump, younger men were more likely to vote for Clinton. For women, the gender gap was reduced with age such that older women were less likely to vote for Clinton than younger women. Figure 5.1 also shows voter preferences for the candidate that would be a better commander in chief. A similar pattern emerged where younger men favor Clinton and middle-aged and older men favored Trump. For women, the preference for Clinton varied by age group such that younger women favored Clinton by the largest margin for the commander in chief role where for middle-aged women the margin was the smallest (see Figure 5.1).

Table 5.2 displays additional characteristics regarding voter preferences about the presidential vote as a function of age, gender, and candidate choice. Table 5.2 shows that for men, regardless of their vote for president, older voters were more likely to strongly favor their candidate than younger voters. However, among older female voters, only Clinton voters (not Trump voters) were more likely to strongly favor their candidate as compared to younger and middle-aged female voters. In regard to qualities that matter most in deciding the vote for president, Clinton voters regardless of gender were more likely to care about "has the right experience" and "has good judgment" whereas Trump voters regardless of gender were overwhelmingly interested in "can bring needed change." Compared to women, men were more interested in a candidate that "can bring needed change"; compared to men, women were more interested in a candidate that "has the right experience." Regarding

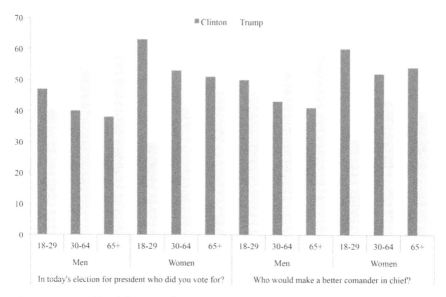

Figure 5.1   Presidential Vote and Commander in Chief Preference by Age and Gender.
Source: Edison Exit Poll (2016)" to bottom of Figure 5.1.

when voters made their decision for whom to vote, most voters made their choice prior to September 2016, regardless of age, gender, or candidate choice. Across voters, there was a trend for older voters to decide earlier than younger voters. In addition, male voters for Clinton decided slightly later than female voters for Clinton. Conversely, female voters for Trump decided slightly later than male voters for Trump.

Democratic Party and Hillary Clinton

Figure 5.2 displays the favorability ratings for both the Democratic Party and Hillary Clinton as a function of age and gender. Women had more favorable views of both the Democratic Party and Hillary Clinton. Favorability ratings were similar across age groups for men. Among women, middle-aged and older voters had less favorable views than younger voters.

Participants also self-reported whether Hillary Clinton was qualified, had the temperament to serve, was honest and trustworthy, what they would feel if she was elected president, and whether her private email use as Secretary of State bothered them Table 5.3. Women were more likely than men to view Hillary Clinton as qualified, that she had the temperament to serve effectively as president, and that she was honest and trustworthy. Regardless of gender, younger voters were more likely than older voters to report that Hillary Clinton was qualified and had the temperament to serve effectively as president. In general and more so among men, voters did not view Hillary Clinton as honest or trustworthy.

Table 5.2 Presidential Voting Characteristics by Age, Gender, and Candidate Choice

| | | Clinton Voters | | | | | | Trump Voters | | | | | |
| | | Men | | | Women | | | Men | | | Women | | |
		YA	MA	OA	YA	MA	OA	YA	MA	OA	YA	MA	OA
Which best describes your vote for president today?	Strongly favor	36	41	56	34	49	61	30	36	50	40	35	41
	Like with reservations	37	32	27	39	33	17	38	32	31	41	34	31
	Dislike	32	25	16	26	16	18	32	30	18	19	29	26
Which qualities matters most in deciding a vote for president?	Care about people like me	23	17	8	19	20	13	11	11	10	18	11	14
	Can bring needed change	17	8	8	23	10	7	75	69	69	69	71	67
	Has the right experience	33	42	49	27	41	49	4	4	5	2	2	2
	Has good judgment	26	31	30	28	26	26	8	12	11	11	11	12
When did you finally decide for whom to vote in the presidential election?	Last few days	10	8	3	9	6	8	5	6	6	11	10	8
	Last week	9	6	4	3	4	1	6	4	5	10	9	3
	October	19	9	8	14	7	7	21	14	12	16	12	11
	September	11	12	19	17	9	16	15	10	12	18	15	15
	Before that	51	64	67	56	71	66	51	65	64	45	53	61

Note: YA: 18–29 years, MA: 30–64 years, OA: 65+
Source: Edison Exit Poll (2016).

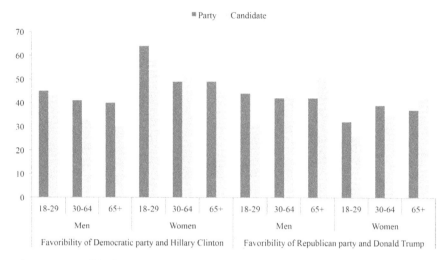

Figure 5.2 Political Party and Candidate Favorability by Age and Gender. *Source*: Edison Exit Poll (2016)" to bottom of Figure 5.2.

Voters reported whether they would feel excited, optimistic, concerned, or scared if Hillary Clinton were elected president. Compared to men, women were more likely to report feeling excited if Hillary Clinton were elected. Compared to women, men were more likely to report feeling concerned if Hillary Clinton were elected. Finally, male voters, regardless of age, were more likely than women to report that Hillary Clinton's use of private email while Secretary of State bothered them "a lot." In addition, middle-aged and older women were more bothered than younger women.

Republican Party and Donald Trump

Figure 5.2 also displays favorability for the Republican Party and Donald Trump as a function of age and gender. Compared to women, men generally had higher favorability ratings for both Donald Trump and the Republican party. For both men and women, younger voters had less favorable views of Donald Trump than older voters. Favorability ratings for the Republican party were stable for men across age groups; however, among women, middle-aged and older voters were more favorable for the Republican party than younger women.

Lastly, participants self-reported whether Donald Trump was qualified, had the temperament to serve, was honest and trustworthy, what they would feel if he were elected president, and whether his treatment of women bothered them Table 5.3. In general, ratings were low to moderate for qualifications, temperament, and honesty and trustworthiness. Male gender and older age were both associated with viewing Trump as qualified, having the temperament to serve, and as more honest and trustworthy.

Table 5.3 Candidate Opinions and Preferences

		Men			Women		
		YA	MA	OA	YA	MA	OA
Hillary Clinton							
Do you think Hillary Clinton is qualified?		58	45	39	63	54	52
Do you think Hillary Clinton has the temperament to serve effectively as president?		57	49	48	67	58	55
Do you think Hillary Clinton is honest and trustworthy? (Y)		33	31	31	41	40	45
If Hillary Clinton is elected president, would you feel:	Excited	9	11	13	22	22	23
	Optimistic	33	25	25	36	24	25
	Concerned	29	26	23	24	24	15
	Scared	25	34	37	15	28	33
Does Hillary Clinton's use of private email while SecState bother you?	A lot	49	53	53	28	40	47
	Some	24	15	11	26	18	14
	Not much	16	13	14	27	20	15
	Not at all	10	17	21	18	21	21
Donald Trump							
Do you think Trump is qualified? (Y)		35	45	49	20	35	37
Do you think Trump has the temperament to serve effectively as president? (Y)		30	41	43	24	31	36
Do you think Trump is honest and trustworthy? (Y)		26	37	42	23	30	38
If Donald Trump is elected president, would you feel:	Excited	13	15	16	10	13	12
	Optimistic	22	33	32	17	26	23
	Concerned	34	19	23	25	18	14
	Scared	30	31	29	45	41	48
Does Donald Trump's treatment of women bother you? (Y)	A lot	47	40	38	66	57	49
	Some	27	28	20	13	16	17
	Not much	17	14	17	7	13	13
	Not at all	8	16	25	13	13	18

Note: YA: 18–29 years, MA: 30–64 years, OA: 65+.
Source: Edison Exit Poll (2016).

Voters self-reported whether they would feel excited, optimistic, concerned, or scared if Donald Trump were elected president. If elected president, male voters were fairly split between optimistic, concerned, and scared. Female voters regardless of age were most likely to report feeling scared. Finally, voters were asked whether Donald Trump's treatment of women bothers them. Younger age and female gender were both associated with being bothered "a lot" by Trump's treatment of women.

DISCUSSION

This chapter explored the role of age across the adult lifespan, gender, and their intersection in terms of voting behavior and candidate preferences. This analysis included an examination of whether norms from previous research and past elections were upheld in the 2016 presidential election. Past work has mainly examined the gender gap and the potential for a "senior vote" as separate issues (e.g., Norrander and Wilcox 2008, Binstock 2009). In this chapter we identified that while there are main effects of age and gender, a closer examination reveals interactional effects such that the gender gap was qualified by age in voting behavior. According to the polling data analyzed in the current study and consistent with the gender gap identified in recent decades (Klein 1984, Kaufmann 2002, Norrander and Wilcox 2008), women were more likely to vote for Hillary Clinton, view her as the better commander in chief, and have higher favorability ratings for both her and the Democratic party. Men were more likely to vote for Trump, view him as the better commander in chief, and have higher favorability ratings for the Republican party and Donald Trump. With the exception of the high ratings for the Republican party for men regardless of age, the gender gap in candidate preferences was largely qualified by age. Middle-aged and older men were more likely to vote for and felt more favorable toward Donald Trump than younger men. In addition, middle-aged and older women were less likely to vote for and reported less favorability toward Hillary Clinton than younger women.

In addition, there were also a number of main effects of age and gender as separate constructs. First, voters, especially male voters, did not view Hillary Clinton as honest or trustworthy. Consistent with RCT (Eagly and Karau 2002), feelings of dishonesty or lack of trust may have been a form of backlash for a more experienced female candidate (Rudman et al. 2012). Second, women, regardless of age, reported feeling scared at the prospect of Trump as president and excited at the prospect of Clinton as president. Male voters, on the other hand, reported feeling more scared or concerned with Hillary Clinton as president but were not overwhelmingly excited at the prospect of Donald Trump. Male voters' reported negative feelings regarding the female candidate in 2016 may reflect perceived threats to social norms that for men, particularly middle-aged and older men for whom gender norms may be more engrained, implicitly represent a loss or shift in power (Connell 2005).

Third, male voters were more likely to report being bothered by Clinton's use of private email and female voters were more likely to report being bothered by Trump's treatment of women. Fourth, male voters for Clinton decided slightly later than female voters for Clinton while female voters for Trump decided slightly later than male voters for Trump. The overall negative feelings toward the use of private email as well as the hesitancy in deciding on a candidate may have also been an indication of the reluctance of some male voters to accept a female in a leadership role. Among women, reports of feeling scared, concerns about Trump's treatment of women, and their hesitancy in deciding on a candidate may have represented a period of wrestling with feelings of cognitive dissonance (Festinger 1962) between behaviors (voting for Trump) and beliefs (negative feelings regarding a per-ceived anti-female candidate).

Fifth, in terms of the role of age in particular, there was a trend for older voters to decide earlier and more strongly favor their candidates compared to younger voters (with the exception of older female Trump voters who did not strongly favor their candidate). Finally, regardless of age or gender, Trump voters valued "change" in their choice for president and Clinton voters valued "experience" in their choice for president.

The finding of a gender gap in the 2016 presidential election is consistent with recent elections where women tend to favor the Democratic candidate and men tend to favor the Republican candidate (Norrander and Wilcox 2008, Kellstedt, Peterson, and Ramirez 2010). As previously mentioned, this gender gap was qualified by age such that younger and older voters differed substan-tially. Younger male voters leaned more toward the Democratic candidate and older female voters leaned toward the Republican candidate. Previous research has documented that voters aged 65 and older lean Republican (Binstock 2009). However, in the 2008 election, the cohort of voters younger than 65 (at the time of the election) did not lean Republican (Binstock 2009). Those voters, now over age 65, tended to lean Republican in the 2016 elec-tion and therefore may have shifted right in their voting behavior. This shift would suggest an age effect (rather than a cohort effect). Future work using longitudinal analysis is needed to better differentiate age versus cohort effects in subsequent elections. Regarding the 2016 presidential election, younger male voters favored Clinton, and it is unclear whether this pattern will con-tinue and thus reduce the gender gap over time.

In the current election, middle-aged and older male voters had the highest ratings for Donald Trump, and older women were also more Republican-leaning in their votes than other groups. While there may be shifts in ideology that occur with age, there may also be generational differences that can help to explain voting behavior across these age groups. Older adults are more likely to be pray, attend church regularly, and consider religion as important to their lives (Pew Research Center 2015), and past work has tied religiosity with voting Republican (Norrander & Wilcox 2008). In the 2016 election, Donald Trump was viewed as having behaviors inconsistent with Christian values. However, as the major political party candidate for the Republicans, Trump received widespread support from evangelical voters and organizations who opposed Hillary Clinton and sought to fill the vacant Supreme Court seat with a conservative justice. In addition, this election was unique in that it included a female political candidate for a major political party for the first time. Research that has examined the role of religiosity and political ideology has shown that traditional gender roles are tied to religiosity, and in particular, biblical literalism and gendered views of the divine (i.e., a masculine God); therefore, stereotypical gender roles may contrast with women's involvement in politics as authoritative figures (Cassese and Holman 2016, 2017). Looking forward, younger generations are not only less religious, but are also more educated (Vespa 2017) both of which are tied to liberal-leaning ideology (Norrander and Wilcox 2008). In future generations, these shifts may have implications for not only the gender gap but also the ties between evangelism and conservative politics.

As summarized above, women were excited at the prospect of Hillary Clinton which aligns with past work suggesting that women's involvement in the political process can act as a motivator (Karp and Banducci 2008). However despite this, as well as reports of feeling scared at the prospect of Donald Trump as president and bothered by his treatment of women, for some women, particularly middle-aged and older women, this excitement did not translate into endorsement. Middle-aged and older women were less favorable to Hillary Clinton and more favorable to Donald Trump than were younger women in terms of voting behavior and preference for commander in chief. Among older women, traditional views regarding the roles of men and women may have been referenced in making the choice for president despite questions about likeability. This may be evidenced by female voters for Trump deciding later who to endorse for president as well as older female voters for Trump being less confident in their choice for president. Younger adults, conversely, may have more experience with women in leadership roles and thus are more comfortable with an agentic female in an authoritative role. This suggests that the endorsement and acceptance of gender norms may differ across the lifespan and that RCT (Eagly and Karau 2002) may operate differently depending on the age of the voter. This is complicated by some researchers suggesting that the explicit bias against female candidates is "no longer a major obstacle" (for review see Ditonto, Hamilton, and Redlawsk 2014). The evidence from our analyses of polling data as well as recently reviewed research suggests that this process of bias for female candidates is an implicit (Mo 2015) rather than an explicit process.

Looking forward, research is needed to better understand whether the gender gap is upheld in future elections. This work should also include analyses as to the racial, ethnic, and religious factors that further differentiate female and male voters as well as younger, middle-aged and older voters. The limited work that has examined voting trends among minority populations has illustrated that great heterogeneity exists within the voting electorate across the lifespan and among an increasingly diverse population of older voters. For example, while older White voters leaned Republican in the 2008 U.S. presidential election (58% endorsed John McCain), only 6 percent of older Black voters and 31 percent of older Latino voters endorsed John McCain (Binstock 2009).

There are some limitations in this analyses that should be noted. As in all self-reporting, there may be bias in answers reported. However, respondents completed exit polls privately and anonymously which would be associated with reduced social bias. Also, the study included only voters and future work is needed to better understand the role of voter turnout and the characteristics and concerns of non-voters in general, as well as how it relates to issues of age and gender. As mentioned above, issues of socioeconomic status, race, ethnicity, religiosity, geographic location, and a more detailed age breakdown are needed to further elucidate voting patterns. Among both gender and age groups, there is a false assumption of homogeny among age and gender groups (Schulz and Binstock 2008). An increasingly diverse society necessitates better data and research to understand voting behavior in future elections.

Future work should examine ideology and specific political issues in addition to party and candidate preference (Norrander & Wilcox, 2008). In the 2016 presidential election, there was strong support for Bernie Sanders as a Democratic candidate, an increase in independent voters, and support for the independent candidates was greater compared to recent elections (Gallup 2016) due in part to an increasing partisan divide and possible dislike for either major political party candidate. Endorsement of these candidates by voters raises a few questions including the likeability of the major political party candidates in the 2016 presidential election and issues regarding ideology and the "messaging" of the Democratic and Republican National Parties.

Political issues (e.g., reproductive rights, health care) are often more complex and multifaceted than identification to party. Men and women may identify with different issues when forming their ideologies, party and candidate preference. In addition, with respect to age and voting behavior, future voting behavior will be influenced by key issues such as the state of the economy, proposed changes, and the status of health care (and in particular, Medicare), and the state of benefit programs such as Social Security. In terms of age-related factors and voting behavior, research is needed to better understand retirement preparation and perceptions regarding the sustainability of Social Security in relation to the "senior vote." This may be another factor that demonstrates the intersectionality of age and gender. As Schulz and Binstock (2008) describe, gender differences exist in terms of wealth and retirement knowledge between older women and older men. Middle-aged and older women are at a particular risk in terms of financial health in retirement due to traditional gender biases that have existed throughout their lifespan at home and in the workplace that have contributed to less accumulated wealth. Therefore, protection of social programs such as Social Security and Medicare may be an especially important issue for women and individuals of lower socioeconomic status (Schulz and Binstock 2008) As part of the ongoing health-care debate, future work will also need to consider the provision of care and payment for long-term care, in particular. In 2014, it was estimated that 15 million family members provided informal care to a relative with dementia and costs for health care, long-term care, and hospice care totaled $226 billion (Alzheimer's Association 2015). There has been an ongoing debate regarding the need to ration care for older adults and the moral issues surrounding this rationing (for review see Schulz and Binstock 2008). In future elections, this debate will likely continue and increasingly require discussion and agreement across multiple generations.

In conclusion, this chapter aimed to contribute scholarly analyses of the role of age, gender, and their intersection in relation to voting behavior and preferences toward the 2016 presidential candidates and in doing so, illustrate the role that these factors did play in the election despite a lack of coverage regarding their influence. Polling data as well as theoretical and empirical analyses provide support to age, gender, and age by gender interactions in predicting voter behavior. Future work is needed to better understand these issues as we look forward to the 2020 midterm elections and beyond.

REFERENCES

Alcindor, Yamiche. 2016. "Hillary Clinton Gains Some Ground Among Young Voters, Poll Finds." The New York Times, October 26, 2016, Election 2016. Accessed June 15, 2017. https://www.nytimes.com/2016/10/27/us/politics/hillary-clinton-gains-some-ground-among-young-voters-poll-finds.html?_r=0.

Aronson, Pamela. 2003. "Feminists or "Postfeminists"? Young Women's Attitudes Toward Feminism and Gender Relations." *Gender & Society* 17 (6):903–922.

Asch, Solomon E. 1956. "Studies of Independence and Conformity: I. A Minority of One Against a Unanimous Majority." *Psychological Monographs: General and Applied* 70 (9): 1–70.

Alzheimer's Association. 2015. "2015 Alzheimer's Disease Facts and Figures." *Alzheimers and Dementia* 11 (3):332–84.

Binstock, Robert. 2000. "Older People and Voting Participation: Past and Future." *The Gerontologist* 40 (1):18–31.

Binstock, Robert. 2009. "Older Voters and the 2008 Election." *The Gerontologist* 49 (5):697–701. doi: 10.1093/geront/gnp100.

Binstock, Robert. 2012. "Older Voters and the 2010 U.S. Election: Implications for 2012 and Beyond*?" The Gerontologist* 52 (3):408–17. doi: 10.1093/geront/gnr118.

Cassese, Erin C, and Mirya R Holman. 2016. "Religious Beliefs, Gender Consciousness, and Women's Political Participation." *Sex Roles* 75 (9-10):514–527.

Cassese, Erin C, and Mirya R Holman. 2017. "Religion, Gendered Authority, and Identity in American Politics " *Politics and Religion* 10 (1):31–56.

Connell, Raewyn W. 2005. "Change among the Gatekeepers: Men, Masculinities, and Gender Equality in the Global Arena." *Signs* 30 (3):1801–1825. doi: 10.1086/427525.

Ditonto, Tessa M, Allison J Hamilton, and David P Redlawsk. 2014. "Gender Stereotypes, Information Search, and Voting Behavior in Political Campaigns." *Political Behavior* 36 (2):335–358.

Eagly, Alice H, and Steven J Karau. 2002. "Role Congruity Theory of Prejudice Toward Female Leaders." *Psychological Review* 109 (3):573.

Festinger, Leon. 1962. A Theory of Cognitive Dissonance. Vol. 2. Stanford, CA: Stanford University Press.

Fry, Richard. 2016. "Millenials Overtake Baby Boomers as America's Largest Generation." Pew Research Center, April 25, 2016, FactTank: News in the Numbers. Accessed May 30, 2017. http://www.pewresearch.org/fact-tank/2016/04/25/millennials-overtake-baby-boomers/.

Gallup. 2016. "Democratic, Republican Identification Near Historical Lows." January 11, 2016. Accessed June 28, 2017. http://www.gallup.com/poll/188096/democratic-republican-identification-near-historical-lows.aspx?g_source=Politics&g_medium=newsfeed&g_campaign=tiles.

Heckhausen, Jutta. 1997. "Developmental Regulation Across Adulthood: Primary and Secondary Control of Age-Related Challenges." *Developmental Psychology* 33 (1):176–187.

Huddy, Leonie, and Nayda Terkildsen. 1993. "Gender Stereotypes and the Perception of Male and Female Candidates." *American Journal of Political Science* 37: 119–147.

Joshi, Aparna. 2014. "By whom and when is women's expertise recognized? The interactive effects of gender and education in science and engineering teams." Administrative Science Quarterly:0001839214528331.

Karp, Jeffrey A, and Susan A Banducci. 2008. "When Politics is Not Just a Man's Game: Women's Representation and Political Engagement." *Electoral Studies* 27 (1):105–115.

Kaufmann, Karen M. 2002. "Culture Wars, Secular Realignment, and the Gender Gap in Party Identification." *Political Behavior* 24 (3):283–307.

Kellstedt, Paul M, David AM Peterson, and Mark D Ramirez. 2010. "The Macro Politics of a Gender Gap." *Public Opinion Quarterly* 74 (3) 477–498.

Klein, Ethel. 1984. Gender Politics From Consciousness to Mass Politics. Cambridge, MA: Harvard University.

Milgram, Stanley, Leonard Bickman, and Lawrence Berkowitz. 1969. "Note on the drawing power of crowds of different size." *Journal of Personality and Social Psychology* 13 (2):79–82.

Mo, Cecilia Hyunjung. 2015. "The Consequences of Explicit and Implicit Gender Attitudes and Candidate Quality in the Calculations of Voters." *Political Behavior* 37 (2):357-395. doi: 10.1007/s11109-014-9274-4.

Montanaro, Domenico. 2016. "7 Reasons Donald Trump won the presidential election." NPR, November 12, 2016, Politics. Accessed June 15, 2016. http://www.npr.org/2016/11/12/501848636/7-reasons-donald-trump-won-the-presidential-election.

Norrander, Barbara, and Clyde Wilcox. 2008. "The Gender Gap in Ideology." Political Behavior 30 (4):503–523.

Ortman, Jennifer M, Victoria A Velkoff, and Howard Hogan. 2014. "An Aging Nation: The Older Population in the United States." Washington, DC: U.S. Census Bureau: 25–1140.

Patient Protection and Affordable Care Act. Public Law 111-148, U.S. Statues at Large (2010).

Pew Research Center. 2015. "America's Changing Religious Landscape." May 12, 2015. Accessed June 20, 2017. http://assets.pewresearch.org/wp-content/uploads/sites/11/2015/05/RLS-08-26-full-report.pdf.

Plutzer, Eric. 2002. "Becoming a Habitual Voter: Inertia, Resources, and Growth in Young Adulthood." *The American Political Science Review* 96 (1):41–56.

Riemer, Yosef, and Robert H Binstock. 1978. "Campaigning for "The Senior Vote:" A Case Study of Carter's 1976 Campaign." *The Gerontologist* 18 (6):517–524.

Rucker, Phillip. 2016. "For Millenial Voters, the Clinton Vs. Trump Choice 'Feels like a Joke'." Washington Post, August 13, 2016, Politics. Accessed June 15, 2016. https://www.washingtonpost.com/politics/for-millennial-voters-the-clinton-vs-trump-choice-feels-like-a-joke/2016/08/13/306d85a2-609c-11e6-8e45-477372e89d78_story.html?utm_term=.ecd669df71c8.

Rudman, Laurie A, Corinne A Moss-Racusin, Julie E Phelan, and Sanne Nauts. 2012. "Status Incongruity and Backlash Effects: Defending the Gender Hierarchy Motivates Prejudice Against Female Leaders." *Journal of Experimental Social Psychology* 48 (1):165–179.

Schulz, James H, and Robert H Binstock. 2008. Aging Nation: The Economics and Politics of Growing Older in America. Baltimore, MD: Johns Hopkins University Press.

Social Security Administration. 2014. "Income of the aged chartbook, 2012 (SSA Publication Number 13-11727)." April 2014. Accessed June 26, 2017. https://www.ssa.gov/policy/docs/chartbooks/income_aged/2012/iac12.pdf.

Snyder, R. Claire. 2008. "What Is Third-Wave Feminism? A New Directions Essay." Signs: *Journal of Women in Culture and Society* 34 (1):175–196. doi: 10.1086/588436.

U.S. Census Bureau, 2012. "Voting and Registration in the Election of November 2012 (Report Number P20-568)," May, 2013. Accessed June 15, 2017. https://www.census.gov/data/tables/2012/demo/voting-and-registration/p20-568.html.

Vespa, Jonathon. 2017. The Changing Economics and Demographics of Young Adulthood: 1975-2016. U.S. Census Bureau. April 2017. Accessed June 20, 2017. https://www.census.gov/content/dam/Census/library/publications/2017/demo/p20-579.pdf.

Chapter 6

Contempt and Anger in the 2016 U.S. Presidential Election

Kyle Mattes, Ira J. Roseman, David P. Redlawsk,
and Steven Katz

"Ben Carson is a complete and total loser!" says Donald Trump. But this one-liner about his opponent in the 2016 Republican Party presidential primaries is not from a campaign speech, nor is it a tweet. It is a promotional spot NBC intended to air for Trump's then-upcoming gig as host of Saturday Night Live.[1]

The joke, of course, is the similarity to Trump's actual campaign rhetoric. "Jeb [Bush] is a loser," said Trump in February 2016.[2] Trump also repeatedly referred to Bush as a low-energy individual. "You know what is happening to Jeb's crowd right down the street?" Trump asked. "They're sleeping."[3] In prior years, a common refrain in Republican primaries had been that the other candidate(s) were not conservative enough, meaning that they did not have sufficiently conservative positions on important political issues. But when Trump attacked his opponents, he rarely focused on their policy initiatives. Instead, Trump appeared to target his opponents' inferiority as people. He told voters that Senator Ted Cruz was "a lying guy. A really lying guy."[4]; that Senator Marco Rubio was "little"; that Senator Lindsay Graham was "a total lightweight."[5] These insults continued into the general election, as Trump lambasted "Crooked Hillary."

Are such insults the vagaries of a rather unusual presidential candidate, or instead a calculated political strategy? Though it could be said that Trump had a unique delivery, personal attacks of this kind are not new to politics.[6] The 2nd U.S. president, John Adams, when he ran against Thomas Jefferson in 1800, was called a "hideous hermaphroditical character which has neither the force and firmness of a man, nor the gentleness and sensibility of a woman" (Cummins 2007). However, in contrast to other modern elections, personal insults flooded the 2016 election landscape. In the Republican primaries, Marco Rubio labeled Trump "a con artist."[7] A Ted Cruz ad disparaged Rubio as "just another pretty face."[8] In a debate, Rubio claimed that New Jersey governor Chris Christie preferred to keep campaigning rather than respond to a snowstorm in his home state. In response, Christie sarcastically asked, "Is that one of the skills you get as a United States senator? ESP?"[9] In the general election, ads for Hillary Clinton labeled Trump as a con man and a fraud. Her campaign sought to convince voters that Trump was "temperamentally unfit" for the presidency.[10]

What do these attacks have in common? In a word, *contempt*. Psychologists regard contempt as an emotion which is "the feeling when one judges another person as an inferior human being" (Fischer 2011, 77). The attacks described above tried to make voters feel contempt toward, and look down upon, an opposing candidate. There is a good theoretical reason for this approach. Contempt is a "rejection" emotion, elicited by appraisals of another person as unworthy, inferior, or beneath some standard (Miller 1997; Roseman 2018). Contempt is associated with the desire to have nothing to do with that person (Fischer and Roseman 2007) *and* to get other people to reject them too (Haidt 2003; Roseman 2018), the latter being especially important to politics. Voting against candidates for whom you feel contempt will help minimize their impact. So, you might expect political scientists to have regularly studied the role of contempt in politics. But this is not the case.

EMOTIONS AND POLITICS

While there is much agreement among scholars that emotions play a pivotal role in elections, disagreements persist on how to categorize them. There are two main approaches (Redlawsk & Pierce 2017). The dimensional approach identifies two emotional vectors: positive and negative. The dimensions themselves are the focus because advocates of this perspective theorize that all the emotions of each type (positives or negatives) have similar effects. For example, anger and fear, both being negative emotions, are combined within the "negative" dimension (e.g., Lodge and Taber 2013). On the other hand, proponents of the discrete perspective argue that there are multiple emotions with distinct effects on voting and other forms of political participation (e.g., Marcus, Neuman, and MacKuen 2000). While clearly the emotions themselves can be classified as positive or negative, this approach argues that specific emotions of the same dimensionality may still have unique and distinguishable effects that are lost by combining them into simple positive/negative vectors. In this chapter we focus on this discrete approach, examining potential differences between two negative emotions, anger and contempt. In doing so we extend as well as test the discrete approach in the context of election campaigns.

In recent election cycles, the media have focused on anger—whether the candidates sound angry, whether angry voters will turn out and/or demand change, and so on. To date, political science research on negative emotions has also focused on anger and on fear (or anxiety). Fear and anger are the only two negative emotions about which there are questions in nearly all iterations of the American National Election Studies. Dimensional theorists (e.g., Lodge and Taber 2013) have viewed them primarily as examples of negative emotions. Marcus et al. (2000) presented evidence indicating that they ought to be distinguished, insofar as "anxiety" (which encompasses fear) and "aversion" (which includes anger, as well as contempt, disgust, and related feelings) made independent contributions to evaluations of presidential candidate Bill Clinton.

Since this Affective Intelligence Theory pioneered the discrete emotion approach in political science, a number of studies have shown the benefit of distinguishing anger from other negative emotions, and have documented its impact. Anger fueled the Tea Party movement (Sparks 2015) and opposition to health care reform (Banks 2014), and it is a driving force behind partisanship in general (Huddy et al. 2015). Moreover, comparisons of negative emotions have shown anger is more influential than fear in predicting high-effort political participation (e.g., working for a campaign or donating money) and voting in presidential campaigns (Finn and Glaser 2010; Valentino et al. 2011).

Thus, the conclusion that anger plays an important role in politics is inescapable. But we propose that contempt is also important, and that new and important findings may emerge if anger and contempt—which have increasingly been separated in emotions research outside political science—are similarly differentiated by political scientists. A brief comparison between the two emotions will help explain our theory.

Anger is an "attack" emotion (Frijda 1986). Angry people often want to confront their target and force that person to change behavior (Potegal and Qiu 2010; Sell et al. 2009). So, with anger there exists the possibility of resolution or reconciliation (e.g., if the target person would stop what he or she is doing). Anger ebbs and flows; it is a relatively short-term emotion. In contrast, as noted above, contempt is a rejection emotion. Contemptuous people often want nothing to do with their target, and reconciliation is less likely (Fischer and Roseman 2007). More so than anger, contempt predicts relationship deterioration (e.g., Gottman and Levenson 1992). Contempt tends to be a longer-term emotion. For example, Romani et al. (2013) found that anger felt in response to perceived corporate wrongdoing predicted actions designed to penalize but maintain a relationship with a company. However, contempt predicted actions designed to discredit or hurt the company and ultimately disengage from it.

Appraisal theories suggest that voters get angry at politicians when they attribute to them outcomes that seem unfair (e.g., Tong 2010). Voters feel contempt for politicians that seem incompetent or corrupt and thus undeserving of public office. Sometimes anger is felt about a negative outcome (e.g., a trade deal that hurts workers like me) and contempt simultaneously about the failings (being a "terrible negotiator" or a "crooked" candidate) alleged to be producing that outcome. Many voters would argue that bad outcomes can be altered, but bad people cannot.

PREVIOUS RESEARCH ON CONTEMPT IN POLITICS

We have mentioned the limited availability of studies analyzing the impact of contempt on election outcomes. One reason is that the American National Election Study (ANES), that is the source of much data for political scientists, routinely asks questions about anger, fear, pride, and hope, but not contempt. Even so, the few extant studies of political contempt give reason to believe it is worthwhile examining its distinct effects.

In 1995, an ANES pilot study asked about contempt felt toward presidential candidates. Using the pilot data, Johnston, Roseman, and Katz (2014) analyzed the relationship between ratings of each candidate's leadership, specific negative emotions, and evaluations of the candidates (feeling thermometers ranging from 0 to 100). They found that for 1996 Democratic candidate (and incumbent president) Bill Clinton, both anger and contempt (but not fear) independently mediated the effect of leadership perceptions and thermometer evaluations. In contrast, for Republican candidate Bob Dole, anger and fear (but not contempt) mediated the relationship between leadership and thermometer score.

A second study asked undergraduates to view excerpts from the 2008 presidential campaign debates between Senator Barack Obama and Senator John McCain (Roseman et al. 2013). This study found that for Democratic candidate Obama, both viewer contempt and anger mediated the relationship between perceived undesirable qualities of Obama and thermometer evaluations. However, only anger mediated the same relationship for McCain. Thus, in two different elections, contempt as well as anger influenced how perceptions of a Democratic presidential candidate affected evaluations of that candidate. Whereas for Republican candidates, anger but not contempt was important.

A third study extended this research beyond presidential elections, and found that contempt mattered for Republican as well as Democratic candidates, depending on contextual factors. Redlawsk, Roseman, Mattes, and Katz (2016) surveyed voters during the 2014 U.S. Senate elections in Iowa and New Jersey, testing the relationship between six felt emotions—anger, contempt, anxiety, enthusiasm, hope, and admiration—and vote intentions. Contempt predicted voting against both Democrat Bruce Braley and Republican Joni Ernst in Iowa. Anger also predicted voting against Braley, while anxiety also predicted voting against Ernst. Furthermore, of the three negative emotions, contempt was the most significant predictor for both candidates. In New Jersey, contempt was the most important negative emotion predicting voting against Republican Jeff Bell, but had little impact on the probability of voting for Democrat Cory Booker. Why the difference? One possibility: in the hotly contested Iowa race, the airwaves were saturated for months with negative ads, which often try to evoke contempt. But in the relatively uncontested New Jersey race, Democrat Booker aired very few TV ads, and Republican Bell aired none.

Extending our work further, we carried out another study during the 2016 presidential primaries, examining whether contempt and anger had differential effects on support for GOP candidates in the first-in-the-nation Iowa Caucuses (Redlawsk, Roseman, Mattes, and Katz 2017). We found clear evidence that Iowa GOP voters perceived contempt coming *from* the candidates, with Donald Trump well ahead of his opponents in this respect. They also felt contempt *toward* candidates, and candidates benefited from contempt felt toward rivals. Even in this intraparty context, where voters share partisan identification and thus some social identity with the candidates, we found contempt and anger had different and unique effects, both on candidate evaluation and the vote.

The rise of Donald Trump in the 2016 presidential election provides an opportunity to examine differences between contempt and anger in a campaign where directly expressing contempt for his opponents became a core feature of Donald Trump's rhetoric. In no previous election of which we are aware has a candidate so blatantly and persistently dismissed multiple opponents as characterologically inferior. While we have previously found that voters perceive contempt in negative ads (Redlawsk et al. 2016), the rhetoric in the ads themselves and the candidate speeches in 2014 Iowa came nowhere close to the 2016 presidential election. This leads us to ask the following questions: To what extent did voters perceive contempt, anger, and other emotions in the 2016 general election? And, to what degree did those perceptions affect voters' responses to the candidates? Rather than relying on generalized feelings as typically asked in surveys, in our online survey we presented voters with two real-life campaign ads—one from the major super PAC supporting Hillary Clinton and the other from the Trump campaign—to directly gauge emotional responses to the campaigns each candidate was carrying out.

We believe that a key purpose of many negative campaign ads is to push voters toward holding an opponent in contempt—not just to make voters feel anxious or angry or afraid, but to make them dismissive of the opponent.

Often this process is relatively subtle, as candidates may sense some risk in "mudslinging" attacks the character of their opponents. Even so, if we are correct, viewers of negative ads should perceive contempt as being expressed in those ads. In this study, we showed participants two political negative advertisements, one attacking Hillary Clinton and the other attacking Donald Trump. We expect that those who perceive more contempt toward the candidate attacked in the ads will feel less favorable toward that candidate, exactly as the ad's sponsor would want. Given what we know about the nature of contempt, if candidates are successful in generating that feeling, we expect this opinion change to be significant and possibly stronger than the effect of perceiving anger. At the same time, we are also interested in whether the Trump and Clinton campaigns, to the extent their ads generate contempt for the other, also risked backlash for perhaps going too far in their attacks.

RESEARCH DESIGN AND THE COOPERATIVE CONGRESSIONAL ELECTION SURVEY (CCES)

Our data were collected as part of the Cooperative Congressional Election Survey (CCES) that is administered biannually to coincide with the presidential and midterm elections in the United States.[11] About half of the survey consists of common content questions that ask for respondents' demographic information and their general political attitudes, and the results are available to the public at large. The remainder of the questionnaire consists of smaller modules that are designed and purchased by individual researchers or research teams interested in more specific questions; these results are proprietary. The questions in each module are asked to a relatively small subset (1000) of the CCES respondents. Our data come from such a module.

The CCES survey is a two-part panel study administered both before and after the election. Most of the questions are asked in the pre-election phase, which is administered in September and October of the election year. In the post-election phase, which is administered in November, the same respondents are asked questions that are usually related to results of the recently completed election. The final sample from the 2016 CCES pre-election survey had 84,292 respondents, of whom 64,000 (76.64%) also completed the post-election survey.[12] Of the 1000 respondents in our pre-election module, 801 (80.1%) the post-election survey.[13]

To test the effects of contempt and other emotions in 2016 presidential campaign ads, we selected two frequently-aired advertisements from the general election campaign—one from each side—randomizing the order in which the ads were viewed by respondents. The ad attacking Clinton, "Careless," begins with CNN host Wolf Blitzer repeating the phrase "extremely careless" from the FBI report on Clinton, then uses a montage to make it appear that FBI director James Comey and the Washington Post are refuting Clinton's claim that her answers were truthful; it ends with the words "careless, reckless, crooked." The Clinton ad, "What a Con Man," features Trump promoting his past business ventures. After each one, it places a red stamp with a single word—such as "FAILED," "SCAM," and "FRAUD,"—to describe the eventual result, and ends with the visual "DONALD TRUMP IS A CON MAN."[14]

The goal of these ads appears to be lowering the viewer's opinion of the opposing candidate—not only in leadership ability, but also as a person. But do these ads make viewers *feel* contempt? It's difficult to judge immediate emotional responses within the context of a survey. However, we believe that viewers at least ought to *perceive* the contempt displayed in the ads.

After each ad, we asked a series of questions about perceived emotions: "How much [EMOTION] was expressed toward [CANDIDATE] in this video?" We asked about anger, contempt, fear, and—in case these negative ads backfired—admiration. The four possible responses ranged from a "none at all" to "a large amount," which we converted into a four-point scale designating "none at all" as one.[15]

RESULTS

Before we turn to our examination of campaign ads, it may be useful to get a sense of the emotional context of the campaign as measured by commonly used questions asking what we call *ever-felt* emotional reactions to the candidates. We asked respondents in the pre-election wave of the CCES to tell us how often they felt each of six discrete emotions for each Trump and Clinton: anger, fear, contempt, hope, pride, and enthusiasm. Both the order of the candidates and the order of the emotions were randomized. The question had two parts. Initially, respondents were asked: "Has [CANDIDATE NAME], because of the kind of person s/he is or because of something s/he has done, ever made you feel [EMOTION]?" with Yes or No as the available responses. Those who answered yes were asked a follow-up question: "How often would you say you've felt [EMOTION]?" with possible responses of Never, Occasionally, About half the time, Most of the time, and Always.

We placed those responding no to the initial question in the "never" category of the second question to create a scale of responses, from one (Never) to five (Always). Figure 6.1 displays the means and standard errors for each emotion for each candidate. The evidence is clear that both candidates had a knack for bringing out the negative. Each of the negative emotions for both candidates had a higher score than any of the positive emotions. The most-felt emotion in the election was anger toward Trump; the score of 2.53 falls

Frequency of felt emotions

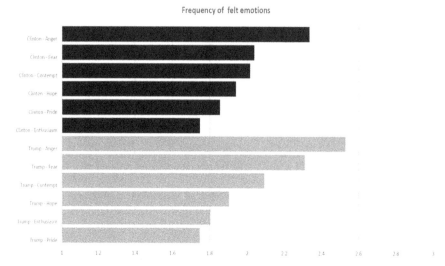

Figure 6.1   Ever-felt Emotions in the 2016 CCES module.

between the categories of "Occasionally" and "Half the time." Given the modal response of No/Never for every emotion, we consider this an indication that the electorate directed a good deal of anger toward Trump. Trump also scored relatively high on fear (2.31) and contempt (2.09). Reactions to Clinton were not far behind; she evoked anger scored at 2.33, fear at 2.04, and contempt at 2.01. None of the positive emotions, for either candidate, reached the 2.00 mark, though hope for Clinton (1.94) and Trump (1.90) came closest.

We now turn to an analysis of the emotions perceived in the campaign ads in the context of this quite negative electoral environment. Table 6.1 summarizes the results of our questions about the campaign ads.

The ads were seen as containing considerable amounts of negative emotions. Contempt, anger, and fear were all perceived as expressed in both ads. On average, viewers perceived contempt significantly more than any other emotion measured in either ad: 3.03 on the 4-point scale (approximately "a moderate amount") for the anti-Trump ad, and 2.98 for the anti-Clinton ad. Anger was next most perceived, at 2.78 on the scale for the anti-Trump ad, and 2.81 for the anti-Clinton ad. Fear was somewhat lower: 2.30 in the anti-Trump ad and 2.59 in anti-Clinton ad. Thus, attack ads are not just cognitively negative: they are seen as expressing negative emotions toward their targets. And, it probably comes as no surprise, but viewers found little evidence of expressed admiration: 1.25 in the anti-Trump ad, and 1.30 in the anti-Clinton ad.

Simply recognizing that negativity occurs in the ads (designed to be attacks, after all) does not tell us the extent to which emotional responses to these ads mattered. To examine this question, we followed the perceived

Table 6.1   Emotions Perceived in Anti-Clinton and Anti-Trump Ads

	Anti-Clinton Ad: "Careless"	Anti-Trump Ad: "Con Man"
Contempt	2.98 (0.06)	3.03 (0.06)
Anger	2.81 (0.06)	2.78 (0.06)
Fear	2.59 (0.06)	2.30 (0.06)
Admiration	1.30 (0.05)	1.25 (0.04)
Change in Favorability toward Target	-0.13 (0.03)	-0.13 (0.03)
Change in Favorability toward Sponsor	-0.06 (0.03)	-0.01 (0.03)

Note: Table entries are means with standard errors in parentheses. Emotion means in the same column differ significantly from each other at $p<.001$.

emotions questions with a question tapping opinion change after watching the ads: "Thinking about the video you just saw, is your opinion of [CANDIDATE] now more favorable, less favorable, or has it not changed?" We asked this about both candidates after each ad was shown. For ease of analysis, we converted the ordinal responses into a three-point scale ranging from less favorable (−1) to more favorable (1). Table 6.1 reports the results of the change in opinion toward Clinton and Trump after watching each attack ad. The ads did significantly lower attitudes toward their intended targets—by −0.13 on our three-point scale, the same for both candidates. It is striking that the ads had a significant effect, even though respondents saw each only once and undoubtedly had developed a trove of attitudes about the candidates and campaign before encountering our survey. This suggests the power of negative ads to influence voters, at least in the short run (Mattes and Redlawsk 2014). As viewers perceived contempt and other emotions expressed in the ads, they lowered their evaluation of the candidate targeted by the ads. But this does not tell us whether contempt and/or anger better explains the opinion change caused by these ads. To more parsimoniously analyze the direct effect of emotions, we combined the data from both ads and then computed the average change in opinion toward the target of the ad—that is, the candidate that was attacked, summarizing across both Clinton and Trump.

To examine the roles of each specific emotion, we ran an OLS regression model using opinion change toward the target as the dependent variable, and the four perceived emotions as independent variables. Results are reported in Table 6.2. The effects are small, but significant, for both anger and contempt (though, not for fear). Perceived anger corresponds to a 0.03 ($p<.001$) decrease in opinion of the target for each point on the scale of increasing emotion. This means that raising perceived anger from lowest ("none at all") to highest ("a large amount") would lower opinions of the attacked candidate by –0.24 on our scale. Unexpectedly, perceived contempt led to an *improved* opinion of the target ($b=0.03$, $p<.05$). What should we make of this difference, not just in magnitude but in direction of the effects of these two discrete emotions? Anger seems to make sense—express anger about the target and voters respond accordingly, reducing their support. But contempt is clearly different. The fact that we see a backlash effect may reflect the nature of contempt in politics. Perhaps some voters who see contempt expressed give more thought to the target (since contempt is an other-regarding emotion) and respond with something akin to "it's disrespectful to talk about the candidate that way" resulting in a rally effect in support for that candidate. This mechanism is, of course, speculation on our part, but the existence of differing effects does support our claim of the importance of differentiating the emotions of contempt and anger.

It is often argued that negative ads create backlash, where the attacker is harmed by the ad more than the intended target, although as Mattes and

Table 6.2   Emotional Response to Campaign Ads Predicting Opinion Change

Perceived Emotion	Opinion change toward attacked candidate
Contempt	0.03**
	(0.01)
Anger	–0.03**
	(0.01)
Fear	–0.01
	(0.01)
Admiration	0.05**
	(0.01)
Constant	–0.23**
	(0.08)
N	726
R-squared	0.05

**$p<0.01$.

Redlawsk (2015) suggest, this effect is dependent on the extremity of the ad. Here, we can measure backlash as opinion change toward the attacker on our three-point scale. Table 6.1 reports the results for each candidate: backlash for the anti-Clinton ad was -0.06, while backlash for the anti-Trump ad was not significant (-0.01). When we summarize across both candidates, the ads caused a minor, but statistically significant, backlash effect on the attacker; opinions of the attacker dropped by -0.04 on the scale, as compared to the -0.13 decrease for the target. We next performed a t-test comparing the opinion changes for attacker and target, and we found this difference to be statistically significant at the p<.001 level. At least within the context of our survey, the candidates gained more than they lost from running the two attack ads, even as they generated a host of emotional responses, including contempt.

CONCLUSION

Prior theory and research on negative emotions and voting have emphasized a small subset of these emotions—anger, and fear or anxiety. We investigated whether an additional emotion, contempt, should be added to theories and research on the determinants of candidate evaluations.

We find evidence that voters *perceive* contempt expressed in political communications, as shown by their responses to two negative advertisements from the 2016 presidential election. From responses to the ever-felt emotion questions, we also know that voters are inclined to *feel* contempt toward the candidates. Furthermore, we have evidence that contempt is relevant to political outcomes—those who perceived anger or contempt in the negative ads were also likely to change their evaluations of the attacked candidates.

Finally, we find that not all negative emotions are alike. Anger and contempt are clearly distinct in our study, felt and perceived at different levels and having different effects on candidate evaluations. Though this suggests altering prevailing models of emotions and voting, it comports well with theory and research in psychology, which suggests that anger and contempt, being quite different emotions, might uniquely contribute to our understanding of political outcomes.

In our 2016 Iowa Caucus study (Redlawsk et al., 2017), we found that contempt, while *felt* by fewer caucus goers than anger, was independently associated with lowered probabilities of voting for leading candidates. Moreover in that study our analyses suggested the leading candidates benefited from contempt *felt* toward their rivals. In contrast, in the present study contempt *perceived* in ads was associated with increased favorability toward the target. Perhaps voters who *perceive* an ad as especially contemptuous are those who do not feel as much contempt toward its target as an ad expresses. That could explain how *perceiving* an ad as contemptuous could correlate with sympathy for the target and backlash against its sponsor, even if *felt* contempt has a negative impact and the ad decreases the target's favorability.

To summarize, we found that the little studied emotion of contempt was perceived most in Republican and Democratic campaign ads, and felt toward candidates by many voters; and that contempt perceived in ads unexpectedly predicted increased favorability toward the target candidate in which might be a backlash against using such an appeal. As with our 2016 Iowa Caucus study, observed independent effects of contempt and anger support discrete emotion theories of emotions and voting, and suggest it is important to add contempt to prevailing theories. They also argue for adding questions measuring contempt to surveys that attempt to understand and predict electoral outcomes, such as the American National Election Studies.

Considering the differences discussed above in the impact of contempt across candidates and elections, we suggest that the effects of contempt on voter evaluation of candidates and subsequent vote choice (as with other emotions that have been studied) are contingent on the election, the specific candidates, and the perceived competitiveness of the campaign. Based on our findings, we suggest that more researchers include contempt in studies of the emotional content of campaigns, and its impact on the perception of candidates for office and election results.

NOTES

1. Dr. Ben Carson ultimately became a member of President Trump's cabinet.

2. Retrieved from http://www.washingtontimes.com/news/2016/feb/8/donald-trump-jeb-bush-trade-loser-insult-ahead-nh-/.

3. Retrieved from http://www.cnn.com/2015/08/19/politics/donald-trump-mitt-romney-choked-2012/.

4. Retrieved from http://time.com/4224871/donald-trump-south-carolina-ted-cruz-liar/.

5. Retrieved from http://www.washingtontimes.com/news/2015/jul/21/donald-trump-lindsey-graham-total-lightweight/.

6. Of course, the history of such attacks predates 2016. For example, in 1968, an ad for the Hubert Humphrey presidential campaign featured the on-screen text "Agnew for Vice-President?" amid the sound of uncontrollable laughter. Retrieved from http://www.cbsnews.com/pictures/memorable-campaign-ads/6/.

7. Retrieved from http://www.cnn.com/2016/02/26/politics/marco-rubio-donald-trump-morning-show-attacks/.

8. Retrieved from http://thehill.com/blogs/ballot-box/presidential-races/269136-cruz-ad-on-rubio-vote-for-more-than-pretty-face.

9. Retrieved from https://www.washingtonpost.com/news/the-fix/wp/2016/02/06/transcript-of-the-feb-6-gop-debate-annotated/.

10. https://www.theguardian.com/us-news/2016/sep/30/clinton-trump-temperamentally-unfit-lead-alicia-machado.

11. More information about the survey, along with data from past years, can be found at https://cces.gov.harvard.edu/.

12. Retrieved from https://cces.gov.harvard.edu/news/cces-pre-election-survey-2016.

13. Of these, the gender breakdown was 56 percent male, 44 percent female. Mean age was 50±16. Seventy-three percent of our 801 respondents classified themselves as white, 10 percent as black, 10 percent as Hispanic, and 3 percent as Asian.

14. The Clinton attack on Trump can be found at https://www.youtube.com/watch?v=A_xkd_hWojc and the Trump attack on Clinton is at https://www.youtube.com/watch?v=XZP3clAgpuQ.

15. A smaller group of our respondents (764) were shown the videos, and of these, 726 answered all of the subsequent questions about emotions in the ad and the candidates' favorability. There were no significant demographic differences between the 764 shown the video and the full sample of 1000.

REFERENCES

Banks, Antoine J. 2014. "The Public's Anger: White Racial Attitudes and Opinions toward Health Care Reform." *Political Behavior* 36 (3): 493–514.

Cummins, J. 2007. Anything for a Vote: Dirty Tricks, Cheap Shots, and October Surprises. Quirk Books.

Finn, Christopher, and Jack Glaser. 2010. "Voter Affect and the 2008 US Presidential Election: Hope and Race Mattered." *Analyses of Social Issues and Public Policy* 10 (1): 262–275.

Fischer, Agneta. 2011. "Contempt: A Hot Feeling Hidden Under a Cold Jacket." In *Re-Constructing Emotional Spaces: From Experience to Regulation*, eds. Trnka Radek, Karel Balcar, and Martin Kuška, 77–89. Prague: College of Psychosocial Studies Press.

Fischer, Agneta., and Ira J. Roseman. 2007. "Beat Them or Ban Them: The Characteristics and Social Functions of Anger and Contempt." *Journal of Personality and Social Psychology* 93 (1): 103–115.

Frijda, N. 1986. *The Emotions*. New York: Cambridge University Press.

Gottman, John M., and Robert W. Levenson. 1992. "Marital Processes Predictive of Later Dissolution: Behavior, Physiology, and Health." *Journal of Personality and Social Psychology* 63 (2): 221–233.

Haidt, Jonathan. 2003. "The Moral Emotions." In *Handbook of Affective Sciences*, eds. Richard J. Davidson, Klaus R. Sherer, and H. Hill Goldsmith, 11:852–870. New York: Oxford University Press.

Huddy, Leonie, Lilliana Mason, and Lene Aarøe. 2015. "Expressive Partisanship: Campaign Involvement, Political Emotion, and Partisan Identity." *American Political Science Review* 109 (1): 1–17.

Hutcherson, Cendri A., and James J. Gross. 2011. "The Moral Emotions: A Social–functionalist Account of Anger, Disgust, and Contempt." *Journal of Personality and Social Psychology* 100 (4): 719–737.

Iyengar, Shanto, and Sean J. Westwood. 2015. "Fear and Loathing across Party Lines: New Evidence on Group Polarization." *American Journal of Political Science* 59 (3): 690–707.

Johnston, Gabriel, Ira Roseman, and Steven Katz. 2014. "Discrete Emotions Mediate Perceptions of Presidential Candidates: A Study Using a Nationally Representative Sample." Poster presented at the 26th Annual Convention, Eastern Psychological Association, Boston, MA.

Kuppens, Peter, Iven Van Mechelen, Dirk JM Smits, and Paul De Boeck. 2003. "The Appraisal Basis of Anger: Specificity, Necessity and Sufficiency of Components." *Emotion* 3 (3): 254–269.

Lodge, Milton, and Charles S. Taber. 2013. *The Rationalizing Voter.* Cambridge, UK: Cambridge University Press.

Marcus, George E., W. Russell Neuman, and Michael MacKuen. 2000. *Affective Intelligence and Political Judgment.* Chicago: University of Chicago Press.

Mattes, Kyle, and David P. Redlawsk. 2015. *The Positive Case for Negative Campaigning.* Chicago: University of Chicago Press.

Miller, William I. 1997. *The Anatomy of Disgust.* Cambridge: Harvard University Press.

Potegal, Michael, and Peihua Qiu. 2010. "Anger in Children's Tantrums: A New, Quantitative, Behaviorally Based Model." In *International Handbook of Anger*, eds. Michael Potegal, Gerhard Stemmler, and Charles Spielberger, 193–217. New York: Springer.

Redlawsk, David P., and Douglas R. Pierce. 2017. "Emotions and Voting." In *The SAGE Handbook of Electoral Behaviour*, edited by Kai Arzheimer, Jocelyn Evans, and Michael S. Lewis-Beck, 406–432. London: Sage.

Redlawsk, David P., Ira J. Roseman, Kyle Mattes, and Steven Katz. 2016. "Losers, Liars, and Low-energy Individuals: Examining Contempt and Anger as Factors in Candidate Evaluation." Paper presented at the annual meeting of the American Political Science Association, Philadelphia, PA.

Redlawsk, David P., Ira J. Roseman, Kyle Mattes, and Steven Katz. 2017. "Emotions, Candidate Evaluations, and Voting in the 2016 GOP Iowa Caucuses." Manuscript submitted for publication.

Romani, Simona, Silvia Grappi, and Richard P. Bagozzi. 2013. "My Anger Is Your Gain, My Contempt Your Loss: Explaining Consumer Responses to Corporate Wrongdoing." *Psychology & Marketing* 30 (12): 1029–1042.

Roseman, Ira J., Brian M. Johnston, Sean Garguilo, James L. Floman, Andrew D. Bryant, Gabriel Johnston, & Melanee K. Nugent. 2013. "Emotions Mediate Perception of Candidates in Presidential Debates." Poster presented at the 25th Annual Convention, Eastern Psychological Association, New York, NY.

Roseman, Ira J. 2018. "Rejecting the Unworthy: The Causes, Components, and Consequences of Contempt." In *The Moral Psychology of Contempt* edited by Michelle Mason. London: Rowman & Littlefield.

Sell, Aaron, John Tooby, and Leda Cosmides. 2009. "Formidability and the Logic of Human Anger." *Proceedings of the National Academy of Sciences* 106 (35): 15073–15078.

Sparks, Holloway. 2015. "Mama Grizzlies and Guardians of the Republic: The Democratic and Intersectional Politics of Anger in the Tea Party Movement." *New Political Science* 37 (1): 25–47.

Valentino, Nicholas A., Ted Brader, Eric W. Groenendyk, Krysha Gregorowicz, and Vincent L. Hutchings. 2011. "Election Night's Alright for Fighting: The Role of Emotions in Political Participation." *The Journal of Politics* 73 (1): 156–170.

Part II

POLITICAL PARTIES: DID 2016 UNDERMINE THE CONVENTIONAL WISDOM ON THE INFLUENCE OF PARTIES IN ELECTIONS?

Chapter 7

Endorsements in the 2016 Invisible Primary

Still a Useful Indicator?

Jack D. Collens and Emily O. Wanless

In a 2015 CNN focus group with supporters of Donald Trump, Susan Demelus said, "We've got people in positions of power who I know for a fact are liars. Liars […] I don't believe any one of [the politicians], not one. I believe Donald. I'm telling you, he says what I'm thinking."[1] The 2016 election cycle saw a number of voters expressing support for candidates who did not receive the support of party elites and, as Ms. Demelus's quotation demonstrates, many voters expressed anger at and distrust towards their own party's leaders. While some voters have always opposed elites within their parties, 2016 is unique in that one party—the Republicans—nominated and then elected a candidate who both lacked endorsements from party leaders and drew a number of "counter-endorsements," statements from elites expressing outright opposition to his candidacy. That Trump ultimately won his party's nomination caused a degree of anxiety among scholars of presidential nominations, as the conventional wisdom in that field would hold that elite opinion can help influence voter's decision-making in a meaningful way. Meanwhile, Democratic voters were split between a candidate who received an overwhelming majority of her party leaders' endorsements and a candidate who received few endorsements and—until he announced his candidacy—was not even a Democrat. While Clinton ultimately won the nomination in the end, Sanders's successes and the continued rift between what some might call "mainstream" Democrats and the "Sanders wing" of the party have raised a number of questions about the future impact party leaders can have. These two nomination campaigns raise a number of questions, including whether the assumptions underlying key arguments by scholars of the influence of elite opinion on the mass public are no longer valid.

This study seeks to tie these candidates' surprising successes to the conventional wisdom offered by two theoretical veins of American politics—the "party decides" theory of presidential nominations and the decline of trust in government theory. If both Bernie Sanders and Donald Trump appealed to the types of voters least likely to trust political elites, this may explain why endorsements for Hillary Clinton or the clear anti-Trump signals ("counter-endorsements") from Republican elites failed to move large numbers of voters away from Sanders and Trump, respectively.

Postmortem analyses following the 2016 presidential primaries appeared grim for the "party decides" theory of presidential nominations (Cohen, et al. 2008), one of political science's most discussed theories in recent times. Conventional wisdom stemming from this theory maintains that endorsements from influential party stakeholders provide a signal to voters indicating who has the support of the party. When one candidate accumulates a critical mass of elite endorsements, this indicates a candidate's broad acceptability to a party's factions, which then cues voters and leads to primary victories. However, in 2016 we saw a potential rejection of this conventional wisdom. While the Republican Party fail to unite behind any one candidate, a number of high-profile figures within the party vigorously objected to the ultimate nominee Donald Trump. On the Democratic side, Hillary Clinton received a tidal wave of endorsements, yet struggled to defeat party outsider, Senator Bernie Sanders.

Core supporters of Trump and Sanders appeared to be composed of people who, conventional wisdom would tell us, would be the least likely to trust government. Both the literature and available survey data suggest that evaluations of the economy are significant predictors of trust—respondents who perceive a stronger economy and are optimistic about future economic gains are more likely to trust the government in both parties. Additionally, respondents who indicate a feeling of "connectedness" to government are more likely to trust government. Early supporters of Trump and Sanders appeared to be some of the most economically challenged and marginalized members of the population, exactly the type of voter least likely to trust government.

To ascertain whether the candidacies of Sanders and Trump were buoyed by their core supporters' lack of trust in political elites, a result of declining governmental trust in general, we determine whether the early (pre-Iowa) supporters of each candidate were those least likely to trust government. By considering the "party decides" theory in light of the theories surrounding trust in government, the unexpected successes of Trump and Sanders in 2016 begin to make more sense. Results that appear detrimental to the conventional wisdom of the "party decides" theory actually are better explained through application of what the conventional wisdom surrounding trust levels in government says about the ineffectiveness of party elites when governmental trust is low. This study thus provides support for the hypothesis that Trump/Sanders supporters were insulated from the traditional effects of elite endorsements due to their lack of trust in government (and, presumably, political elites).

We begin by examining political science research on both the "party decides" theory of presidential nominations and the determinants of political trust. Following this review, we will turn to recent survey data (from the 2012 ANES and 2016 ANES Pilot Study) to identify the common predictors of trust in government within each party. Conducted at the end of the "invisible primary" phase (January 2016), the Pilot Study survey allows us to examine how potential voters felt before the first results were uncovered, but after the most influential endorsements had been reported by the media. We will conclude with a discussion of the implications of this particular "invisible primary" phase nomination season on the broader theoretical understanding regarding the role of the political elite in presidential selection. While these findings cannot speak to the broader implications of declining trust, it appears that candidates who appeal specifically to those voters least likely to trust government will find little reason to worry about a lack of elite support.

THE "CONVENTIONAL WISDOM"

Since the publication of *The Party Decides* by Marty Cohen, David Karol, Hans Noel, and John Zaller in 2008, scholars of American presidential elections have devoted considerable attention to applying the logic of that seminal text to contemporary nomination campaigns. Moreover, political pundits have discovered the arguments laid forth by Cohen and colleagues, employing them to better understand ongoing events. Punditry websites such as FiveThirtyEight and the *New York Times*'s The Upshot prominently featured graphics tracking the number of endorsements each candidate earned prior to and during the 2016 nomination contests. In discussing their new trackers, both sites either directly or indirectly cited *The Party Decides* (Bycoffe 2015; Aisch, et al. 2015; Vavreck 2015). Clearly, then, *The Party Decides* has made its way into the consciousness of American political punditry and represented—at the start of the 2016 election cycle—the "conventional wisdom" of how presidential nominees are chosen.

In this section, we review the (relevant) central arguments of *The Party Decides* and the works that preceded and built upon it. In doing so, we hope to provide an accurate representation of the current "conventional wisdom" among presidential nomination scholars. We then discuss the limitations of this approach and how these limitations may help to explain why the 2016 nomination battles provoked so much consternation among pundits and scholars alike.

The Party Decides was built upon a foundation created by dozens of earlier scholars. It is not our intention to delineate the genealogy of the book's central theses, but the relevance of some of these earlier works to our current study merits discussion here. First, Kam (2005) uncovers evidence that more politically aware people are less likely to rely on party (or elite) cues when forming issue opinions than the less politically aware. Extending this research to the sphere of candidate evaluations and vote intention, then, we can infer that less politically aware voters may be more susceptible to influence by elite endorsement than their more aware counterparts. This helps to uncover the mechanism by which elite endorsements may influence voter decision-making.

One of the clearest antecedents for *The Party Decides* was the work of Wayne Steger. In earlier works, Steger examined presidential primary campaigns and found that endorsements by party leaders "thus appear to have a potent effect signaling the partisan electorate as to which candidates should be supported even prior to the caucuses and primaries" (2007, 97). Ultimately, elite endorsements influence voters by sending a cue to voters regarding a candidate's viability and broader support. Fitting this research into the context established by Kam (2005), in the more strategic environment of primary voting, even politically aware voters may ultimately opt to vote for a candidate farther from their ideal point than another option. This is because—though these voters do not base their preferences on elite cues—their decision-making in this environment is less driven by ideological preference and more by candidate viability. Elite endorsements can inform such perceptions of viability.

The authors of *The Party Decides* build on this earlier research by incorporating their own theory of political parties. Parties—in their view—are best thought of as coalitions of policy demanders. These policy demanders exert influence over the political process by choosing nominees for public office and holding officeholders accountable through the nomination system. Under this formulation, then, parties seek to control the nomination process even when formal rules render direct influence impractical or impossible. Moreover, these intense policy demanders prefer to coordinate in advance of a nomination battle to choose a nominee behind whom they will marshal their combined resources. Thus, their efforts are aimed at reducing the options available to voters to their preferred choice(s) and—assuming they have not reduced the options to only their preferred choice—directing resources in support of their choice. Examples of these resources may include funds, endorsements, and activist support. Endorsements thus help to advance the policy demanders' preferred candidates.

Importantly, for these efforts to have their intended effects, the policy demanders must coordinate to help a preferred candidate. While the factions within the coalition of policy demanders may have diverse preferences, a candidate acceptable to all factions may emerge. This candidate will receive a wave of endorsements during the "invisible primary" phase and then see additional media coverage, funds, and further endorsements. Ultimately, this candidate should receive more delegates and win the nomination.

To test their theories, Cohen, et al. examine all candidates for the major-party nominations for president from 1980 to 2004. They study the standing and resources of candidates before the first contest (in Iowa), including poll results, endorsements from party elites, funds, and media coverage (in the last quarter of the invisible primary) to determine each factor's impact on candidate delegate share (measured in a variety of ways). The authors find that endorsements have the greatest effect on ultimate delegate counts, providing support for the idea that endorsements offer an important path to victory for candidates in the invisible primary phase of the nomination contest (2008, 285).

In work building off of the arguments made in *The Party Decides*, Summary (2010) finds that endorsements by sitting members of Congress and governors increased a candidate's state-level vote share in the 2008 Democratic primary season, providing additional evidence for Cohen, et al.'s (2008) argument that endorsements *can* have state-level effects (though they find that most of the effects are found at the national level). Importantly, Cohen, et al. (2008) and Summary (2010) both find that the state-level effects of endorsements are conditional on a number of other factors.

Kousser, et al. (2015) examined California's 2012 state primary election and found that the endorsement of the Democratic Party led to significant increases in vote share of the endorsed candidate. Although this study only examined candidates for state-level offices and the effects of the most salient party elite (the California Democratic Party), the logic is still similar to that offered by Cohen, et al. (2008). In particular, Kousser and his coauthors find that the effects in California were concentrated only among Democratic and independent voters and that only traditional, labor-oriented Democratic candidates enjoyed the benefits of the endorsement (as opposed to pro-business Democrats). These results suggest that the broader effects of endorsements are still not well understood in political science. Although Cohen, et al. (2008) find that endorsements help, they do not distinguish between different types of candidates or how the effects may not be uniform across voters.

This study seeks to speak to that last concern. One potential limitation of the theories advanced in *The Party Decides* is that the authors assume that voters trust elites and the signals they send. They state, "If voters trust their party leadership, endorsements might have great influence. But if voters are ignorant of leader endorsements, or simply independent minded, endorsements might not make two cents worth of difference" (2008, 278). That they ultimately find that endorsements have strong effects does not dismiss this concern. It is still possible that large numbers of voters disregard elite signals because they simply do not trust those elites. Later, Cohen, et al. even acknowledge this potential limitation of their study: "The degree to which voters think for themselves in politics, as against following the advice of others whom they trust, is an absolutely central question [...] on which we wish we could have shed more light in this study" (2008, 359). Thus, the authors concede that voters may still make up their own minds, disregarding the signals sent by those they trust. This leaves open an intriguing question: What happens when voters actively distrust their party elites? These voters may still reach the same conclusion as those party elites for ideological reasons, but it is also likely that they will choose to support the strongest "outsider" candidate. It is to these possibilities we now turn our attention.

We begin by reviewing the literature on trust in government, as a way to uncover the determinants of trust most commonly uncovered in the literature. We then test these determinants by examining the 2012 American National Election Study. In particular, we examine the determinants of trust in government *within* each party. Once we have established the common determinants of trust in government, we examine the determinants of support for the two "outsider" candidates (who did not receive many elite endorsements in 2016 or—in the case of Republican Donald Trump—received strong "counter-endorsement" messages from elites) using the 2016 NES Pilot Study, conducted before the Iowa caucuses. We expect that the types of voters least likely to trust political elites will be those most likely to offer early support for Donald Trump (among Republicans) and Sen. Bernie Sanders (among Democrats). This would suggest that endorsements are only important for voter decision-making among those voters who trust government elites and the signals they send.

Trust in Government

In 1958, the American National Election Studies began asking respondents to comment on their trust in government (Vavreck 2015). These early surveys found that people in the 1960s trusted government and perceived officials to be skilled, principled, and as a result, beneficial to the nation as a whole (Dalton 2005). The net result was high levels of approval for government. In that initial survey, 73 percent of respondents fell into either of the two "trust" categories, with the remaining 27 percent identified with one of the two "untrusting" categories.[2] However, in recent years those percentages have practically switched. In 2014, Pew Research (the public opinion organization asking questions on levels of trust in government during non-presidential election years) found only 24 percent of respondents indicated some level of trust. Citizens now perceive government to be filled with dishonest politicians focused on their own interests rather than what is in the best interest of the country (Dalton 2005).

These survey responses exemplify the trend we see in levels of governmental trust by the American people. Trust levels were greatest in the late 1950s and early 1960s, with 75 percent of respondents indicating a trust in government shortly after President Johnson assumed the presidency upon President Kennedy's assassination. Trust levels declined throughout the Johnson, Nixon, Ford, and Carter Administrations, bottoming out in 1980 (Citrin and Luks 2001). By this time, 75 percent of respondents fell into the two "untrusting" categories. Surprisingly, the ramifications of the Watergate scandal were not the only cause for the dramatic decline in public confidence, as trust levels had already dropped by twenty-three points by 1972 (Alford 2001). Trust in government rebounded slightly with the Reagan Administration, but has seen a rather steady decline since September 11, 2001. This trend of a declining trust in government is not exclusive to the United States. Trust levels have been on the decline among almost all advanced industrialized democracies (Dalton 2005; Norris 1999; Pharr and Putnam 2002).

If the declining trust in government cannot be attributed to the massive scandal of Watergate, nor is it exclusive to the United States, what does account for the public's faith in government? The answer to this question has been a source of scholarly debate since the 1970s. Initial explanations maintained various demographic characteristics were the source for decline, with disparities among racial, educational level, and/or income reflecting a growing distrust of government performance. For example, levels of public trust in government correlated with social reactions like the Blacklash of the 1970s (Alford 2001).

However, as these demographic markers did not consistently trend with levels of trust in government, scholars sought alternative explanations. From the very beginning, the debate over what impacts trust levels centered on whether declining trust levels corresponded to a long-term change in political culture (Miller 1974), or by short-term responses to the political environment (Citrin 1974). Miller (1974) maintained the public's waning trust in government resulted from a change in the country's political culture, which was increasingly rejecting the political regime. For Miller, the political regime is society's core set of beliefs, values, and rules that govern political behavior. Dissatisfaction of members of both political parties, as well as the consequential nature of big picture, long-term factors like suspicion of power, served as evidence for this rejected political regime theory, and the corresponding decrease in government trust levels.

Arguing that decreasing levels of trust in government were spurred by reactions to the current political environment, Citrin (1974) attributed dissatisfaction to incumbents, not necessarily both political parties. Specifically, survey respondents indicated dissatisfaction for the party in power (both the president and Congress). Additionally, short-term evaluations of economic and social issues were more influential than long-term forces (see also Vavreck 2015).

The debate on what drives levels of political trust continues today, but largely remains divided around these ideas of holistic, systemic dissatisfaction beyond the current political environment and a referendum on the current political environment. Specifically, this dichotomy has been discussed in a number of ways. Orren (1997) distinguished between long-term forces, such as distribution of power and authoritative figures, views of the health of political institution, and society's political culture, and short-term forces, like national conditions or policy output. Tyler and Degoey (1996) argue when discussing trust it is important to consider the type of trust. Is the growing dissatisfaction a result of a decline in relational trust, a failure of intentions, or instrumental trust, measured by an inability to produce desired outcomes (see also Barber 1983 for a discussion on the gap between expectations and perceived outcomes)? Similarly, Chanley, Rudolph, and Rahn (2000) find that trust levels correlate with expectations and outputs surrounding economic, government, and societal performance.

However, Hetherington and Rudolph (2008) and Chanley (2002) take it one step further, maintaining the drop in levels of governmental trust results from a shift in what Americans use to evaluate government performance. Historically, Americans have utilized international issues to gauge success, issues sparking patriotism, unity, and subsequently, led to positive connotations of the country and administration. However, today's evaluations stem from perceptions derived from the government's handling of frequently contentious and divisive domestic issues. Americans only utilize economic factors when the economy is struggling, and typically consider domestic crime rates over international incidents.

Finally, scholars have looked to explain declining trust by considering a populace's connectedness to the government versus their current evaluations of it (Cook and Gronke 2005). Comparing the results of the National Election Survey and the General Social Survey, the authors find that trust is impacted by current evaluations of government and skepticism toward the efficacy one has within the political system. For example, personal economic conditions influence satisfaction with governance (Cook and Gronke 2005; Lipset and Schneider 1987; Newton and Morris 2000) and representation (Bartels 2005), while connectedness, as measured by feelings of interpersonal trust, impacts the attitudes about society generally, and the role government plays within it (Brehm and Rahn 1997; Cook and Gronke 2005).

Building off of this idea of trust levels driven by connectedness rather than simply short-term evaluations of the current political context, Cramer's research on the recall election of Wisconsin governor Scott Walker proposes that trust in government is explained by the politics of resentment (2016). Particularly applicable to the 2016 Election and the resulting explanations for a Trump victory, Cramer notes a significant rural-urban divide that exists in Wisconsin (and elsewhere) that promotes a certain distrust of government. This rural-urban divide not only divides people by a different belief system, but also creates a feeling of resentment based on the perceptions of government attentiveness. Specifically, the rural populations in this country feel the party establishment is focused almost exclusively on the urban population, and most certainly at the expense of the rural population. Cramer maintains that rural residents feel their rightfully owed resources are not allocated and their values not championed. The net result of this resentment toward the current representation and governance is a distrust of government and an overarching desire for less government.

Regardless of how we frame the debate surrounding the cause of declining levels of government trust, conventional wisdom from the field of study draws two main conclusions. First, demographics, such as income, education, and race do not matter in the prediction of trust levels. Second, personal perceptions drive the lenses in which government is evaluated. Party identification ideology, especially in the context of the ruling party, and economic evaluations matter most to when determining trust levels. In the next section, we apply this logic to the question of the 2016 nomination cycle.

DATA AND METHODS

To examine the relationship between trust in government and support for 2016's two clearest "outsider" candidates, we begin by confirming the determinants of trust in government using the 2012 American National Election Study. Although this is from 2012, we do not have a more comprehensive survey with all of the necessary variables from any time closer to the beginning of the 2016 presidential primary season. The 2016 ANES Pilot Study—which we later use to test for early support for Trump and Sanders—does not ask about trust. While we could use the full 2016 ANES, this survey was fielded after Donald Trump and Hillary Clinton had won their respective nominations and voters had been exposed to the continued rhetoric of Trump, Sanders, and the other "anti-establishment" candidates. We anticipate that this rhetoric may have led their supporters to further distrust political elites. To avoid any such contamination, we chose the 2012 ANES survey, the most recent survey with all necessary variables.

The 2016 ANES Pilot Study was fielded from January 22 to January 28, 2016. Important for our purposes, this timing coincides with the very end of the "invisible primary" period. We use this study—rather than the 2016 ANES Time Series study—because it will measure the earliest supporters of Trump and Sanders. This allows us to examine the core supporters for each candidate, presumably before others have begun supporting them because of their electoral successes, but after party elites have expressed their opinions about these candidates. Unfortunately, this survey lacks a question about government trust. As such, we must examine whether the *types* of voters who distrust government elites are the same *types* who support Trump or Sanders. We concede that this is an imperfect instrument, but it should uncover any connection between trust in political elites and support for the candidates who lacked endorsements (or even were "counter-endorsed" in Trump's case).

While the existing literature on trust emphasized the role of partisanship in determining trust, we are primarily interested in which voters *within* each party are least likely to trust government. Thus, we look to other factors, including income, ideology, economic outlook and perceptions, interest in and attention to politics, the adequacy of government services, perceptions of racial bias, presidential job approval, patriotic sentiment, and various demographic factors such as race, gender, and age. Table 7.1 displays the variables used in all analyses. While the 2012 ANES and 2016 Pilot Study use similar variables, they are often measured differently, so the table contains information about measurement as well. Readers should note that several variables are coded in reverse—for example, higher values of the trust variable indicate less trust in government, higher values of importance of American identity indicate lower importance, etc.

Based on our reading of the literature on political trust, we expect better evaluations of economic performance and outlook to correlate positively with trust, within both parties. We expect that approval of President Obama's job as president will positively predict trust, as this would substitute for partisanship within the parties. Finally, we anticipate strong identification as an American to positively correlate with trust in government. Identifying with one's government is a clear sign that you feel connected to it, and research shows the more connected one feels to government, the more they trust that government to be serving the needs of its constituents. Besides these predictors, we have no strong expectations for the other variables, as the literature is unclear as to their potential effects. We have included many of them because they were mentioned in at least one of the several prior studies on political trust or because they represent basic demographic information that should be included in any individual-level study of public opinion.

We use ordered logit to regress political trust on each of these factors within each party, categorizing as Republicans (Democrats), all self-identified Republicans (Democrats), and Republican (Democratic) leaners. Importantly, we also use the same factors when examining the 2016 Pilot Study data, employing standard logistic (logit) regression to estimate a model predicting Trump/Sanders support. Thus, while the list of covariates in each

Table 7.1   Measurement and Means of Variables Used

Variable	2012 ANES Measurement	Mean	2016 Pilot Study Measurement	Mean
Trust	1=Always 4=Never	2.86		
Candidate support (R: Trump; D: Sanders)			0=No support 1=Support	R: 0.23 D: 0.31
Voted in past	0=Did not vote 1=Voted 2008	0.78	0=Did not vote 1=Voted 2012	0.79
Plan to vote	0=0–20% likely 4=81–100%	3.30	Percentage likelihood	85.70
Registered to vote	0=Not registered 1=Registered	0.88	0=Not registered 1=Registered	0.89
Pays attention	1=Always 5=Never	2.63	1=Most of time 4=Hardly at all	1.80
Rally attendance	0=No 1=Yes	0.06	1=Extr likely 5=Not likely at all	3.68
Contribution	0=No 1=Yes	0.13	0=No 1=Yes	0.21
Income	1=Under $5000 28=$250,000+	13.35	1=Under $10000 16=Over $500000	5.66
Economic performance	1=Much better 5=Much worse	3.13	1=Much better 5=Much worse	3.05
Economic outlook/ opportunity	1=V. likely to imp 5=V. unlikely	2.64	1=None 5=A great deal	2.63
Adequacy of govt. services	1=Many fewer 7=Many more	3.88	1=Reduce 7=Increase	4.08
Pref. treatment for blacks	1=Favors whites 3=Favors blacks	2.19	1=Favors whites 7=Favors blacks	3.61
Obama job approval	1=Approve str 5=Disapprove str	2.81	1=Appr extr str 7=Disap extr str	4.19
Conservatism	1=Extr liberal 7=Extr conservative	4.17	1=Extr liberal 7=Extr conservative	3.94
American identity	1=Extr impt 5=Not at all impt	1.83	1=Extr impt 5=Not at all impt	2.14
Nonwhite	0=White, non-Hisp 1=Nonwhite	0.41	0=White, non-Hisp 1=Nonwhite	0.27
Education	1=Less than HS 5=Graduate degree	2.97	1=No HS 6=Postgraduate	3.22
Age	Respondent's age	49.44	Respondent's age	48.06
Male	0=Female 1=Male	0.48	0=Female 1=Male	0.48

model is imperfect, it is the best list which—according to theory—should influence both dependent variables. If our theory that the voters least likely to trust government are those most likely to express a 2016 candidate preference contrary to their party elites' stated preferences holds, we should see the same variables predicting lower trust predicting higher support for Trump and Sanders.

RESULTS AND DISCUSSION

Table 7.2 displays the results of the models of both trust and candidate support. Looking first at the predictions of trust for both Democrats and Republicans, it is evident that stronger evaluations of the economy's recent performance predict stronger trust in government (recall that both trust and economic performance are coded such that higher values equate to greater pessimism). Among Republicans, the probability of a respondent answering that they trust those in government to do what is right at least most of the time falls more than 15 percent (from a predicted 24% to a predicted 8%, holding all other variables at their medians) as the respondent moves from feeling the economy is much better than a year ago to much worse than a year ago. For Democrats, the decrease is by slightly more than 10 percent (from a predicted 28% to a predicted 17%). We also see that, across both parties, stronger approval of President Obama's job performance predicts stronger trust in government, with moving from strongly approving to strongly disapproving decreasing both Republicans' and Democrats' predicted likelihood of trusting government at least most of the time by about 15 percent. Finally, in both parties the importance of being American to one's identity predicts stronger trust in government. Moving a respondent from feeling that being American is extremely important to not at all important reduced Republicans' trust by little more than 5 percent and Democrats' trust by little more than 10 percent.

For Republicans, those respondents who believe their economic outlook is unlikely to improve saw reduced trust, as did those who believe government social spending is excessive and that it favors blacks over whites. We also see that more conservative Republicans are more likely to trust government than more moderate Republicans. For Democrats, those attending rallies were more likely to trust government. Surprisingly, those Democrats who made political contributions in the past 12 months were less likely to trust government than those who had not. We also see that poorer, nonwhite, and older Democrats were more likely to trust government. While the coefficient for nonwhite may surprise some, the presence of a black president in the

Table 7.2 Predictors of Trust and Candidate Support

Variable	Republicans		Democrats	
	Trust	Trump	Trust	Sanders
Voted past election	**−0.494***	**−0.960****	0.028	−0.457
	(0.266)	**(0.461)**	(0.167)	(0.417)
Plan to vote in next election	0.038	−0.001	0.008	0.014**
	(0.082)	(0.009)	(0.057)	(0.007)
Registered to vote	0.481	−0.523	−0.135	0.615
	(0.379)	(0.814)	(0.259)	(0.586)
Pays attention to politics	−0.075	0.134	0.022	−0.240
	(0.073)	(0.185)	(0.051)	(0.157)
Rally attendance	−0.205	−0.065	−0.384**	0.237**
	(0.285)	(0.101)	(0.184)	(0.097)
Political contribution	0.077	0.172	0.293**	0.376
	(0.216)	(0.346)	(0.149)	(0.277)
Income	−0.007	−0.014	0.014**	−0.012
	(0.010)	(0.037)	(0.007)	(0.038)
Economic performance	0.301**	−0.104	*0.154***	0.081
	(0.079)	(0.156)	*(0.062)*	(0.124)
Economic outlook/ opportunity	**0.206****	**−0.197***	−0.009	*−0.487***
	(0.056)	**(0.121)**	(0.043)	*(0.133)*
Adequacy of govt. services	−0.264**	−0.045	−0.029	0.067
	(0.058)	(0.093)	(0.041)	(0.080)
Pref. treatment for blacks	0.393**	0.152	−0.060	−0.094
	(0.148)	(0.095)	(0.197)	(0.087)
Obama job approval	0.264**	0.076	0.311**	−0.121
	(0.072)	(0.130)	(0.059)	(0.085)
Conservatism	−0.180**	−0.116	0.033	−0.233**
	(0.070)	(0.120)	(0.042)	(0.088)
American identity	0.195**	−0.325**	**0.146****	**0.211****
	(0.082)	(0.154)	**(0.052)**	**(0.096)**
Nonwhite	−0.211	−1.027**	**−0.464****	**−0.938****
	(0.184)	(0.499)	**(0.111)**	**(0.265)**

Table 7.2   Predictors of Trust and Candidate Support (continued)

	Republicans		Democrats	
Variable	Trust	Trump	Trust	Sanders
Education	–0.049	–0.135	0.057	–0.005
	(0.069)	(0.086)	(0.049)	(0.081)
Age	–0.001	0.004	–0.007*	–0.018**
	(0.004)	(0.009)	(0.004)	(0.008)
Male	0.058	–0.018	0.042	0.277
	(0.140)	(0.256)	(0.100)	(0.228)
Constant		2.341		–0.478
		(1.670)		(1.210)
N	1581	326	2131	444
Cut–point 1	–3.098		–3.195	
Cut–point 2	–0.312		–0.399	
Cut–point 3	4.980		4.412	

Bolded figures represent clear support for our hypotheses across identical variables (predicting both candidate support and trust in government). Italicized figures represent support for our hypotheses across similar variables predicting both. Thus, while restrospective evaluations of the economy predict trust among Democrats, prospective evaluations predict support for Sanders. While not identical variables, the results – taken together – are supportive of our hypothesis that similar factors will predict trust and support for Sanders.
Note: Estimates are ordered logistic (trust) and logistic (candidate support) regression coefficients, standard errors in parentheses. *$p \leq 0.10$, **$p \leq 0.05$
Source: 2012 ANES (trust), 2016 ANES Pilot Study (candidate support).

White House likely contributed to higher levels of government trust among nonwhite Democrats.

Based on the findings related to political trust, we should expect higher support for Donald Trump among Republicans who: perceived poor economic performance and outlook; believed government social spending is excessive and favors blacks; disapproved strongly of President Obama's job as president; were less conservative; and placed greater importance on being American.

We should expect higher support for Sen. Bernie Sanders among Democrats who: do not attend political rallies; had not recently contributed to a candidate; were of a higher income; were more pessimistic about the economy; disapproved of the job Barack Obama was doing as president; and were white.

Turning now to the results in Table 7.2 for the models of candidate support, the four significant predictors of Trump support among Republicans are: whether they voted in 2012 (decreases the probability of Trump support); economic outlook (stronger outlook decreases Trump support); felt that being American was important to their identity (increased Trump support); and were nonwhite (decreased Trump support). Table 7.3 depicts the marginal effects of each of these variables on the probability that the respondent would support Trump (holding all other variables at their medians/means). Moving each of the

Table 7.3 **Marginal Effects on Candidate Support (Significant Variables Only)**

Variable	ΔPr(Trump Support)	ΔPr(Sanders Support)
Voted in last election (0→1)	–0.236	
Intention to vote (70→100)		+0.105
Rally attendance (1→5)		+0.232
Economic outlook/opportunity (1→5)	–0.189	–0.450
Conservatism (1→3)		–0.113
American identity (1→5)	–0.251	+0.193
Nonwhite (0→1)	–0.211	–0.230
Age (41→65)		–0.107

four significant predictors of Trump support from their minimum to maximum values, we can see that the strongest substantive predictor of Trump support is the importance of being American to one's identity, as movement across the full range decreases the predicted likelihood that the respondent will support Trump by more than 25 percent. Next is whether the respondent voted in 2012 (reduces likelihood of Trump support by nearly 24%), and whether the respondent is nonwhite (reduces Trump support by 21%). Finally, a respondent believing there is a great deal of opportunity for the average American to get ahead (economic outlook/opportunity) is 19 percent less likely to support Trump than a respondent saying there is no such opportunity, all else equal.

Among Democratic respondents to the 2016 NES Pilot Study, significant predictors of support for Sanders include intention to vote in 2016, rally attendance, economic outlook/opportunity, conservatism, the importance of being American to one's identity, the respondent's race, and the respondent's age. Again, Table 7.3 demonstrates the effects of changes in each significant independent variable on the probability the respondent will support Sanders. Substantively, economic outlook/opportunity is the strongest predictor of Sanders support, as those perceiving a great deal of opportunity for the average person to get ahead were 45 percent less likely to support Sanders than those believing there is no such opportunity. Other strong predictors include rally attendance (decreases Sanders support by 23%, as a 5 indicates the respondent is very unlikely to attend a rally), the respondent's race (nonwhites were 23% less likely to support Sanders), and the importance of being American to one's identity (moving from most to least important increased Sanders support by 19%).

Comparing these results to the results from the model predicting trust among Republicans, we see little overlap. The figures in bold in the first two columns of Table 7.2 display those that predict both trust and Trump support in the correct direction (predicting less trust and more likely to support Trump). Looking at the 2012 ANES, those respondents who voted in 2008 and who had pessimistic feelings about the economy were less likely to report that they trusted those in government to do what is right. In the 2016 ANES, those who voted in 2012 and who felt pessimistic about the economy were more likely to support Trump.

Thus, there is some evidence that the types of voters who distrust government elites were the types to support Donald Trump in spite of elite signals against Trump. Unfortunately, many other significant predictors of trust (the adequacy of government services, perceived racial bias, and conservatism) do not predict Trump support in any significant way. Moreover, the importance of being American to one's identity predicts higher trust *and* greater support for Trump. As such, the results for Republican voters are decidedly mixed.

Among Democrats, there is more overlap between predictors of trust and predictors of Sanders support. As seen by the bolded results in the last two columns of Table 7.2, two variables clearly predict lower trust and higher likelihood of supporting Sanders: the importance of being American to one's identity and the respondent's race. In fact, these were the third and fourth most substantively significant predictors of trust and ended up being strong predictors of Sanders support as well. One other variable to note is economic outlook/opportunity. Although this variable did not reach significance in predicting trust, economic performance did (and it was the second most substantively important variable for predicting trust among Democrats, after Obama job approval). Thus, if we view both evaluations of previous economic performance and economic outlook/opportunity as two measures of the same underlying concept—general perceptions of the American economy—the types of voters who are bullish on the economy are more likely to trust government elites (which coincides well with prior literature on trust) and less likely to support Sanders. Indeed, economic outlook/opportunity is, by far, the strongest substantive predictor of support for Sanders among Democratic voters, as seen in Table 7.3.

Thus, although other predictors of trust among Democrats do not predict Sanders support (or, in the case of rally attendance, actually predicts Sanders support *and* higher trust), the most substantively important predictors of trust (including economic perceptions, the importance of being American to one's identity, and the respondent's race) predict Sanders support such that the types of Democrats least likely to trust government elites are the most likely to support Sanders.

CONCLUSION

While *The Party Decides* has certainly earned the status "conventional wisdom," the 2016 elections provided some important clarifications and refinements of the theories presented by Cohen, et al. (2008). As Steger (2016) notes, in light of the 2016 nomination contests, it is clear that elites do not always coordinate—when and why they do so remains in question. He also argues that elite influence is largely limited in the current era to "weeding out the chafe from the seed before the caucuses and primaries" (714). Our research provides an additional potential caveat. While Republican elites did not coordinate to endorse one candidate, they clearly coordinated in an effort to stop businessman Donald Trump. That they were ineffective in doing so provides evidence that their powers of influence are limited and that these limitations are exacerbated with a wider field and no clear alternative. Democratic elites did coordinate, but the unwillingness of a large portion of the Democratic electorate to support Hillary Clinton—and the deep resentment many Democratic voters felt toward the DNC after November—provides evidence that the waning power of elite endorsements is bipartisan.

While our work provides strong evidence that Democratic voters who distrusted elites were particularly prone to support Sanders, the evidence among Republicans was decidedly mixed. One possible explanation is that the "outsider" or "anti-establishment" vote may have been divided between Trump and Sen. Ted Cruz of Texas. Nonetheless, we find some evidence that Republicans inclined to distrust elites may have been more likely to support Trump. Perhaps Trump's unique platform spoke more to some of these types of voters than others. Similarly, among Democrats, Sanders's platform was very clearly an "outsider" and "anti-establishment" platform. His successes suggest a potential further rift in the Democratic electorate, as other candidates (such as Massachusetts Sen. Elizabeth Warren) emphasize the issues of concern to those who feel the American economy cannot work for them. As we have seen, these are exactly the types of voters inclined to disregard elite preferences, so no amount of elite endorsements will sway their decisions if one of these candidates remains in the field. That the Democratic Party is witnessing more of its candidates down-ballot emphasizing issues of economic inequality and a "rigged" system may end up creating difficulties if those elites intend to coordinate to support another candidate. On the Republican side, there is little evidence thus far to suggest that a strong wave of candidates is emerging who appeal specifically to those Republican voters least likely to trust elite opinion. As such, Republican elites may have an easier time coordinating and influencing voters in the future than Democratic elites.

Our research provides evidence that a key assumption of *The Party Decides* may be breaking down for at least one of the two major parties. While this requires reading and applying conventional wisdom a bit differently, it does not undermine the central arguments of Cohen, et al. (2008)—elites often attempt to coordinate to support their preferred presidential candidate, but are often unable to and, when they do, they are often successful in steering the electorate to their preferred candidate. As we have demonstrated, for some types of voters and some types of candidates, endorsements will be less success-ful. Thus far, this has not clearly led to elites being "rolled" by voters, but recent events in the Democratic Party make that party more likely to oppose the wishes of its elites. In the meantime, however, we find no clear evidence that endorse-ments are any less useful for the average candidate or nomination campaign.

NOTES

1. Lee, M.J. and Kait Richmond. 2015. "I Am a Trump Supporter: Voters Speak Out." *CNN* December 11. Accessed online December 11, 2015. http://www.cnn.com/2015/12/10/politics/donald-trump-supporters-speak-out/.

2. The survey question gave participants five responses to choose from when asked, "How much of the time do you think you can trust the government in Wash-ington to do what is right—just about always, most of the time, only some of the time, or none of the time."

REFERENCES

Aisch, Gregor, Wilson Andrews, Alicia Parlapiano, and Derek Willis. 2015. "Who's Winning the Presidential Campaign?" *New York Times Upshot*, September 15. Accessed June 27, 2017. https://www.nytimes.com/interactive/2016/us/elections/presidential-candidates-dashboard.html.

Alford, John R. 2001. *Political Attitudes in America: Formation and Change.* San Francisco: W.H. Freeman.

American National Election Studies. 2012. "Trust the Federal Government, 1958-2012."

Barber, Bernard. 1983. *The Logic and Limits of Trust.* New Brunswick, NJ: Rutgers University Press.

Bartels, Larry M. 2005. "Homer Gets a Tax Cut: Inequality and Public Policy in the American Mind." *Perspectives on Politics* 3(1): 15-31.

Brehm, John and Wendy Rahn. 1997. "Individual-Level Evidence for the Causes and Consequences of Social Capital." *American Journal of Political Science* 41(3): 999-1023.

Bycoffe, Aaron. 2015. "The Endorsement Primary." *FiveThirtyEight.com*, July 14. Accessed June 27, 2017. https://projects.fivethirtyeight.com/2016-endorsement-primary/.

Chanley, Virginia A. 2002. "Trust in Government in the Aftermath of 9/11: Determi-nants and Consequences." *Political Psychology* 23(3): 469-483.

Chanley, Virginia A., Thomas J. Rudolph, and Wendy M. Rahn. 2000. "The Origins and Consequences of Public Trust in Government." *Public Opinion Quarterly* 64(3): 239-256.

Citrin, Jack. 1974. "Comment: The Political Relevance of Trust in Government." *American Political Science Review* 68(3): 973-988.

Citrin, Jack and Samantha Luks. 2001. "Revisiting Political Trust in an Angry Age." In *What is it about Government that Americans Dislike?*, edited by John R. Hibbing and Elizabeth Theiss-Morse, 9-27. New York, NY: Cambridge University Press.

Cohen, Marty, David Karol, Hans Noel, and John Zaller. 2008. *The Party Decides: Presidential Nominations Before and After Reform.* Chicago: University of Chicago Press.

Cook, Timothy E. and Paul Gronke. 2005. "The Skeptical American: Revisiting the Meanings of Trust in Government and Confidence in Institutions." *Journal of Politics* 63(3): 784-803.

Cramer, Katherine J. 2016. *The Politics of Resentment: Rural Consciousness in Wisconsin and the Rise of Scott Walker.* Chicago, IL: University of Chicago Press.

Dalton, Russell J. 2005. "The Social Transformation of Trust in Government." *International Review of Sociology* 15 (1): 133-154.

Hetherington, Marc J. and Thomas J. Rudolph. 2008. "Priming, Performance, and the Dynamics of Political Trust." *Journal of Politics* 70(2): 498-512.

Kam, Cindy D. 2005. "Who Toes the Party Line? Cues, Values, and Individual Differences." *Political Behavior* 27(2): 163-182.

Kousser, Thad, Scott Lucas, Seth Masket, and Eric McGhee. 2015. "Kingmakers or Cheerleaders? Party Power and the Causal Effects of Endorsements." *Political Research Quarterly* 68(3): 443-456.

Lipset, Seymour Martin and William Schneider. 1987. *The Confidence Gap: Business, Labor, and Government in the Public Mind.* Baltimore, MD: Johns Hopkins University Press.

Miller, Arthur A. 1974. "Political Issues and Trust in Government: 1964-1970." *American Political Science Review* 68(3): 951-972.

Newton, Kenneth and Pippa Morris. 2000. "Confidence in Public Institutions: Faith, Culture, or Performance?" In *Disaffected Democracies: What's Troubling the Trilaterla Countries?* Eds. Susan J. Pharr and Robert D. Putnam. Princeton, N.J.: Princeton University Press.

Norris, Pippa. 1999. *Critical Citizens: Global Support for Democratic Government.* New York: Oxford University Press.

Orren, Gary. 1997. "Fall from Grace: The Public's Loss of Faith in Government." In *Why People Don't Trust Government*, edited by Joseph S. Nye, Philip D. Zelikow, and David C.King. Cambridge MA: Harvard University Press.

Pew Research Center. 2014. "Public Trust in Government: 1958-2014."

Putnam, Robert and S. Pharr. 2002. *Democracy in Flux: Social Capital in Contemporary Societies.* New York: Oxford University Press.

Steger, Wayne P. 2007. "Who Wins Nominations and Why? An Updated Forecast of the Presidential Primary Vote." *Political Research Quarterly* 60(1): 91-99.

Steger, Wayne P. 2016. "Conditional Arbiters: The Limits of Political Party Influence in Presidential Nominations." *PS: Political Science & Politics* 49(4): 709-715.

Summary, Bryce. 2010. "The Endorsement Effect: An Examination of Statewide Political Endorsements in the 2008 Democratic Caucus and Primary Season." *American Behavioral Scientist* 54(3): 284-297.

Tyler, Tom R. and Peter Degoey 1996. "Trust in Organizational Authorities." In *Trust in Organizations: Frontiers of Theory and Research*. Eds. Roderick M. Kramer and Tom R. Tyler. Thousand Oaks, CA: Sage Publications.

Vavreck, Lynn. 2015. "2016 Endorsements: How and Why They Matter." *New York Times Upshot*, July 29. Accessed June 27, 2017. https://www.nytimes.com/2015/07/30/upshot/2016-endorsements-how-and-why-they-matter.html.

Chapter 8

Intraparty Democracy and the 2016 Election

Julia Azari and Seth Masket

The subject of democracy within political parties became a heated one in 2016. From Donald Trump's claims that some states' delegate selection processes were rigged against him (Richardson and Sherfinski 2016) to the complaints of Bernie Sanders' supporters that closed primaries (King 2016) and superdelegates (Everett and Kim 2016) stacked the deck against their candidate, voters and caucus-goers focused heavily on internal democracy. The idea of making political parties more participatory and transparent goes back further than the 2016 election cycle, however. To a degree, the history of nomination politics since the early twentieth century is a story of opening the process up to voters. The major American political parties today are probably more procedurally democratic than they have ever been.

Thus it is not without irony that the most recent presidential election produced a result that violated a great many substantive ideas about democracy. From his campaign promises to jail his opponent to his pre-election lamentations that general electoral contests were rigged to his vows to strip citizens of their rights for expressing unpopular political views, Donald Trump proved to be one of the most hostile presidential candidates toward basic democratic norms in the modern age. How did such democratic parties produce such an anti-democratic result?

In this chapter, we argue that this is not just a simple matter of bad luck. Nor is this outcome entirely the product of a substantive shift in preferences among party rank-and-file—in this case, toward Trump's positions and away from those held by more conventional candidates. The results were also created by institutional change. The parties' moves toward internal party democracy, we maintain, helped to create an environment in which a candidate like Trump could succeed. We believe that several aspects of party democratization are responsible for the inability of the Republican Party to thwart Trump's candidacy. For this chapter, however, we focus specifically on the evolution of presidential primary debates.

We focus on two recent developments in primary debates: the adoption of polling threshold requirements for candidate participation, and changes the Republican National Committee made to presidential primary debates in the wake of the 2012 election. We focus on the Republicans for several reasons. There is the obvious reason that the Republican nomination contest in 2016 will likely continue to fascinate and frustrate party politics scholars for years to come, and the relevance of Donald Trump's insurgent candidacy to notions of intraparty democracy is difficult to miss. The Republican nomination field has also featured a wide range of candidates, including a number who were well outside the political mainstream, for several election cycles, making the contemporary Republican Party an illustrative case for how parties address competition and inclusion within party ranks. We evaluate the extent to which these changes have simultaneously reinforced and undermined intraparty democracy in the pursuit of party and candidate goals.

CONVENTIONAL WISDOM

Two related areas of conventional wisdom intersected during the 2016 primary season. Conventional wisdom—or perhaps more accurately, popular understanding—of democracy is that its main element is broad participation. As we will demonstrate, the standard generally applied to parties as internal democracies is grassroots participation in party decisions. However, political scientists have developed other ways to define democracy's core elements. Democracy requires robust and consistent institutions, and its citizens—who is allowed to participate—must be clearly defined.

Our argument also challenges the conventional wisdom that within political parties, loosening elite control will help create outcomes that better reflect the preferences of party rank-and-file, and produce broader satisfaction with party decisions about whom to nominate for president. In the 2016 Republican nomination contest, this conventional wisdom did not hold. A democratized process with weak party control and loosely conceived institutional rules produced a chaotic situation, and ultimately a historically unpopular nominee who went on to be a historically unpopular president. In an analysis of the rules structuring Republican primary debates and the role those debates played in the 2016 nomination process, we claim that the conventional wisdom in 2016 was wrong about democracy and about parties.

Conventional Wisdom about Party Democracy

It is quite common for candidates, political observers, and party leaders to describe American political parties as democratic institutions. That is, the major decisions a party makes—especially over the nomination of candidates for high office—are expected to be in accordance with the wishes of rank-and-file members, the "citizens" of a party. We witnessed a good deal of such language employed during the presidential nominating contests in both major parties in 2016, as both parties were riddled with complaints about fairness and openness in caucuses and primary elections.

On the Democratic side, one of Senator Bernie Sanders' chief complaints was that the party's superdelegate system (which grants party votes to office-holders as unpledged party delegates) was inherently anti-democratic and thus illegitimate. He implored superdelegates to vote with the pledged delegates in their states. "I think that the superdelegates in those states [where I have won] should respond to what their constituents [want]," Sanders said in the spring. "Superdelegates are supporting Clinton in states that I have won in a landslide. I think that is wrong" (Neidig 2016). Sanders even claimed it would be "outrageously undemocratic" for him to drop out of the race given his support among the Democratic base (Wagner 2016).

A petition directed at the unpledged Democratic delegates in the state of Washington said, "Let the voters decide. Pledge to support the candidate who gets the most pledged delegate votes at the Democratic National Convention. Follow the lead of average Democratic party voters and uphold authentic democracy" (Best 2016). A superdelegate in neighboring Oregon agreed with the sentiment, saying, "Every Democrat I have talked to finds the unpledged delegate system offensive. I don't think my vote ... should invalidate the vote of thousands of voters" (Greenfield 2016).

The same sort of language infiltrated discussions over the 2016 nomination process, especially as some within the party began to organize against Donald Trump as he began to emerge as the popular choice among primary voters. As Republican donor Peter Kalikow (2016) said in the summer of 2016, "Those who seek to deny Trump victory by changing nomination rules so that a different candidate—who received fewer, or no, delegates— could emerge the nominee are engaging in the type of undemocratic and 'business-as-usual' politics that disgusts the public and that, quite frankly, has led to the popularity of outsiders like Trump." One-time Republican delegate Joshua Claybourn (2016) warned his fellow partisans, "The so-called establishment and the 'Never Trump' movement seek to defend the true Republican Party ideals, but the average GOP voter sees them as Roman citizens saw their senators—elites looking out for themselves and a select few."

This language, depicting parties as democracies and any institutional rule that empowers elites over the rank-and-file as both anti-democratic and illegitimate, is so commonplace today as to be almost unremarkable. The conventional wisdom holds that a party simply must bow to the wishes of its primary voters and caucus-goers. Yet, as we argue in this chapter, this view is not only ahistorical and inaccurate, but it can also result in anti-democratic outcomes.

THE POLITICAL SCIENCE VIEW OF DEMOCRACY

Applying the concept of democracy to political parties is as challenging as it is common. Nonetheless, if parties are going to be described as democracies, it is at least useful to examine just how healthy they are as democracies. But before we can adequately analyze the state and advance of democracy within American political parties, we should be clear about just what we mean by democracy. Although American party politics scholars have often eschewed normative questions surrounding democracy, an extensive literature in comparative politics tackles the topic. This literature has long identified multiple facets of democracy that go beyond expanding electoral participation. Much of this body of scholarship focuses on civil rights and liberties and the treatment of racial, ethnic, and religious minorities (see for example Smith and Ziegler 2008; Plattner 2010). Democracy, in other words, has been conceptualized in political science in the context of states and regimes (Collier and Levitsky 1997, Schmitter and Karl 1991), and there has been, to our knowledge, no serious effort to date to reconcile the concepts forged in the comparative and democratic theory literatures with the developments of American political parties.

Schattschneider (1942, 58-9) famously dismissed the notion of parties as democracies and of partisans as "citizens" within the party. In his framework, parties have always been run by a small group who make the key decisions, and then supported by a rank-and-file with little say over the direction of the party:

> It is manifestly impossible for twenty-seven million Democrats to control the Democratic party .... There is no basis in reality for it, and the idea that a few party primaries might enable the rank and file of party membership to control the inner processes of the parties is fantastic .... In what sense is a partisan injured if he is deprived of the right to control an organization toward which he has no duties?

Yet the democratization of the parties has nonetheless continued apace, in many ways confirming many of Schattschneider's fears.

One of the central goals for any democracy is to determine just who its citizens are—who participates in its elections, who benefits from its services, whether rights can be stripped or reinstated based on the behavior of a citizen, whether those rights are innate to a person's birth or bloodline or require some sort of proof of fealty, and so forth. In an essay titled "What Democracy Is ... and Is Not," Philippe Schmitter and Terry Lynn Karl (1991) identify citizens as "a distinguishing characteristic of democracy." Citizens have legal equality, access to participation in the political process, and the ability to run for office themselves. An important implication of these ideas is that democracy requires clear boundaries about who is entitled to participate in politics, including running for office. If parties are to properly be considered democracies, then it should be noted that they have largely failed to address this key question of citizenship.

Indeed, as American parties have become more democratic, they have largely done so by extending rights and privileges without defining responsibilities and costs. This openness is unique among Western political parties on several levels. Parties in France and the UK are only beginning to explore primary elections to select candidates and party leaders. In the United States, on other hand, many states allow voters to participate in "open" primaries regardless of affiliation. In places that do require party affiliation for participation in "closed" primaries, voters need only register as a member of a party—not pay dues or participate in any other way.

These developments illustrate the core value that has undergirded much of the party democratization process in U.S. politics: openness and broad access. We do not dispute that this is an important democratic value; however, an extensive literature on the concept of democracy and the process of democratization demonstrates that this is just one value of many. As this research reminds us, democracies require institutions, rules, and norms to succeed. If political parties are democracies, then they are not exempt from these requirements.

Parties have partially addressed some of the concerns of citizenship in their conduct of nomination contests. Each state or state party defines who may or may not participate in its primaries and caucuses. But these participation rules vary wildly across states and time periods. In some states, one must have publicly declared membership in a party for several months before being able to participate in its primary elections. In others, one need not even declare membership in a party to participate in its primary.

In such an environment, it is difficult to define in a national sense just who the parties consider their citizens. If key party decisions like the nomination of candidates for high level offices may be made by those who decline to register as party members or even choose to register as members of another party, then party citizenship is a muddy concept at best.

These problems extend to another important and developing area of party nominations—the use of primary debates for presidential candidates. As we explain below, primary debates, which were held inconsistently and with a wide range of rules and expectations just a few decades ago, have quickly been institutionalized and are now a regular feature of presidential election cycles. But parties have had a difficult time determining who may or may not participate in these events. As these events have played a more critical role in determining who the nominee will be in a given cycle, the potential for a perverse outcome has become more likely.

It is our contention that this was the key to understanding Donald Trump's surprising nomination in 2016. The rapid rise in the number of Republicans running for office was not peculiar to presidential races (Masket 2016). But the presidential debate system was not equipped to deal with this situation. Essentially everyone with any name recognition was considered qualified for participation. What's more, the two-tiered debate system many networks used in the early debates gave additional prominence to those candidates with greater name recognition.

On top of this, the large number of candidates dramatically increased the challenge for party elites of deciding upon and coordinating efforts behind a favorite candidate. There were several governors, senators, outsiders, people with established conservative credentials, people with strong electoral histories, etc., making it difficult to identify an obvious coordination point. This lack of insider coordination and an open debate system that gave prominence for those with greater name recognition created a ripe environment for a wealthy and well-known candidate to win many early contests and, ultimately, the nomination.

Primary debates illustrate the problems of democracy and institutionalization. Debates showcase some central aspects of democracy. These events allow voters to respond to candidates and they push candidates to engage on policy issues (at least in theory). However, primary debates have evolved in a somewhat arbitrary manner, with different entities making rules about inclusion, speaking time, and location. As a result, the parties themselves have had relatively little control over one of the most public facets of party politics.

DEBATES

Our study of internal party democracy focuses on the development of presidential primary debates. We look at primary debates for several reasons. First, the institutional literature on political parties has neglected debates to a large degree. Importantly, debates challenge many of the key principles that characterize the literature on parties as institutions: coordination and elite control over nominations. The mere existence of primary debates suggests a degree of unpredictability and openness.

Second, the development of rules governing debates shows parties wrestling with the democratic concepts in which we are interested. They leave behind a number of clear metrics, including the formal thresholds for inclusion in the debate and the list of participants. They reveal parties struggling with how much of a voice to give to minor candidates seen as having little chance at the nomination and how much to protect favored candidates from potential criticism.

The linkage between debates and participation is intuitive: more debates, with more candidates, should broaden the scope of participation. Rules that curtail the number of debates or limit who can participate in them will be perceived by actors concerned with the appearance of democratic legitimacy as trade-offs, and will be pursued only when the benefits of restriction are perceived by these actors to be worthwhile.

Restrictive debate rules, particularly thresholds, attempt to delineate who belongs in the party and who does not. Nearly every election cycle brings forth a few fringe candidates with tenuous affiliations to the parties whose nominations they seek. Those fringe candidates present a potential threat to the party brand, possibly undermining it and causing party loyalists to waiver in their support. Excluding such candidates in order to protect the party brand will be a goal that drives the use of debate thresholds.

The coordination goals of parties make uncertain outcomes a costly trade-off. Risk-averse actors, including party leaders, will prefer to limit competition and minimize uncertainty about the outcome of the nomination process. What are the implications for debate rules? One possibility is that more candidates and more debates make for greater uncertainty, increasing the unpredictability of the nomination contest. However, the presence of multiple candidates on the debate stage may actually confer an advantage on the frontrunners. Candidates like Mitt Romney in 2012—or even Donald Trump in 2016—may benefit from not facing their main rivals directly in early debates. Based on this reasoning, we hypothesize that low debate thresholds, despite fitting conventional understandings of democracy, contributed to the eventual nomination of an unconventional, anti-democratic, and unpopular candidate.

While, as we mention above, party leaders may wish to enforce boundaries about which candidates can be associated with the party or expound up on their views on the party's debate stage, party elites may also have incentives to keep representativeness in mind. Unifying the party after the nomination season has concluded often requires reaching out to losing candidates, and may require reaching out to particular factions, such as libertarians or evangelical Christians. In other words, party leaders have competing incentives to narrow the ideological range of the candidates participating in a debate in order to protect the party's reputation, and to include a range of perspectives in order to avoid defection and intraparty fighting.

Debates have the potential to influence nominations regardless of whether we believe it is primary voters or party elites that determine the outcomes. Former House Speaker Newt Gingrich, Norrander (2015b, 97) argues, "was saved on more than one occasion by a feisty debate performance" in 2012, while Rick Perry's "lackluster" debate performance likely contributed to the demise of his candidacy that year.

By the 1990s, primary debates had changed in a number of ways. Among these changes was that in the 1992 Democratic primary debates, more of a "team" identity had emerged among participants (Kendall 2000). This is commensurate with findings on party polarization, as intraparty contests today likely encompass a narrower ideological range of candidates than they did in the mid-twentieth century, and as partisan activists have become more hostile toward members and beliefs of the rival party over that same time period. Benoit *et al.* note that in contrast with the 1948 radio debate, the 1980 Republican primary debate featured substantial attacks on Democrats—nearly half of the attacks uttered were directed at the other party rather than the candidates on stage (Benoit *et al.* 2002, 40).

Our study focuses on two important shifts in the development of presidential primary debates. The first is the adoption of overt participation qualification rules for candidates, usually in the form of minimal polling thresholds. These have occurred in recent contests across both parties. The second development is the Republican National Committee's assertion of primary debate rules following the 2012 election.

Participation Thresholds

Candidate participation thresholds in presidential primary debates are actually a relatively new innovation, first implemented widely in 2008.[1] Unlike general election presidential debates, which have been governed by a bipartisan commission for three decades and have been relatively stable in their rules and practices, norms for primary debates have developed only in fits and starts. Indeed, these rules continue to develop to the present day.

While some primary debates existed prior to the reforms of the early 1970s, these were haphazard and just as likely to be interpartisan as intrapartisan. For example, in May of 1967, Democratic senator Robert Kennedy and Republican governor Ronald Reagan, both seen as possible presidential candidates for 1968, participated in a televised debate answering a series of questions from an international panel of students about the Vietnam War (Kengor 2007).

Every presidential election cycle after 1968 featured some sort of primary debates among the presidential candidates. These occurred for both major parties, with the exception of the reelection-seeking incumbents' party. But until fairly recently, these events were not treated as quadrennial rituals of democracy so much as campaign devices, to be employed selectively by candidates. Debates would sometimes take place between just the two poll-leaders, or sometimes among a larger field of candidates if one or more of the poll-leaders saw a tactical advantage to inviting more people. There was little need for thresholds as candidates or local media hosts would invite whomever they wanted.

In a famous example, Ronald Reagan challenged George H. W. Bush to a debate in New Hampshire in February of 1980, and the *Nashua Telegraph* agreed to host it. When Senator Bob Dole, also running for president, complained to the Federal Election Commission that this event was giving an advantage to just two candidates, the FEC agreed and informed the *Telegraph* that it couldn't pay for such an event. Reagan then offered to pay the $3,500 fee himself and invited other candidates. The *Telegraph* still ran the event as a two-person affair, relegating Dole, Howard Baker, and other candidates to the audience. Dole yelled complaints from the back of the room, but was otherwise not able to participate in the debate. The other candidates expressed anger at Bush and the newspaper, with Baker saying, "I don't begrudge him [Bush] the role of frontrunner, if that is what he is. But he wears the crown mighty unbecomingly." Dole complained that Bush "stiffed us, with the help of the paper" (Smith 1980).

Debates in 1972, the first cycle of the post-reform era, were similarly haphazard. Many began as two-candidate affairs, with Hubert Humphrey challenging George McGovern to debates, and other candidates sometimes being invited later (Lydons 1972). Most debates involved extensive deliberations between campaigns. A New Hampshire debate that year was limited to just the five candidates appearing on the state's Democratic primary ballot; candidate Wilbur Mills, who was organizing a write-in campaign, was excluded from the debate (Kovach 1972). Meanwhile, Representative Shirley Chisholm had been excluded from some debates hosted by ABC and CBS. A federal court then ordered those networks to provide her with equal time on other news programs (*New York Times* Staff 1972).

One of the most explicit early discussions of candidate participation qualifications was associated with the planning of a Democratic debate at Dartmouth College in 1984. The event, sponsored by the House Democratic Caucus and largely planned out by Representative Chuck Schumer and television producer Norman Lear, was most likely the first time a formal party organization took on the role of running a presidential debate, viewing it as serving a party purpose. At the time, there were 71 candidates who had filed papers with the Federal Election Commission to be a candidate for the Democratic nomination for president. The Democratic Caucus set rules for the event that "excluded minor candidates," although it is not clear today just how they distinguished major from minor ones. The "no rules" debate consisted of eight "major" candidates—Walter Mondale, John Glenn, Gary Hart, Fritz Hollings, Alan Cranston, Reubin Askew, George McGovern, and Jesse Jackson—and was moderated by talk show host Phil Donahue (Clendinen 1984). For primary debates over the next two decades, participation was generally limited to the "major" candidates, with the hosting media organizations determining just what that term meant.[2]

For Republicans, 2008 appears to represent the transition point from more free-form primary debates to more structured rules about inclusion. Republicans held twenty debates, starting in May 2007 and ending with a final debate in February 2008, in what was then the midst of the primary cycle. We were only able to find three instances of formal thresholds for participation in the debates.

Fox News sponsored the second debate of the 2008 season, on May 15, 2007, and established a threshold of 1 percent in South Carolina and national polls. Participation in this debate was fairly broad as a result, with minor candidates such as former Virginia governor Jim Gilmore, then-senator Sam Brownback, and Rep. Tom Tancredo. However, one candidate, businessman John Cox, filed a lawsuit after Fox decided to base its inclusion decision on a poll on which Cox did not appear. Cox had come in first place in one South Carolina straw poll, which should have qualified him for participation under the rules. A judge ruled that the primary debate was not a public forum and thus the party could choose to exclude candidates at will (Davenport 2007).

This was not the last round of tension over debate exclusion in the 2008 election cycle. Leading up to the New Hampshire primary, Fox News sponsored a debate in the famous early primary state. In the *New York Times*, Michael Falcone reported that Texas Libertarian Ron Paul was excluded from the Fox debate despite a strong performance in the Iowa caucuses and active, successful fundraising efforts (Falcone 2008). This exclusion was notable for its selective use of polls to determine which candidates met the thresholds. It also violated an important norm of inclusion in New Hampshire primary politics, thus prompting the state party to pull out of its partnership sponsoring the debate with Fox.

These incidents (which, notably, both involve Fox News) complicate the narrative that debate thresholds were introduced as a way to either establish a consistent set of standards to be applied to all candidates or exclude minor candidates. Instead of raising thresholds to keep out fringe players, the network appears to have cherry-picked the polls it used, crafting its criteria to exclude specific candidates. These potential violations of democratic norms prompted different responses from different institutions. While the response of the courts was that parties and media companies are private entities with the right to decide whom to include (a typical legal approach to intraparty issues), the New Hampshire state party came down on the side of competition and an even playing field. In particular, this clash between Fox News and the New Hampshire Republican Party illustrates the loosely confederated nature of American political parties, and thus the barriers to, and need for, stronger institutionalization.

Although we do not have any direct evidence of the impact of these incidents, subsequent debates seemed to have clearer standards. In 2012, several media outlets provided very specific lists of polls that would qualify for debate inclusion.[3]

Tables 8.1 and 8.2 describe the structures of the 2012 and 2016 debates. The 2016 table covers the prime time debate only, not the "undercard" debates that were held in order to accommodate the expansive field of candidates. We offer a few observations and one caveat. First, the caveat: the information regarding participation thresholds in the 2012 debates is likely incomplete. In contrast with the 2016 debate season, in which media outlets eagerly reported debate rules, including thresholds, this was a much smaller part of the story in 2012.

Second, as far as our current data show, in both years the participation threshold increased as the field narrowed—as candidates suspended their campaigns leading up to and after the early contests. We also note the possibility of a connection in 2012 between debates co-sponsored by state parties and higher participation thresholds.

It is worth examining just whom these debate thresholds excluded. Did they keep competitors with a legitimate chance of challenging front-runners off the debate stage? Is there evidence of a systematic loss of perspectives within the party? The simple answers to these questions appear to be: no and maybe.

Tables 8.3 to 8.5 illustrate that winnowing does far more to empty out debates than do thresholds. These tables list the Republican presidential candidates in 2008, 2012, and 2016, respectively, along with their ideal points (calculated as DIME CF (Bonica 2013) scores in the first two cycles and CrowdPac scores in the most recent). The tables are coded such that candidates eliminated from debates through winnowing appear in bold and those excluded by polling thresholds appear in italics.

In these crowded and somewhat volatile fields of candidates, no candidate excluded from early debates went on to gain strength in the polls. This did not even happen in the case of Carly Fiorina, who began the 2016 season in the undercard debate but went on to be a formidable presence in later prime time debates. Nevertheless, she never gained serious strength in the polls, nor did she win a primary or caucus.

Table 8.1 Details on 2012 Republican Primary Debates

Date	Location	Host	Sponsor/organizer	1% or lower thres-hold	More than 1% thres-hold	Alternative criteria
5/5/11	Greenville SC[1]	Peace Center	Fox News, South Carolina Republican Party	x		Filed with FEC and South Carolina
6/15/11	Goffstown NH[2]	Saint Anselm College	CNN, WMUR, New Hampshire Union-Leader		x	
8/11/11	Ames IA[3]	Iowa State U.	Republican Party of Iowa, Fox News, Washington Examiner	x		Filed with FEC
9/7/11	Simi Valley CA[4]	Reagan Pres. Library	Reagan Foundation, NBC News, Politico		x	
9/12/11	Tampa FL[5]		Tea Party Express		x	No clear criteria found
9/22/11	Orlando FL[6]		Fox News, Google, Republican Party of Florida			
10/11/11	Hanover NH[7]	Dartmouth				Filed with FEC, raised at least $500,000, received "measurable support" in the polls
10/18/11	Las Vegas NV		CNN/Western Republican Leadership Conference		x	
11/9/11	Auburn Hills MI	Oakland U.	CNBC/Michigan Republican Party			Unable to find debate criteria
11/12/12	Spartan-burg SC	Wofford College	CBS News, National Journal, South Carolina Republican Party			Unable to find debate criteria
11/22/12	Wash-ington DC					Unable to find debate criteria
12/10/11	Des Moines IA[8]	Drake U.	ABC News, ABC5/WOI-DT TV, The Des Moines Register and Republican Party of Iowa		x	
12/15/11	Sioux City IA[9]		Fox News and the Republican Party of Iowa		x	
1/7/12	GoffstownNH[10]	St. Anselm College	ABC News, Yahoo!, WMUR		x	
1/8/12	Concord NH		NBC			Unable to find debate criteria
1/16/12	Myrtle Beach, SC		Fox News/Wall Street Journal			Unable to find debate criteria

Date	Location		Sponsor		
1/19/12	CharlestonSC		CNN/ Southern Republican Leadership Conference		
1/23/12	Tampa FL[11]		NBC News, National Journal, Tampa Bay Times	x	x —Candidates could also qualify by placing in the top four in Iowa caucuses or New Hampshire primary
					x—Candidates must be on the ballot in Florida and be among the top 4 in Iowa Caucuses, New Hampshire primary or South Carolina primary
1/26/12	Jackson-ville FL[12]	U. of North Florida	CNN and Hispanic Leadership Network		
2/22/12	Mesa AZ		CNN, Arizona GOP		

1 "Fox News Announces Entry Criteria for May 5 South Carolina GOP Debate," http://press.foxnews.com/2011/04/fox-news-announces-entry-criteria-for-may-5-south-carolina-gop-debate/

2 CNN Political Unit, "Criteria for the New Hampshire Debate," CNN.com, June 3, 2011. http://politicalticker.blogs.cnn.com/2011/06/03/criteria-for-the-new-hampshire-republican-presidential-debate/

3 Jennifer Jacobs, "Rules Outlined for Republican Debate on August 11," *Des Moines Register*, July 23, 2011. http://caucuses.desmoinesregister.com/2011/07/23/rules-finalized-for-the-iowa-republican-debate-on-aug-11/

4 "Eligibility Standards for the Sept. 7 Republican Candidates Debate at Reagan Library," Politico.com, August 18, 2011. http://www.politico.com/story/2011/08/eligibility-standards-for-the-sept-7-republican-candidates-debate-at-the-reagan-library-061676

5 Mark Preston, "GOP Hopefuls Will Face Off in CNN Tea Party Debate," CNN.com, September 1, 2011. http://politicalticker.blogs.cnn.com/2011/09/01/gop-hopefuls-will-face-off-in-cnn-tea-party-debate/?on.cnn=1

6 Although we were unable to locate clear criteria for this debate, the reporting suggests that it was by invitation, and that Gary Johnson was invited despite the objections of the Florida Republican Party. Nate Ashworth, "Fox News/Google Republican Debate Tonight at 9pm ET," Election Central, uspresidentialelectionnews.com, September 22, 2011. http://www.uspresidentialelectionnews.com/2011/09/fox-newsgoogle-republican-debate-tonight-at-9pm-et/

7 "Debate Criteria," Republican Presidential Debate at Dartmouth, http://www.dartmouth.edu/debates/about/criteria.html

8 Jason Noble, "Mitt Romney Will Attend GOP Candidate Debates in Iowa Next Month," *Des Moines Register*, November 29, 2011. http://caucuses.desmoinesregister.com/2011/11/29/mitt-romney-will-attend-gop-candidate-debates-in-iowa-next-month/

9 Ibid

10 "Criteria for ABC News Debate in New Hampshire on January 7, 2012" ABCNews.com, December 15, 2011. http://abcnews.go.com/blogs/headlines/2011/12/criteria-for-abc-news-debate-in-new-hampshire-on-january-7-2012

11 "The NBC NEWS/National Journal/Tampa Bay Times Republican Presidential Candidates Debate, Jan 23, 2012: Eligibility Criteria," http://www.nbcnews.com/id/20114724/ns/politics-the_debates/t/nbc-news-national-journal-tampa-bay-times-republican-presidential-candidates-debatejan/#.WVV4jjOZORs

12 Felicia Sonmez, "Florida Republican Debate in Jacksonville: Live Updates," Washington Post, January 26, 2012. https://www.washingtonpost.com/blogs/election-2012/post/florida-republican-debate-in-jacksonville-live-updates/2012/01/26/gIQAv2P3TQ_blog.html?utm_term=.3286e8f21198

Table 8.2 Details on the 2016 Republican debates

Date	Location	Host	Sponsor/organizer	1% or lower thres-hold[13]	More than 1% thres-hold	Alternative criteria
8/6/15	Cleveland OH[14]		Fox	x		
9/16/15	Simi Valley CA[15]	Reagan Pres. Library	CNN, Reagan Presidential Foundation		x	x—Criteria amended to include top 10 candidates. Candidates required to have filed with FEC and have at least one campaign aide working in two of four "early contest" states.[16]
10/28/15	Boulder CO[17]	U. of Colorado			x	
11/10/15	Milwaukee WI[18]		Fox Business		x	
12/15/15	Las Vegas NV[19]		CNN, Facebook		x	
1/14/16	CharlestonSC[20]		Fox Business			X—top 6 candidates in national polls or top 5 in either New Hampshire or Iowa polls
1/28/16	Des Moines IA[21]		Fox News			X—top 6 candidates in national polls or top 5 in either New Hampshire or Iowa polls
2/6/16	Man-chester, NH[22]	Saint Anselm College	ABC			Top 3 in Iowa Caucuses, top 6 in recognized New Hampshire polls, or top 6 in recognized national polls

2/13/16	Greenville SC[23]	Peace Center	CBS	Top 5 in NH popular vote, top 3 in IA popular vote, or top 5 in SC and national polls and at least 3% in NH or IA contests or SC or national polls.
2/25/16	Houston, TX[24]	U. of Houston	CNN, Telemundo	At least 5% in popular vote in NH, IA, SC, or NV.
3/3/15	Detroit, MI[25]		Fox News	At least 3% in five most recent national polls.
3/10/16	Miami, FL	U. of Miami	CNN	No criteria found

[13]Because of the large number of candidates in 2016, several debate hosts held an "undercard" debate prior to the main event. All threshold numbers are for the main debate.

[14]Mike Allen, "Fox Lowers Threshold for Early Debate," *Politico.com*, July 28, 2015. http://www.politico.com/story/2015/07/fox-republican-debate-lowers-threshold-120748

[15]"CNN Debate: Candidate criteria for September 16, 2015," CNN.com, September 1, 2015. http://www.cnn.com/2015/09/01/politics/cnn-debate-rules-september-16/index.html

[16]Ibid

[17]"CNBC Republican Debate Criteria," September 30, 2015. http://www.cnbc.com/2015/09/30/cnbc-republican-debate-criteria.html

[18]Ashley Parker, "Fox Business Network Details Criteria for Nov. 10 Debate and Plans Undercard," *New York Times*, October 27, 2015. https://www.nytimes.com/politics/first-draft/2015/10/27/fox-business-news-details-criteria-for-nov-10-debate-and-plans-undercard/

[19]Eugene Scott, "Stage Set for final GOP Debate of 2015," *CNN.com*, December 14, 2015. http://www.cnn.com/2015/12/13/politics/republican-debate-gop-stage/index.html

[20]Fox Business Network Announces Entry Criteria for GOP Primary Debates on Jan. 14," December 22, 2015. http://www.foxbusiness.com/features/2015/12/22/fox-business-network-announces-entry-criteria-for-gop-primary-debates-on-jan-14.html

[21]"Fox News Channel Announces Criteria for Upcoming Republican Presidential Primary Debate," January 2016. http://press.foxnews.com/2016/01/fox-news-channel-announces-criteria-for-upcoming-republican-presidential-primary-debate/

[22]"ABC Announces Criteria for New Hampshire Republican Debate," January 27, 2016. http://abcnews.go.com/Politics/abc-news-announces-criteria-hampshire-republican-debate/story?id=36550263

[23]"CBS News Announces Republican Debate Criteria," February 9, 2016. http://www.cbsnews.com/news/criteria-for-cbs-news-republican-debate/

[24]Eli Watkins, "CNN's Wolf Blitzer will Moderate Republican Debate in Houston," *CNN.com*, February 19, 2016. http://www.cnn.com/2016/02/10/politics/wolf-blitzer-gop-debate-houston/

[25]Josh Feldman, "Fox News Announces Criteria for Next Week's Big GOP Debate,"*Mediaite.com*, February 26, 2016. http://www.mediaite.com/online/fox-news-announces-criteria-for-next-weeks-big-gop-debate/

Table 8.3   2008 Candidates and Ideal Points

Candidate	Ideal Point
Brownback	**1.02**
Gilmore	**.95**
Giuliani	.562
Huckabee	1.23
Hunter	***.916***
McCain	.68
Paul	*1.57*
Romney	.878
Tancredo	**1.23**
Thompson	**1.06**

Note: Ideal points are DIME (CF) scores (Bonica 2013).
Bold—excluded from one or more debates by winnowing
Italics—excluded from one more debates by thresholds

Table 8.4   2012 Candidates and Ideal Points

Candidate	Ideal Point
Bachmann	**1.34**
Cain	**1.29**
Huntsman	***0.586***
Gingrich	1.11
Johnson	*1.1*
Paul	1.57
Pawlenty	**0.971**
Perry	**1.08**
Romney	0.879
Santorum	0.912

Note: Ideal points are DIME (CF) scores (Bonica 2013).
Bold—excluded from one or more debates by winnowing
Italics—excluded from one more debates by thresholds

In 2012, debate thresholds excluded Utah governor Jon Huntsman at least once, along with libertarian Gary Johnson. The ideological scores in Tables 8.4 and 8.5 (derived from different sources) place Johnson among mainstream conservative candidates, although his identity as a libertarian and his positions on some issues, such as drug legalization, suggest that he might bring a distinct perspective, and represent a specific wing of the party.

We provide a visual analysis of both ideology and threshold effects in Figure 8.1 This figure displays the median ideal point of the field of Republican presidential candidates across 2008, 2012, and 2016. Each data point represents the moment a candidate drops out of the race, calculated as the number of days since August 1st of the year preceding the election. The data point shows the median ideal point of the field at that time. Gray dots indicate

Table 8.5   2016 Republican Presidential Candidates and Ideal Points

Candidate	Ideal Point
Bush	**4.9**
Carson	**8.4**
Christie	*2.6*
Cruz	9.6
Fiorina	*6*
Graham	*4.2*
Gilmore	*6.3*
Huckabee	*6.3*
Jindal	*5.1*
Kasich	4.5
Pataki	*.9*
Paul	**10**
Perry	*6.9*
Rubio	5.7
Santorum	*4.7*
Trump	1.5
Walker	**7.9**

Note: Ideal points from CrowdPac.com.
Bold—excluded from one or more debates by winnowing
Italics—excluded from one more debates by thresholds
Source: https://web.archive.org/web/20151030015253/https://www.crowdpac.com/elections/2016-
   presidential-election.

candidates eliminated from debates due to polling thresholds. These figures do not suggest any systematic ideological pattern for polling threshold eliminations. With the exception of Ron Paul's late dropout in June of 2008, which moved the median ideal point substantially leftward, the eliminations of other threshold-affected candidates do not appear to have substantially shifted the field.

There are several points of significance to take away from this. First, as Gary Johnson's ideological score from 2012 suggests, quantitative scores might not capture the most important dimensions of inclusion and participation by candidates who represent different constituencies within the party.[4] Johnson—and, for that matter, Ron Paul, who also identifies as a Libertarian—fell in the middle of more conventional Republicans using this measure.

Second, if we confine our analysis to these scores for the moment, the evidence that even higher debate thresholds systematically exclude certain perspectives is fairly thin. In 2016, both winnowing and thresholds excluded some of the more centrist candidates from the main stage. But, especially in 2016, there nevertheless existed a range of ideological positions. The questions underlying the legitimacy of these exclusions go back to fundamental issues about who should be included among the "population" or "citizens" of a party. It is plausible to claim that candidates like Huntsman did not reach

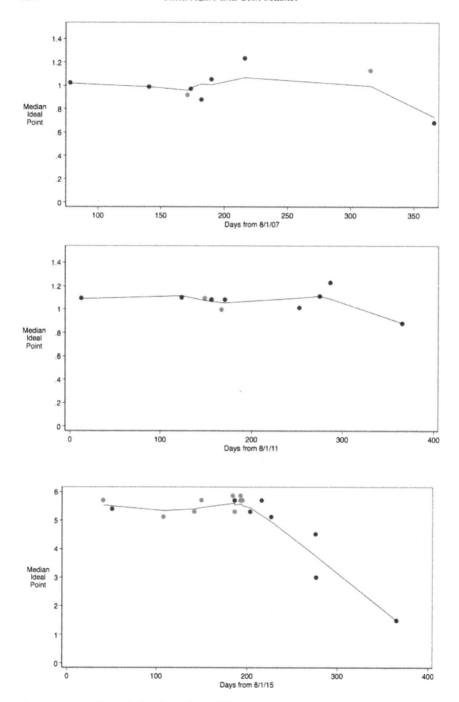

Figure 8.1   Median Ideal Points of Republican Presidential Candidate Pools in 2008, 2012, and 2016.

the modest thresholds established by debate organizers because their positions were not representative of important constituencies within the party.

Finally, it is not clear that an underlying logic of party democracy—of inclusion, or, alternately, exclusion — drove the rules about debates in either 2012 or 2016. It is difficult to ignore the prominent role Fox News has played during these cycles, possibly functioning as an informal gatekeeper for the GOP, but as yet we do not have concrete evidence that this was the intention of anyone at the news organization. Instead, the reforms enacted in these years focused on resolving some of the logistical problems that debates posed for candidates, and to institutionalize the practice of debates. Far from the free-form events like the 1987 cross-partisan affair, the 2012 and 2016 debates adhered to clearer and more consistent rules in the past. Nevertheless, these institutionalization efforts were too little, too late to prevent Trump's nomination.

The RNC's Debate Takeover

We observe a notable shift in the norms and rules of presidential primary debates shortly after the 2012 presidential election. In the wake of the Republican loss at the presidential level, the Republican National Committee commissioned its Growth and Opportunity Project, widely known as the party's "post-mortem" report (Barbour *et al.* 2013). This report included many recommendations to make the party more competitive for future elections, including advice on reaching out to a more demographically diverse set of voters and utilizing better data analytics in campaign work. Also included in the report were suggestions about taking greater control over presidential primary debates. Such a move seemed entirely logical to then-RNC Chief Strategist Sean Spicer (2016): "This [a primary debate] is people seeking the nomination of our party … and the party has no role in a major aspect of it. It just seemed on its face very silly."

As the report framed it, the presidential primary debates of 2008 and 2012 were problematic. They'd featured an unwieldy number of debates—21 and 20 in 2008 and 2012, respectively, whereas there'd been only 13 in 2000 and never more than 7 prior to that. What's more, the schedule for these debates was arranged haphazardly, usually as a result of decisions by the hosting media organizations, and occasionally in conjunction with state parties. These schedules were often inconvenient for the candidates and sometimes undermined their campaigns. Just prior to the 2012 New Hampshire primary, ABC News hosted a candidate debate on the night of Saturday, January 7th, in Goffstown, and NBC News hosted one the very next morning in Concord. The dates, times, and locations of such debates might be announced with as little as 48 hours' notice (Cairncross 2016).

This created a dilemma for candidates. None wanted to ignore a debate invitation, as debates presented candidates with an unusual opportunity for free exposure and a largely unmediated voice. Furthermore, passing up on a debate allowed a candidate's competitors to gain further attention. However, accepting a debate invitation often meant disrupting a planned campaign schedule and traveling to another state. "The candidates are afraid to say no," explains Frank Fahrenkopf (2016), a former chair of the RNC.

While debates are generally seen as a useful tool for candidates, they can be highly disruptive to a campaign. As Fahrenkopf explains, preparing for a debate generally absorbs the candidate and several staffers (including one or more who will stand in as mock opponents) for days before the debate occurs. As a result, "You've lost two to three days off the campaign trail. Then you have the day of the debate, which is also off the campaign trail. Then for the next two or three days, you have to explain what happened in the debate. You freeze the campaign for a week." This undermines campaign speeches, meetings with voters and activists, and other more grassroots activities that can be critical in early contest states.

Party leaders perceived an additional problem with the 2012 debate cycle, in that moderators were seen as having an agenda substantially different from those of candidates and viewers. They saw moderators as appealing to a national audience and sometimes trying to embarrass candidates for their conservative stances, even though the purpose of the event was seen as providing Republican primary voters with information needed to cast a party vote. "The frustration that you had coming out of 2012," explains RNC chief executive officer Sean Cairncross (2016), was "things like the 19 questions George Stephanopoulous asked Mitt Romney about the war on women. Setting aside the partisan hit job aspect, that's not a Republican party primary question. That's not what the primary voters are trying to get a sense of."

Interviews suggested an additional problem associated with 2012: former U.S. House Speaker Newt Gingrich. Gingrich was not especially popular among party elites. He had virtually no prominent endorsements to his name, and apart from some generous super PAC funding from Sheldon Adelson, he had neither funds nor much of a campaign infrastructure on which to spend them. Gingrich was, however, seen as particularly skilled in the primary debate environment. In particular, he was able to turn criticisms by several debate moderators, including Fox News' Juan Williams and CNN's Jonathan King, into successful attacks on the press during some South Carolina debates, helping him win primaries in that state and in Georgia. These debates and primaries created a late surge for Gingrich even as most other candidacies were sputtering and the party was beginning to rally behind Mitt Romney.

As Fahrenkopf explains, "I think after the 2012 experience, where people stayed in longer than perhaps they should have, out came a very damaged

Mitt Romney …. The fact that Newt Gingrich stayed in as long as he did and beat up on the candidate, I just didn't think that the system worked very well." Spicer agrees, "Clearly in 2012, Newt Gingrich in particular was very helped by the debate process, and a couple of candidates were hurt by it. They had flat performances. Tim Pawlenty … was expected to do very well and he just didn't come out of the box strong. Otherwise he was a very very strong and appealing candidate …. They dragged on a process for Romney that otherwise didn't have to get dragged on."

The overwhelming message from respondents was that the 2012 debates created several problematic situations. First, they aided Newt Gingrich, whom they saw as a poor general election candidate who would not represent the party well and whose candidacy was already functionally dead. Second, they undermined and needlessly tarnished Mitt Romney, with whom party elites were generally comfortable. Third, to the extent insiders were not comfortable with Romney, they were looking for candidates like Tim Pawlenty or Rick Perry, accomplished governors with solid conservative credentials. The debates essentially destroyed those candidates' chances based on just a handful of incidents. From the perspective of party strategists, a better primary debate system would be one that allows candidates to get their messages to primary voters but doesn't necessarily undermine strong candidates in favor of demagogues.

In the wake of the Growth and Opportunity Project, the RNC asserted some control over primary debates in three specific ways:

1. It limited the number of party-sanctioned debates and required ample intervals between them.
2. It prescribed the geographic locations of those debates.
3. It insisted on conservative panelists joining other network moderators.

In terms of its immediate goals, the party succeeded. There were only 12 primary debates in 2016, just over half the number from 2012, with several weeks between them. The debates moved around to key primary and caucus states and never repeated a state. And network panelists were joined by conservative voices like Hugh Hewitt, Rick Santelli, and Mary Katharine Ham, who posed different sorts of questions than those posed by other panelists. This change didn't necessarily meet with universal approval by conservatives (Borchers 2015), and there are remaining questions about just how broad a range of party sentiment the new panelists captured (Lord 2015), but it undoubtedly changed the tenor of the debates.

One thing the party's 2012 reforms notably did not address was polling thresholds for inclusion in debates. The reforms did not substantially affect the ease or difficulty of participation, leaving the networks in charge of determining who could participate in them. The resulting debates in 2016 were, in many ways, the most procedurally developed and consistent ever, but were also the most crowded.

Participation thresholds for the seven "undercard" debates were nearly nonexistent, and for the primetime debates they were quite low, often around 3 percent. Raising the threshold to even 5 or 6 percent would have substantially narrowed participation, forcing Trump to face off against a smaller number of opponents. It is impossible to know for sure, but it seems possible that such a chance would have altered the calculus for coordination, allowing the party to mobilize around a different nominee.

As seems quite obvious, Donald Trump, with minimal endorsements from within the party and little fealty to long-standing party doctrines on domestic or foreign policy, was not the preferred candidate for the nomination. Indeed, Trump seemed to play the role that Gingrich had four years earlier, drawing attention to a candidacy that lacked funding, party support, or campaign infrastructure. What's more, due to the large number of candidates and other internal party challenges (Mischiefs of Faction 2016), party insiders never concentrated support on a preferred candidate, as they tend to do (Cohen *et al.* 2008). Gingrich, for all his debating skills, could not overcome Romney's institutional advantages; Trump had no such obstacle in his way. Among 2016's great ironies was that institutional changes designed to prevent the rise of a non-ideological demagogue only ended up abetting it. From the perspective of party democracy, the case of 2016 suggests that while conventional wisdom calls for broader inclusion in the nomination process, a coherent decision-making process requires more structure and institutionalization. For Republican elites, many of the 2012 reforms were too little, too late, and did not target key aspects of the process, such as thresholds.

CONCLUSIONS

Intraparty democracy remains the subject of much hand-wringing and little genuine analysis. This chapter represents our preliminary effort to systematically gather quantitative and qualitative data about the ways in which parties attempt to control the primary debate process, and to place these findings in the context of a broader theoretical framework about parties as democracies.

From our preliminary evidence, we draw a few tentative conclusions. First, we note that while primary debates have become institutionalized with a number of democratic norms built into them, parties and debate sponsors have largely failed to address issues of participation. Interviews revealed that the party organization and the campaigns were driven by pragmatic considerations as much—if not more—than concerns about curbing competition within the party. We also observe that, despite several high profile exclusions, there appears to be little concentrated effort to limit debate participation, especially early in the season. This reflects a broader reluctance by parties to formally define citizenship.

These findings suggest a party system that has incompletely adopted democracy as its guiding model for internal governance. And just as a nation can find itself in compromising situations when it cannot decide who is and isn't among its citizenry, so can a party produce perverse outcomes when it doesn't define who its members and prospective nominees are. The Republican Party has, in recent decades, developed an impressive informal system for guiding voters' choice toward certain types of nominees. But this system was compromised in 2016 by a crowded field of candidates the party had few formal tools for culling and a primary debate system predisposed toward the broadest definition of citizenship. Such an environment was ripe for a wealthy and well-known candidate, even one whose commitment to the party was weak at best. In this sense, the surprising developments of the 2016 race were years in the making.

NOTES

1. Importantly, any presidential debate includes some sort of participation threshold requirement, whether stated overtly or not. The 2016 Republican field was notable for its size—17 candidates—but the debates still omitted 120 other Republicans who had filed papers with the FEC before the first debate.

2. One excluded minor Democratic candidate, California Democrat Larry Agran, was arrested in 1992 for interrupting a debate he claimed he should have been part of. He lost his subsequent lawsuit. "Former Candidate Loses Lawsuit Over 1992 Arrest," *New York Times*. Metro News Briefs, July 10, 1997.

3. See, for example, "Criteria for ABC News Debate in New Hampshire on January 7, 2012," by ABC News, December 15, 2011. http://abcnews.go.com/blogs/headlines/2011/12/criteria-for-abc-news-debate-in-new-hampshire-on-january-7-2012/.

4. We additionally acknowledge the difficulty of assigning an ideal point to Donald Trump, many of whose policy stances were notoriously vague, who had no legislative voting record, and who had an unusually small number of donations. The very moderate ideal point used here (1.5) comes from early in the campaign, although CrowdPac later calculated it as 5.1 as more conservative donors began backing him.

REFERENCES

Barbour, Henry, Sally Bradshaw, Ari Fleischer, Zori Fonalledas, and Glenn McCall. 2013. "Growth and Opportunity Project." Report of the Republican National Committee. Accessed March 17, 2017. http://goproject.gop.com/rnc_growth_opportunity_book_2013.pdf.

Benoit, William L. 2002. *The Primary Decision: A Functional Analysis of Debates in Presidential Primaries*. Vol. 1062, no. 5623. Santa Barbara: Greenwood Publishing Group.

Benoit, William L., Mitchell S. McKinney, and Michael T. Stephenson. 2002. "Effects of Watching Primary Debates in the 2000 US Presidential Campaign." *Journal of Communication* 52 (2): 316–331.

Best, Charlie. 2016. "Washington State Unpledged Delegates: Let Voters Decide!" Moveon.org petition. Accessed March 17, 2017. https://pac.petitions.moveon.org/sign/washington-state-unpledged?r_by=333771.

Bonica, Adam. 2013. Database on Ideology, Money in Politics, and Elections: Public version 1.0 [Computer file]. Stanford, CA: Stanford University Libraries. Accessed March 17, 2017. http://data.stanford.edu/dime.

Borchers, Callum. 2015. "What Do Republicans Have To Show For Their Debate Moderator Complaints? Hugh Hewitt … Again." *Washington Post's The Fix*. December 15. Accessed March 17, 2017. https://www.washingtonpost.com/news/the-fix/wp/2015/12/15/what-do-republicans-have-to-show-for-their-debate-moderator-complaints-hugh-hewitt-again/.

Cairncross, Sean. 2016. Telephone interview with author, conducted August 3rd.

Claybourn, Joshua. 2016. "Dumping Trump Would Be Undemocratic And Counterproductive." *The Federalist*. July 13.

Clendinen, Dudley. 1984. "Eight Democrats are Enticed into a No-Rules Debate." *New York Times*. January 12.

Cohen, Marty, David Karol, Hans Noel, and John Zaller. 2008. *The Party Decides: Presidential Nominations before and after Reform*. Chicago Studies in American Politics. Chicago: University of Chicago Press.

Collier, David and Steve Levitsky. 1997. "Democracy with Adjectives: Conceptual Innovation in Comparative Research." *World Politics* 49 (3): 430–451.

Davenport, Jim. 2007. "Judge Denies Bid to Stop GOP Debate," *Associated Press*, May 11. Columbia, SC.

Dominguez, Casey B.K. 2011. "Does the Party Matter? Endorsements in Congressional Primaries." *Political Research Quarterly* 64 (3): 534–544.

Everett, Burgess and Seung Min Kim. 2016. "Sanders' Anti-Superdelegate Push Gains Steam in Senate." *Politico*. June 21.

Fahrenkopf, Frank. 2016. Telephone interview with author, conducted August 12th.

Falcone, Michael. 2008. "New Hampshire GOP Backs Out of Fox Forum," *New York Times*, January 5.

Greenfield, Jeff. 2016. "Why We Need Those 'Anti-Democratic' Superdelegates." *Politico*. May 28.

Greenwald, Glenn. 2016. "Perfect End to Democratic Primary: Anonymous Superdelegates Declare Winner Through Media." *The Intercept*. June 7.

Kalikow, Peter S. 2016. "The anti-democratic plot to steal the GOP nomination from Trump." *New York Post*. March 14.

Kendall, Kathleen. 2000. *Communication in the Presidential Primaries: Candidates and the Media, 1912-2000*. Santa Barbara: Greenwood Publishing Group.

Kengor, Paul. 2007. "The Great Forgotten Debate." *National Review*. May 22.

King, Shaun. 2016. "Superdelegates Will Decide Who Wins the Democratic Nomination — but not Until the Convention." *New York Daily News.* May 19.

Kovach, Bill. 1972. "Debate Planned in New Hampshire." *New York Times.* February 24.

Lawrence, Eric, Todd Donovan, and Shaun Bowler. 2013. "The Adoption of Direct Primaries in the United States." *Party Politics* 19 (1): 3–18.

LoBianco, Tom. 2016. "Trump Children Unable to Vote for Dad in NY Primary." CNN. April 12. Accessed March 17, 2017. http://www.cnn.com/2016/04/11/politics/donald-trump-ivanka-vice-president/.

Lord, Jeffrey. 2015. "Where is the Conservative Debate?" *Conservative Review.* August 5. https://www.conservativereview.com/commentary/2015/08/where-is-the-conservative-debate.

Lydons, Christopher. 1972. "Humphrey Proposes Debates to McGovern and He Accepts." *New York Times.* May 19.

Masket, Seth E. 2009. *No Middle Ground: How Informal Party Organizations Control Nominations and Polarize Legislatures.* Ann Arbor: University of Michigan Press.

Masket, Seth. 2016. "The GOP Doesn't Seem to be Cracking Up in Down-Ballot Races." *FiveThirtyEight.* May 9. Accessed March 17, 2017. http://fivethirtyeight.com/features/the-gop-doesnt-seem-to-be-cracking-up-in-down-ballot-races/.

McConnaughy, Corrine M. 2013. *The Woman Suffrage Movement in America: A Reassessment.* Cambridge: Cambridge University Press.

McGhee, Eric, Seth Masket, Nolan McCarty, Steve Rogers, and Boris Shor. 2014. "A Primary Cause of Partisanship? Nomination Systems and Legislator Ideology." *The American Journal of Political Science* 58 (2): 337–51.

Mischiefs of Faction staff. 2016. "What Happened to the GOP?" *Vox.com/Mischiefs of Faction.* May 18. Accessed March 17, 2017. http://www.vox.com/mischiefs-of-faction/2016/5/18/11693158/republican-party-failure.

Neidig, Harper. 2016. "Sanders: 'Extremely undemocratic' to call Clinton the nominee at this point." *The Hill.* May 3.

New York Times Staff. 1972. "U.S. Court Rules Mrs. Chisholm Must Receive Equal Time on TV." June 3.

Norrander, Barbara. 2015a. *Super Tuesday: Regional Politics and Presidential Primaries.* Lexington: University Press of Kentucky.

Norrander, Barbara 2015b. *The Imperfect Primary: Oddities, Biases and Strengths of U.S. Presidential Nomination Politics,* 2nd ed. New York: Routledge Press.

Philipp, Emanuel L. 1910. *Political Reform in Wisconsin: A Historical Review of the Subjects of Primary Election, Taxation and Railway Regulation.* Madison: State Historical Society of Wisconsin.

Plattner, Marc F. 2010. "Populism, Pluralism, and Liberal Democracy," *Journal of Democracy* 21(1): 81–92.

Polsby, Nelson W. 1983. "The Reform of Presidential Selection and Democratic Theory." *PS* 16 (4): 695–698.

Ranney, Austin. 1975. *Curing the Mischiefs of Faction: Party Reform in America.* Jefferson Memorial Lectures. Berkeley: University of California Press.

Redlawsk, David P., Caroline J. Tolbert, Todd Donovan. 2011. *Why Iowa?: How Caucuses and Sequential Elections Improve the Presidential Nominating Process.* Chicago: University of Chicago Press.

Reynolds, John F. *The Demise of the American Convention System, 1880–1911.* Cambridge: Cambridge University Press, 2006.

Richardson, Valerie and David Sherfinski. 2016. "Donald Trump Blasts 'Rigged' GOP System after Latest Setback." *Washington Times.* April 11.

Schattschneider, E. E. 1942. *Party Government.* Piscataway, NJ: Transaction Publishers.

Schmitter, Philippe C., and Terry Lynn Karl. 1991. "What Democracy is... and is Not." *Journal of Democracy* 2 (3): 75–88.

Smith, Hedrick. 1980. "Excluded from G.O.P. Debate, Four Attack Bush." *New York Times.* February 24.

Smith, Jennifer K., and Julia R. Azari. 2015. "The Anti-Party Tradition in American Political Development." Working paper.

Smith, Peter H., and Ziegler Melissa R. 2008. "Liberal and Illiberal Democracy in Latin America." *Latin American Politics and Society* 50 (1): 31–57.

Spicer, Sean. 2016. Telephone interview with author, conducted August 16.

Wagner, John. 2016. "Not continuing to run would be 'outrageously undemocratic,' Bernie Sanders says." *The Washington Post.* March 17.

Ware, Alan. 2002. *The American Direct Primary.* New York: Cambridge University Press.

Weber, Max, 1919. "Politics as a Vocation." Speech delivered at Munich University, 1918.

Chapter 9

Conspiracy Theories in the 2016 Election

Costly Signals or Conventional Wisdom

Matthew Atkinson, Darin DeWitt, and Joseph E. Uscinski

Conspiracies are real events that involve a small group of powerful persons plotting in secret for their own benefit against the common good. Conspiracies happen all too regularly, but because they are easily exposed, they tend to fail (Grimes 2016). Examples in recent history include Watergate and Iran-Contra. *Conspiracy theories* also posit a small group of powerful persons plotting in secret for their own benefit against the common good, but unlike *conspiracies*, conspiracy theories are unsubstantiated claims that may or may not be true (Uscinski and Parent 2014).

We know that Richard Nixon and his underlings violated the Constitution along with several criminal statutes during the period known as Watergate because the appropriate institutions held open hearings, evidence was brought forward for public assessment, and official findings were made. Therefore, Watergate is a conspiracy. Assertions that President Kennedy was assassinated by then-vice-president Johnson, Fidel Castro, or the Mafia, however, are conspiracy theories because they conflict with the authoritative account provided by the appropriate institution in this case, which is the Warren Commission (Levy 2007).

Regardless of their strained relationship with truth, conspiracy theories have long been intertwined in American politics. Before the United States united, settlers believed that witches were plotting with Satan against the colonies. Some of these "witches" were burned alive for their supposed crimes. The American Revolution was fueled in part by conspiracy theories (Middlekauff 2005, Bailyn 1992). Following the brilliant political prose that opens the Declaration of Independence, Thomas Jefferson devolves into a series of baseless accusations against the King of England. Jefferson's original draft contained many more conspiratorial accusations, but his coauthors cut them out (Maier 1998). Since the Revolution, Americans have been alerted to conspiracies by the Illuminati, Freemasons, Jews, Catholics, Muslims, Mormons, monopolists, capitalists, communists, terrorists and many, many more.

Polls suggest that all Americans believe at least one conspiracy theory; most people believe in several (Miller, Saunders, and Farhart 2016, Oliver and Wood 2014a). Conspiracy theories include far-out claims, for example, that a race of shapeshifting interdimensional lizard people secretly rule the planet or that jet exhaust fumes (the white lines we commonly see in the sky following aircraft) are actually airborne poisons intended to kill off much of the world's population. These lines in the sky are commonly referred to by conspiracy theorists as "Chem-trails." About 5 percent of Americans subscribe to each of these conspiracy theories (Public Policy Polling 2013).

Other conspiracy theories are grounded in an acute distrust of opposing political groups, and often serve as proxy fights between partisans. For example, about 25 percent of Americans believe in some form of the "Birther" theory—that President Obama is hiding his true place of origin and faked his birth certificate to usurp the presidency (Berinsky 2012). This conspiracy theory was popular during the 2008 election and became relevant again when Donald Trump attempted to investigate President Obama's "true" heritage. An equal number of Americans believe the "Truther" theory—that President Bush orchestrated or knew in advance about the 9/11 attacks. Interestingly, both of these theories attract believers from largely one party; Republicans tend to subscribe to the "Birther" theory and Democrats to the "Truther" theory (Nyhan 2009).

Still other conspiracy theories surround contemporary policy disputes. For example, a significant portion of Americans believe that climate change is some form of hoax, perhaps perpetrated by unscrupulous scientists or cunning communists (Lewandowsky, Cook, and Lloyd 2016). Many believed in 2010 that "death panels" lay beneath President Obama's health-care plan (Nyhan 2010). These beliefs are largely harbored by Republicans. On the other side of the isle, Democrats frequently express belief in conspiracy theories that accuse Republicans, conservatives, corporations, and the rich of conspiring against the country (Furnham 2013, Goertzel 2010). Democrats' use of conspiracy theories seemed to spike after the 2016 election (Frankovic 2016).

In the years leading up to the 2016 presidential election, conspiracy theories often made headlines. The 2014 Ebola scare drove some Americans to believe that the Ebola virus was turning victims into zombies who were then rising from the grave to wreak havoc on the living. Conspiracy mongers like Alex Jones propagated the idea that Ebola was part of a government plot to depopulate the United States (Jones 2014). In 2015, many Texans were concerned that a nearby military training exercise known as Jade Helm was actually the beginning of a federal government takeover (Fernandez 2015), and in 2016 the death of Supreme Court Justice Antonin Scalia drove many to believe that President Obama had assassinated the Justice to take control of the Supreme Court (Uscinski 2016). Conspiracy theories are a normal part of American democracy and more commonplace than extraordinary (Miller and Saunders 2016).

Despite their generally poor reputation in regard to truth, conspiracy theories can alert people to coming danger and steer leaders toward good behavior by holding them accountable for wrongdoing. In this context, conspiracy theories can be a net positive. Just consider Bob Woodward and Carl Bernstein at *The Washington Post* who followed a conspiracy theory to eventually brought down a corrupt president, Richard Nixon. But such benefits are not sometimes without costs.

Conspiracy theories sometimes lead people to act on dubious information, engage in scapegoating and, worse, attempt and commit violence and murder. Take Timothy McVeigh, for example—he believed the government was plotting to take away rights, so he conspired against the government by killing 168 and injuring more than 600. In 2016, a man with a loaded weapon walked into a pizza parlor intending to uncover a secretive child sex ring operated by high ranking members of the Democratic Party (we will return to this episode later). And, in 2017, a man opened fire on Republican members of Congress while they were practicing for a charity baseball game, shooting four people. Initial reports suggest the perpetrator was driven by anti-Trump conspiracy theories. The cases are, of course, extreme and unusual. Everyone believes at least one conspiracy theory but the vast majority of people do not commit either violence or conspiracy-inspired violence. But when such cases do arise, they are of little surprise to social scientists, who find that those who are the most drawn to conspiracy thinking are also the most accepting of violence and the most willing to conspire themselves to reach their ends (Douglas and Sutton 2011, Uscinski and Parent 2014).

The more common consequence of conspiracy theories is that people make mundane decisions based upon them. This is of concern because when people make decisions based upon dubious information, their resultant actions can be ill-advised and regrettable. For example, conspiracy theories influence people to make poor decisions about their health (Oliver and Wood 2014b), their sexual behavior (Bird and Bogart 2003), and the environment (Douglas and Sutton 2015). Of particular concern to this chapter is how conspiracy theories influence decision-making in politics.

In what remains of this chapter, we examine what social scientists know about conspiracy theories and how these theories have tended to operate in our national politics, and in particular, our presidential campaign politics. We then turn to the 2016 presidential election and argue that while some amount of conspiracy theorizing will always be present in our politics and that all presidential elections will feature conspiracy theories, 2016 was different from previous elections. We show that conspiracy theories played a more prominent role and were used very differently—particularly by elites—in 2016 when compared to prior elections. Relying on literatures from several disciplines, we attempt to explain why conspiracy theories were used both by individuals with alternative ideologies and by political elites. We suggest that conspiracy theories were used as costly signals: the former used conspiracy theories to contact like-minded individuals, the latter to mobilize an oft-ignored segment of the population. We argue that conspiracy theories allowed Donald Trump and like-minded ideological groups to organize and mobilize, thereby overcoming some difficult collective action problems, and eventually win the 2016 presidential election. We conclude by offering some predictions on how this strategy may affect Trump's performance as president.

CONVENTIONAL WISDOM ABOUT UNCONVENTIONAL IDEAS

Conspiracy theories make tantalizing news, and journalists are quick to capitalize on them. News reports are chock full of the latest salacious conspiracy theories, and headlines have been quick to suggest that the country has fallen into a conspiracy theory–induced delirium. In 2017, *The Atlantic* suggested that a conspiracy culture had taken ahold of the nation, "The Normalization of Conspiracy Culture." In 2013, the *New York Times* ran the headline, "No Comment Necessary: Conspiracy Nation." In 2011, the *New York Daily News* breathlessly declared "The United States of Conspiracy: Why, more and more, Americans cling to crazy theories." Reporting like this would give the impression that belief in conspiracy theories has been on the rise over the last decade. The only problem is that journalists have regularly claimed for at least the last 50 years that the United States has gone off the proverbial conspiracy cliff (Uscinski and Parent 2014), and such claims can't be true all the time. There is no evidence to suggest that Americans believed in more conspiracy theories in 2016 than in any previous time period, and the available evidence suggests that conspiracy theories have steadily decreased since the 1960s (Uscinski and Parent 2014).

Many news articles highlighted conspiracy theories in the run up to the 2016 election, and it is also true that prominent politicians propagated and discussed conspiracy theories more in 2016 than in previous years. But that does not mean that more people believed in conspiracy theories or that the people who did believed in more of them in 2016. The evidence that has been provided by social scientists suggests that conspiracy theorizing is rather stable in the United States (Uscinski and Parent 2014). Here is why:

Rather than being easy to convince people that a conspiracy is afoot, it is somewhat difficult (Uscinski, Klofstad, and Atkinson 2016). It is true that some conspiracy theories amass millions of followers, but to put this into perspective, think instead of all the people not convinced by conspiracy theories enough to believe them. Twenty-five percent of Americans believed the "Birther" and "Truther" theories respectively; but seventy-five percent of Americans did not believe each theory. This should not be taken to minimize that a quarter of the public buys into these dubious ideas, but rather that large majorities don't. The reason for this comes down to traditional theories of public opinion (Zaller 1992).

In order for a person to adopt a conspiracy theory, like the "Birther" or "Truther" theories, one first needs to have partisan inclinations that match the logic of the particular conspiracy theory. Birther theories do not convince Democrats and Truther theories have a tough time convincing Republicans. The reason for this is that partisan predispositions keep partisans from believing ideas that implicate their own party. Instead, partisans are more likely to accept ideas that impugn the opposing party (Claassen and Ensley 2016, McClosky and Chong 1985). Second, in order to believe in a conspiracy theory, a person must also be open to conspiratorial logic. Much like how partisans see the world through partisan-tinted glasses, people see the world through a lens that is more or less open to conspiracy theories. Some people have a world view that is very open to conspiracy logic while others have a world view that is closed to almost any insulation of conspiracy (Brotherton, French, and Pickering 2013). Think of this as a continuum, with most people being somewhere in the middle.

When we put together partisanship and conspiracy worldviews, we can explain why most conspiracy theories amass very few followers or run into a ceiling. Conspiracy theories that have a partisan element to them (i.e., the Birther and Truther theories) can't seem to convince more than 25 percent of the population because only people who both have a conducive partisan identity *and* an elevated conspiracy worldview will believe in any given partisan conspiracy theory (Uscinski, Klofstad, and Atkinson 2016). While many are concerned over the Internet's ability to spread conspiracy theories very quickly and to larger audiences than ever before, most people are fickle with their beliefs and aren't quick to fall prey to conspiracy theories.

This is why politicians, and particularly presidential candidates, avoid them in public discourse. Because most people will object to any given partisan conspiracy theory, it is usually not in their favor to traffic in conspiracy theories. In addition, their dubious nature makes it so that propagating conspiracy theories is costly; conspiracy theories have a bad reputation and cast some doubt on the person propagating them (Husting and Orr 2007). For that reason, presidential candidates in modern American history have avoided trafficking in such ideas; there is little to be gained from it. If conspiracy theories do enter campaign discourse, it is usually due to a surrogate (i.e., Harry Reid suggesting that Mitt Romney never paid his taxes). In short, the conventional wisdom on conspiracy theories suggests that conspiracy theories are stable in the United States, and that presidential candidates have good reason to avoid them in their discourse.

THE UNCONVENTIONAL ELECTION

Conspiracy rhetoric seemingly dominated campaign discourse in 2016. That conspiracy theories attracted so much media attention and so much elite discussion made all previous presidential campaigns pale in comparison. Election results were questioned, candidates were accused of subversion, and America's political and economic systems were deemed "rigged." Major presidential candidates—including the eventual winner of the election—discussed at length on national television whether or not Senator Ted Cruz's father assassinated President Kennedy (Haberman 2016). What seemed most out of place was that Donald Trump was able to overcome a party system designed to promote consensus candidates, while endlessly trafficking in conspiracy theories consisting of pseudoscientific claims, exaggerations, and outright lies.

With the sheer prominence of conspiracy theories during the campaign, the 2016 election cycle marked the return of a political style not seen in America since the nineteenth century. As discussions of negative campaigning written in the years before 2016 frequently point out: if you think contemporary campaign tactics are dirty, you would be shocked to learn of the tactics used in the nineteenth century—an era that historians Glenn Altschuler and Stuart Blumin (2001) call the "rude republic." The 2016 election gave us a taste of what those elections were like. Prominent discussions of male hand size, genitalia, and virility in 2016 are reminiscent of the 1800 presidential election in which James Callender—the Alex Jones of his day—faced libel charges as a result of the scandalmongering that helped deliver Thomas Jefferson the presidency.

The use of far-fetched conspiracy theories in 2016 as in the nineteenth century was enabled by the political context. The two eras share several important political features. First, in 2016, ideological polarization is at a contemporary high, reaching extreme levels not seen since the late nineteenth century (Lewis, Poole, and Rosenthal 2017b). Second, the country is profoundly separated into red and blue geographies as it was throughout much of the nineteenth century (Lewis, Poole, and Rosenthal 2017a, c). Third, today's media sector is highly decentralized and laden with ideology in a way that harkens back to the partisan newspapers in the nineteenth century (Russo 1980, Uscinski 2014). These political features serve as necessary conditions for the widespread elevation of conspiracy theories in our political discourse.

Yet political conditions alone do not account for why people participate in sharing conspiracy theories. Here, we use social science theory to propose a new explanation of why political activists find extremely specious conspiracy theories especially useful. The 2016 election presents a conundrum for the existing literature on conspiracy theory propagation; largely because many conspiracy theories proved impressively resilient to the presentation of refuting evidence from a broad and diverse range of elites. We look to signaling theory to explain the spread of dubious conspiracy theories in the 2016 election. Using canonical examples from the signaling theory literature, we illustrate the logic of signaling theory and show how it accounts for the use and spread of (sometimes far-fetched) conspiracy theories in the 2016 election.

Costly Signaling Theory

Individuals with ideas outside the mainstream have a coordination problem. They would like to find each other but their communication is constrained by societal norms. To remain an upstanding member of their local community, individuals who hold unconventional ideas must keep their opinions private. All individuals who wish to undertake collective actions that conflict with mainstream norms experience this predicament. For example, in *The Strategy of Conflict*, economist Thomas Schelling (1980) illustrates the coordination problem faced by a bank robber and a corrupt bank employee, who are constrained by the legal code:

> The bank employee who would like to rob the bank if he could only find an outside collaborator and the bank robber who would like to rob the bank if only he could find an inside accomplice may find it difficult to collaborate because they are unable to identify each other, there being severe penalties in the event that either should declare his intentions to someone who proved not to have identical interests.

The prospective bank robbers and those on the ideological fringe face the same general problem: they need to credibly communicate information that is hidden. While the bank robber does not want to incriminate himself by publicly announcing his attentions to break the law, the individual with a fringe ideology does not wish to advertise the fact that his private beliefs breach societal norms.

In *Job Market Signaling*, Nobel prize-winning economist Michael Spence (1973) uncovers an effective solution to the problem of communicating hidden information—his solution is a costly signal. In Spence's signaling model, an employee would like to credibly communicate to a prospective employer her aptitude for the job, information that the employer is also eager to collect. For the job candidate, pronouncing her capability is insufficient, as candidates with varying skill levels will make identical claims. The claim of aptitude is *cheap talk*—it means nothing. The truly high-quality candidate must find a way of credibly communicating her underlying aptitude, which is hard to directly observe, through a *costly signal* that less qualified candidates cannot mimic. A costly signal is a bachelor's degree from an Ivy League college. For individuals who lack either the inherent talent or commitment to succeed, admission to an elite university and passing grades will be an infeasible achievement. Since educational attainment requires skills that also make for good employees such as cognitive ability and willingness to follow directions, the costly signal of educational attainment allows an employer to hire a high-quality candidate.

In abstract terms, individuals with hidden dispositions find each other by means of costly signals. A costly signal is designed to credibly transmit information about the signaler's underlying type to a receiver. The signaler needs to verify to the receiver that he is not misrepresenting his underlying type. To make the signal credible, the communicative act needs to be associated with a cost that discriminates those who hold the underlying value from either accidental or purposeful mimics. Credible signals are associated with costs that only people who possess the underlying quality can or will choose to bear. In an ideal situation, the signal is cheap to transmit for individuals who hold the underlying value but prohibitively costly for all others. This is precisely what makes the signal truly informative.

In *Codes of the Underworld*, sociologist Diego Gambetta (2009) considers hidden information more broadly than Spence does in his original formulation of signaling theory. Gambetta shows that information may be hidden because it is hard to observe as in the job market signaling example or because it reveals beliefs or actions that exist outside the bounds of polite society, perhaps because those ideas are illegal or violate social norms. With this extension, Gambetta explicitly links Spence's signaling theory to criminal communications, and shows that costly signaling allows criminals to credibly communicate information that is hidden. For example, after FBI agent Donnie Brasco infiltrated the mob, the mafia now requires prospective members to commit murder before entry into the brotherhood is confirmed because murder is a signal of the underlying criminal type that is too costly for an undercover agent to mimic (Gambetta 2009, pg. 23).

Gambetta modifies Spence's original formulation of the signaling model to accommodate the possibility that criminals and other individuals communicating information outside the bounds of polite society must devise their signals with at least some plausible deniability, in case outsiders who do not share the underlying value intercept the message. After all, if outsiders understand the signal, the result is "social embarrassment," "jail or retribution" (pg. 150). Gambetta illustrates this idea by discussing the signaling strategy of street prostitutes (pg. 181):

> Advertising prostitution commonly consists of walking the street at a leisurely pace in eye-catching and skimpy attire. By displaying what is on sale, this signal is allusive enough for those who want that sort of business to understand it but vague enough not to warrant an arrest, for anyone is free to walk the street. Above all, the signal prevents confusion, for ordinary women would not walk around like that. This ensures that a woman with that demeanor and outfit is *really* a prostitute. An ordinary woman would not only fail to obtain any benefit from looking like one but would pay some cost.

Like prostitutes, individuals wanting to bribe public officials have to employ discreet signals that are nearly unambiguous to those looking for them. Gambetta reports that in some countries motorists store large banknotes with their driver's licenses in order to signal their willingness to bribe the police. Gambetta explains why the banknote serves as an efficient signal (pg. 170):

> Even if policemen did not know that the banknote was such a signal to start with, nonetheless it could still denote because it stands as *an icon* of the willingness to pay a bribe. Had the item inserted in the driver's license been a leaf or a photo, the signal could have worked if and only if in some way the policeman had prior knowledge of these other items being used with that meaning, for they do not remind one of a bribe. But a banknote can make it work without prior agreement or precedent—and it is quick. It works by conveying the driver's intention, for it embodies a key aspect of a corrupt transaction: cash.

An Illustration of Costly Signaling: Gang Tattoos

Raymond Fisman and Tim Sullivan (2016a) apply signaling theory to understand how criminals solve their coordination problems. For example, they observe that criminals exhibiting erratic—even masochistic—behavior are often times are engaging in a rational action, by transmitting a costly signal that credibly communicates their toughness and willingness to take risks:

> A new prisoner whacking his head against the wall or jabbing a knife in his own thigh may seem crazy. But he's communicating to his audience of fellow inmates that he won't mind a few cuts or bruises in a confrontation. Compared to a fresh arrival who tries to solidify his place in the prison hierarchy by acting tough or talking tough, in a way, the head banger is the more rational one. At least the message he's sending is credible.

According to Fisman and Sullivan (2016b), costly signaling also explains why it is rational for gang members to get gang tattoos on their faces and necks. Typically, face tattoos are not obtained for aesthetic purposes. Rather, face and neck tattoos serve as a costly signal that credibly communicates information under conditions of plausible deniability. Face and neck tattoos credibly transmit hidden information about an individual's underlying criminal type, including strength, toughness, and gang membership (Gambetta 2009).

A verbal commitment to a life of crime is cheap talk for a prospective gang member and such proclamations lack credibility. Verbal commitments that have a costly component and, thus, count as costly signals include those where a criminal mentions his gang affiliation or previous prison sentence. If membership or prison time can be confirmed, the sender is conveying a credible and costly signal about his underlying trait. Even in this case, however, a neck or face tattoo would be even more convincing. In contrast, because face and neck tattoos are prohibitively costly for those who are not committed to a life of gang membership, face and neck tattoos credibly discriminate between individuals who hold these qualities and those who do not. By bearing such tattoos, one signals his credible commitment to the gang's network and its interests.

The neck tattoo has the ideal properties of a costly signal: it efficiently communicates credible commitment. The signal is efficient because, on the one hand, it is unlikely to be mimicked by people (whether upstanding citizens, police, or informants) who do not share the underlying criminal type: "the uncommitted might consider the future cost of finding legal employment, how he'll be perceived in 'polite' society, or the financial and physical pain involved in removing the works 'F*** the LAPD' from across his chest" (Fisman and Sullivan 2016a). On the other hand, while a face tattoo is not a subtle signal, it still meets Gambetta's criterion of plausible deniability. It credibly signals an individual's gang affiliation, their past crimes, and their prospects for recidivism, but the tattoo itself is not enough to convict its bearer with a crime. By meeting all of these criteria, the costly signal of a face tattoo aids criminals in finding and identifying kindred spirits, while avoiding punishment (in this case, time in jail) associated with such communication. The costly signal outlined by Spence and Gambetta solves the coordination problem advanced by Schelling.

In short, people like to be agreeable and avoid social friction. But likeminded people would also like an efficient way to identify one another. This process is easy if you hold mainstream convictions—you simply advertise your beliefs to others. But suppose you harbor extreme political ideas that exist outside the conventions of polite society—you would prefer not to advertise beliefs that are sanctioned by social norms. How do you find kindred spirits? We argue that conspiracy theories—even seemingly far-fetched ones—are a costly signal used by individuals who hold extreme ideologies in order to advertise their beliefs—under the cover of plausible deniability—and find like-minded individuals who they can open up to behind closed doors. In particular, we think our model explains the propagation of particularly dubious conspiracy theories during the 2016 presidential campaign. We now apply this logic to two cases: Pizzagate, which was a fringe conspiracy theory spread on Reddit, and to Donald Trump's assertion, that seemingly defied all of the rules of campaign politics, that Senator Ted Cruz's father was involved in the assassination of JFK. We choose these two cases to demonstrate the signaling theory because the former shows how this theory works on the Internet—the modern-day water cooler—while the latter shows how signaling works when a political elite is sending the costly signal.

Application: Pizzagate

To understand how costly signaling illuminates the dissemination of fringe conspiracy theories on the Internet, imagine that you participate in a Midwestern coffee klatch with a range of acquaintances. In this group, most everyone leans toward traditional limited government conservatism. But, as someone who harbors extremist views, you would like to find fellow hardliners. To do that, you must devise a costly signal that advertises your views and locates fellow extremists without creating enormous social friction. To remain an upstanding member of the coffee klatch, you cannot endorse fringe ideas about racial politics. But you can repeat a nascent conspiracy theory that Hillary Rodham Clinton orchestrated a child sex ring in a Washington D.C. pizza parlor. By doing so, you come off as wacky to non-believers rather than dangerous, as you would if you endorsed anti-democratic ideas.

The very outlandishness of the idea that Clinton orchestrated a child sex ring serves a useful purpose in this case: it imposes a cost that effectively discriminates between ideological types. Let's consider why. If the signal is not costly, people trying to reduce social friction will be agreeable with the ideological extremist and effective sorting will not transpire. But advocating Pizzagate is costly, so members of the coffee klatch who simply harbor traditional limited government views—as opposed to extreme views outside of the mainstream—will be disinclined to sympathize with or parrot this particularly ludicrous idea, which was roundly condemned by elites across the ideological spectrum.

When an individual who disguises his extreme views shares the Pizzagate conspiracy theory at his coffee klatch, he looks for other individuals who also espouse the idea or are willing to entertain the idea and seek more information. Advocating Pizzagate eliminates the possibility that non-like-minded people will agree with you for the sake of eliminating social friction and, given how dubious the conspiracy theory is, it is unlikely to be seriously espoused—even accidentally—by a conventional conservative, as conventional conservatives do not want to bear the cost of appearing irrational.

The crazier the conspiracy theory, the clearer a signal that one sends to a like-minded receiver. Even if you think it is implausible that Hillary Clinton is running a child sex ring, you understand that like-minded extremists are willing to entertain the possibility during the presidential election campaign and discussing the topic is a good way to connect with them. Ideas like Pizzagate are imbued with symbolic meaning. By saying Pizzagate, you communicate a lot of information about who you are, who you listen to, and who you are in a coalition with. The Pizzagate signal suggests you harbor a strongly conspiratorial worldview and extreme skepticism of our mainstream institutions, politicians, and narratives. It suggests that you despise the opposing party so much that you are willing to entertain the idea that they commit the most despicable acts—including the rape, torture, and sacrificial murder of children. It suggests you receive information from alternative sources of news and that you are in coalition with people who think in similar terms. Communicating that sort of information is far more important than whether or not you think Pizzagate is true, even though some people did come to the conclusion that it was—including one gunman who attempted to investigate the theory.

But of all the possible conspiracy theories, why Pizzagate? Would advocating any ludicrous idea suffice to signal that you are a hardliner? No. Advocating idiosyncratic ludicrous ideas will not facilitate coordination. The challenge of sending a credible costly signal is accomplished only by using those dubious ideas that are imbued with symbolic meaning, which is why some dubious ideas snowball but most do not (Uscinski, DeWitt, and Atkinson 2018). In this case, the signal had to suggest a conspiracy worldview, the rejection of mainstream institutions, policies, and narratives, and a deep hatred of opposing political groups. Advocating random implausible ideas will more likely succeed in signaling that one is delusional rather than the advocate of a fringe ideology.

Application: Ted Cruz's Father Killed JFK

For years, the Republican front-runner and New York billionaire Donald Trump has actively investigated, propagated, or defended many conspiracy theories. He is perhaps the most publicly conspiratorial presidential contender in U.S. history. Trump's use of conspiracy theories for political purposes began with the Birther theory. When Trump's public "investigation" into Obama's past failed to provide evidence of a foreign birth, Trump moved on to suggest conspiracies about Obama's college transcripts. His conspiracy theories about

Obama culminated in the suggestion that Obama was himself affiliated with terror cells. Donald Trump on several occasions prior to this also entertained vaccine conspiracy theories, suggesting on Twitter that vaccines cause autism.

During the campaign Trump propagated conspiracy theories including: that there was a cover-up of the San Bernardino shooting, that the Bush administration allowed the 9/11 terror attacks to occur, that Syrian refugees were ISIS agents, that Mexico was conspiring to ship murderers and rapists across our borders, and that the primaries, convention, and general election were rigged. These are just to name a few. Trump's salience in the media combined with his unabashed use of conspiracy narratives accounted for the led to conspiracy rhetoric infecting American political discourse during 2016.

Trump's conspiracy rhetoric boiled down to a single unifying claim: Political elites have abandoned the interests of regular Americans in favor of foreign interests. For Trump, the political system was corrupt and the establishment could not be trusted. It followed, then, that only an outsider could stop the corruption. The majority of Trump's conspiracy claims were opportunistic: he attached conspiracy theories to every policy area and to every newsworthy event.

Perhaps Trump's most unnecessary conspiracy theory accused Senator Ted Cruz's father of being involved in the JFK assassination. When Trump introduced this idea, his accusation was twofold: that his now-vanquished presidential rival Ted Cruz's father conspired in 1963 to assassinate President Kennedy and that the media conspired to cover up this fact. Trump offered no evidence to back up either assertion, and CNN was quick to admonish him for his accusations toward the media. However, this was a deft use of conspiracy theories by Trump: by suggesting that the evidence had been covered up by the media, he made the lack of evidence count in favor of the conspiracy theory. This conspiracy theory was unnecessary at first glance because Trump propagated it at a time when he was largely guaranteed to win Republican nomination and had thwarted Ted Cruz. There was seemingly no motivation for this theory if it was only intended to attack Cruz.

But, if the conspiracy theory about Ted Cruz's father was used by Trump as a costly signal, then its use makes perfect sense because the theory communicated that Trump was committed to unconventional views at the exact time he was expected to go more mainstream. This theory, and the many that followed, allowed Trump to maintain credibility as an outsider non-mainstream candidate even though he was on the verge of a major party presidential nomination. In addition, attaching a wild conspiracy theory to JFK's assassination allowed Trump to reach across party lines with this unconventional signal because a majority of Americans from both parties believe there was a cover-up in the Kennedy assassination.

In all, Trump's conspiracy theories delivered an unconventional political appeal that effectively engaged groups outside of the party's mainstream. By using conspiracy theories, Trump succeeded in mobilizing a group of people who were less likely to take part in collective action. By focusing his populist appeals on conspiracy rhetoric—rather than substantive policy—Trump galvanized the broad support needed to overcome the party establishment

A Farleigh Dickenson poll shows that Trump's supporters are the most likely to believe in several conspiracy theories as well. They are most likely to have responded that the following conspiracy theories are "definitely true" or "possibly true": that global warming is a fraud, that vaccines cause autism, and that Hillary Clinton knew about Benghazi in advance and allowed the attacks to occur.

Appealing to the conspiracy-minded may be a short-term winning strategy for Trump, but there will be long-term consequences. There is a cost to democracy. Imagine the person who takes Trump's rhetoric at face value: They would traffic in ideas such as: that President Obama is a foreign usurper bent on bringing Islamic terrorism to the United States, that a current senator's father assassinated JFK, that doctors are covering up the link between vaccines and autism, and that Mexico is purposely sending its people here to murder and rape us. These comprise a very dark set of views in which those people, practices, and institutions that we trust the most are all corrupt and untrustable.

Disdain for elites is the common thread uniting the diverse conservative groups outside the Republican establishment. Trump's continued support among these groups is due to his continued use of conspiracy theories, even upon taking office. Trump now has the challenge faced by all leaders who have come to power using conspiracy signals to build their coalition of support: The coalition that brought you to power is not a coalition you can use to govern.

CONCLUSION

The 2016 election cycle saw conspiracy theories rise to prominence in ways not recently witnessed in presidential politics. For example, significant portions of Americans claimed to seriously entertain the possibility that Hillary Clinton orchestrated a child sex ring in a Washington, DC, pizza parlor and that Ted Cruz's father may have shot John F. Kennedy. Far-fetched theories such as these are certainly not new to politics—slanderous allegations of betrayal, murder, and pedophilia have a long tradition. But in modern American history, such dubious rumors have rarely featured prominently in national election campaigns.

The 2016 election upends the conventional wisdom of how conspiracy theories spread. In the leading account, conspiracies gain traction through an information cascade process (Sunstein 2014). Information cascades occur when people with limited knowledge base their beliefs on what other people seem to believe—the perceived wisdom of the crowd—rather than on their own independent judgment. Political rumors propagate when people choose not to think for themselves but instead rely on the actions of the larger crowd to make a decision, such as the decision of whether to accept a conspiracy theory rumor or not. Rumors can spread quickly through this process. However, rumors that spread through this mechanism are also exceedingly fragile. According to Sunstein, "dissent is an indispensable corrective" (Sunstein 2014, pg. 17). In other words, information cascades are easily undone when refuting evidence is made widely available. 2016 suggests this leading account is incorrect: many conspiracy theories spread among ideologically like-minded people despite correcting evidence rather than through a cascading process.

In conclusion, individuals rationally endorse conspiracy theories not only because they believe they are true but also because conspiracy theories can effectively discriminate between individuals with conventional versus fringe views, just as the hideous face tattoo discriminates committed criminals from everyone else. We argue that conspiracy theories such as those about Pizzagate and Ted Cruz's father gained currency during the 2016 presidential election campaign because they helped ideological extremists communicate their beliefs without the risk of being ostracized from mainstream society.

The decision Trump must now make is whether he wants to build the governing coalition that will enable him to accomplish some of his policy goals or whether he will continue to practice the style of politics he has mastered—conspiracy theory politics—and forgo the prospect of significant policy accomplishments. Conspiracy theorists are often tactically brilliant in climbing the greasy pole to leadership, but they're often strategically daft when they get to the top. It's hard to sustain fear for extended periods of time, and it's hard to maintain credibility or craft effective policy when relying on conspiratorial arguments. (See, for example, Venezuela.)

If we look outside the United States, Hitler, Stalin, and Mao propagated many conspiracy theories. This led to the deaths of millions. The current Castro and Kim Jong-un regimes in Cuba and North Korea, respectively, use conspiratorial rhetoric to maintain control. It goes without saying that the political arrangements in World War II–era Germany, Russia and China and contemporary Cuba and North Korea are very different than those in the United States, but what they do suggest is that consolidated power and coalitions built on conspiracy theories don't mix well. Stalin's paranoid purges almost cost him his state (Nazi Germany attacked after he had destroyed much of his officer corps); Hitler's obsession with Untermenschen conjured up an unwinnable war Germany couldn't escape.

Trump's conspiracy theorizing has shown not just that he knows how, but also that he is very willing to use, conspiratorial rhetoric to rally (sometimes violent) support. Note that whether Trump believes his conspiracy theories or not, many of his supporters do, and his past rhetoric could entrap him, bending his behavior toward extreme expectations. Trump's conspiracy-driven policy views could either force him to act or leave him with the consequence of his followers acting where he does not. Go figure: If shadowy, powerful people are working in secret against you for evil purposes, then you need to fight fire with fire.

REFERENCES

Altschuler, Glenn C, and Stuart M Blumin. 2001. *Rude Republic: Americans and Their Politics in the Nineteenth Century.* Princeton, NJ: Princeton University Press.

Bailyn, Bernard. 1992. *The Ideological Origins of the American Revolution.* Cambridge: Harvard University Press.

Berinsky, Adam. 2012. The Birthers are (Still) Back. *YouGov: What the World Thinks.*

Bird, Sheryl Thorburn, and Laura M. Bogart. 2003. "Birth Control Conspiracy Beliefs, Perceived Discrimination, and Contraception among African Americans: An Exploratory Study." *Journal of Health Psychology* 8 (2): 263–276.

Brotherton, Rob, Christopher C. French, and Alan D. Pickering. 2013. "Measuring Belief in Conspiracy Theories: The Generic Conspiracist Beliefs Scale." *Frontiers in Psychology* 4 (Article 279).

Claassen, Ryan L., and Michael J. Ensley. 2016. "Motivated Reasoning and Yard-Sign-Stealing Partisans: Mine is a Likable Rogue, Yours is a Degenerate Criminal." *Political Behavior* 38 (2): 317–335.

Douglas, Karen M., and Robbie M. Sutton. 2015. "Climate change: Why the Conspiracy Theories Are Dangerous." *Bulletin of the Atomic Scientists* 71 (2): 98–106.

Douglas, Karen, and Robbie Sutton. 2011. "Does It Take One to Know One? Endorsement of Conspiracy Theories is Influenced by Personal Willingness to Conspire." *British Journal of Social Psychology* 50 (3): 544–552.

Fernandez, Manny. 2015. "As Jade Helm 15 Military Exercise Begins, Texans Keep Watch 'Just in Case'." *The New York Times*, July 15.

Fisman, Ray, and Tim Sullivan. 2016a. *The Inner Lives of Markets: How People Shape Them? And They Shape Us.* New York: PublicAffairs.

Fisman, Raymond, and Tim Sullivan. 2016b. "The Case for Neck Tattoos According to Economists." *The Atlantic*, June 13.

Frankovic, Kathy. 2016. "Belief in Conspiracies Largely Depends on Political Identity." *YouGov*, December 27. Accessed online March 17, 2017. https://today.yougov.com/news/2016/12/27/belief-conspiracies-largely-depends-political-iden/.

Furnham, Adrian. 2013. "Commercial Conspiracy Theories: A Pilot Study." *Frontiers in Psychology* 4.

Gambetta, Diego. 2009. *Codes of the underworld: How Criminals Communicate*: Princeton, NJ: Princeton University Press.

Goertzel, Ted. 2010. "Conspiracy Theories in Science." *EMBO reports* 11(7): 493–499.

Grimes, David Robert. 2016. "On the Viability of Conspiratorial Beliefs." *PloS one* 11 (1): e0147905.

Haberman, Maggie. 2016. "Donald Trump Accuses Ted Cruz's Father of Associating With Kennedy Assassin." *The New York Times*, May 3.

Husting, Gina, and Martin Orr. 2007. "Dangerous Machinery: "Conspiracy Theorist" as a Transpersonal Strategy of Exclusion." *Symbolic Interaction* 30(2): 127–150.

Jones, Alex. 2014. The Alex Jones Channel. In *Infowars.com*, edited by Alex Jones. YouTube: The Alex Jones Channel.

Levy, Neil. 2007. "Radically Socialized Knowledge and Conspiracy Theories." *Episteme* 4 (02):181–192.

Lewandowsky, Stephan, John Cook, and Elisabeth Lloyd. 2016. "The 'Alice in Wonderland' Mechanics of the Rejection of (Climate) Science: Simulating Coherence by Conspiracism." *Synthese*:1–22.

Lewis, Jeffrey B., Keith T. Poole, and Howard Rosenthal. 2017a. "Vote-View: Democratic Party." Accessed March 17, 2016. https://voteview.com/parties/100/democratic-party.

Lewis, Jeffrey B., Keith T. Poole, and Howard Rosenthal. 2017b. "Vote-View: Parties Overview." Accessed March 17, 2016. https://voteview.com/parties/all.

Lewis, Jeffrey B., Keith T. Poole, and Howard Rosenthal. 2017c. "Vote-View: Republican Party." Accessed March 17, 2016. https://voteview.com/parties/200/republican-party.

Maier, Pauline. 1998. *American Scripture: Making the Declaration of Independence*. New York: Vintage Books.

McClosky, Herbert, and Dennis Chong. 1985. "Similarities and Differences between Left-Wing and Right-Wing Radicals." *British Journal of Political Science* 15(3): 329–363.

Middlekauff, Robert. 2005. *The Glorious Cause: The American Revolution, 1763-1789*. New York: Oxford University Press.

Miller, Joanne M., and Kyle L. Saunders. 2016. "Conspiracy Theories in the United States: More Commonplace than Extraordinary." *Critical Review*:1–10.

Miller, Joanne M., Kyle L. Saunders, and Christina E. Farhart. 2016. "Conspiracy Endorsement as Motivated Reasoning: The Moderating Roles of Political Knowledge and Trust." *American Journal of Political Science* 60(4): 824–44.

Nyhan, Brendan. 2009. "9/11 and Birther Misperceptions Compared." *Brendannyhan.com/blog*. Accessed August 1, 2011.

Nyhan, Brendan. 2010. "Why the "Death Panel" Myth Wouldn't Die: Misinformation in the Health Care Reform Debate." *The Forum* 8 (1):Article 5.

Oliver, Eric, and Thomas Wood. 2014a. "Conspiracy Theories and the Paranoid Style (s) of Mass Opinion." *American Journal of Political Science* 58(4): 952–966.

Oliver, Eric, and Thomas Wood. 2014b. "Medical Conspiracy Theories and Health Behaviors in the United States." *JAMA Internal Medicine* 174(5): 817–818.

Polling, Public Policy. 2013. Democrats and Republicans differ on conspiracy theory beliefs. *Public Policy Polling.* Accessed August 3, 2013.

Russo, David J. 1980. "The Origins of Local News in the US Country Press, 1840s-1870s." *Journalism and Communication Monographs* 65.

Schelling, Thomas. 1980. *The Strategy of Conflict.* Cambridge: Harvard University Press.

Spence, Michael. 1973. "Job Market Signaling." *The Quarterly Journal of Economics* 87 (3): 355–374.

Sunstein, Cass R. 2014. *Conspiracy Theories and Other Dangerous Ideas.* New York: Simon and Schuster.

Uscinski, Joseph E. 2016. "The Psychology Behind Why People Believe Conspiracy Theories about Scalia's Death." *The Washington Post*, February 19.

Uscinski, Joseph E, Darin DeWitt, and Matthew Atkinson. 2018. "Conspiracy Theories and the Internet." In *The Brill Handbook of Conspiracy Theory and Contemporary Religion* edited by Egil Asprem, Asbjorn Dyrendal and David Robinson. Brill.

Uscinski, Joseph E, Casey Klofstad, and Matthew Atkinson. 2016. "Why Do People Believe in Conspiracy Theories? The Role of Informational Cues and Predispositions." *Political Research Quarterly* 69 (1): 57–71.

Uscinski, Joseph E, and Joseph M. Parent. 2014. *American Conspiracy Theories.* New York: Oxford University Press.

Uscinski, Joseph E. 2014. *The People's News: Media, Politics, and the Demands of Capitalism.* New York: New York University Press.

Zaller, John. 1992. *The Nature and Origins of Mass Opinion.* Cambridge, UK: Cambridge University Press.

Part III

2016 CONGRESSIONAL RACES: WHAT IMPACT DID TRUMP HAVE ON CONGRESSIONAL RACES IN 2016?

Chapter 10

Experienced Legislator or Career Politician?

Outsider Rhetoric in the 2016 Election

Christopher Chapp, Dan Hofrenning, Tyler Benning, and Aidan Zielske

Decrying Washington was the sine qua non of Donald Trump's campaign. As Trump summarized at one Charlotte, NC campaign rally, "to achieve this new American future, we must break from the failures of the past. As you know, I'm not a politician. I've never wanted to learn the language of the insiders and I've never been politically correct. It takes far too much time." In many ways, Trump set the tone for others in a crowded field of presidential hopefuls, with many portraying themselves as outsiders—even when they were not. Jeb Bush discussed never living in Washington; he said he did not know his way around the city. Marco Rubio said he was leaving the Senate because he had grown tired of the "political establishment in Washington, DC." Ted Cruz repeatedly excoriated his Congressional colleagues for not fighting hard enough for true conservative ideals. Hillary Clinton stated that she could not "imagine anyone being more of an outsider than the first woman president." Outsider rhetoric seemed to have permeated every presidential campaign, and many media outlets labeled 2016 the year of the outsider.[1]

On the Congressional campaign trail, candidates repeatedly railed against the institution of Congress. With approval of Congress historically low, defending Congress is difficult for incumbents and challengers alike.[2] Accordingly, candidates regularly claimed a lack of governmental experience was a virtue. In the special election to fill the Congressional seat in Montana, a banjo playing populist, Rob Quist, squared off against a tech entrepreneur, Greg Gianforte. In the 2016 race to replace retiring establishment Republican John Kline in Minnesota, a talk radio host defeated a health-care executive. As in Montana, neither had held previous office.

This chapter looks at Congressional campaign rhetoric and appraises the connection with the Trump phenomenon of 2016. Observer after observer described the most recent election as a year like none other. CNN called it an "unprecedented" election.[3] Noted presidential historian Michael Beschloss told PBS that he could find no historical parallels to this election.[4] NPR's Danielle Kurtzleben listed 65 ways in which this election was unprecedented. David Leonard noted the prevalence of outsider candidates assailing the establishment.[5] While many stories were written about the presidential campaign, few journalists explored the level of outsider and anti-establishment rhetoric in Congressional campaigns. Did the amazing success of outsider presidential candidates trickle down and reveal a qualitative upsurge in outsider Congressional campaigns? Was the historic uniqueness of the presidential campaign matched by a new rhetorical tone in Congressional campaigns? Excepting the extreme anti-establishment posture of Trump, were electoral contests in 2016 really an aberration? As political scientists, we read pronouncements like "the year of the outsider" against a long backdrop of research that has sought to understand the ways in which candidates "run for Congress by running against Congress" (Fenno, 1978), suggesting that we ought to be cautious when labeling 2016 as a historically unique election of the outsider. Moreover, it is clear that "incumbency advantage" is still a significant force in Congressional elections, meaning that the virtues of being an outsider need to be weighed against the tangible benefits of political experience.

This chapter addresses these claims, assessing both the extent to which Congressional races in 2016 were unique, and the extent to which this uniqueness owed to the dynamics of the presidential contest. We begin by reviewing the literature on political outsiders, finding no clear consensus with respect to the question of why outsider branding is popular. We develop a unique dataset to test these competing perspectives alongside the main media narratives of the 2016 contest. Specifically, we examine the campaign website "biography" pages from every House of Representatives candidate from the 2014 and 2016 Congressional election and evaluate them for "insider" and "outsider" language. Our analysis makes three main contributions. First, we argue that, at least in Congressional campaigns, 2016 was not especially remarkable in terms of outsider rhetoric. Second, although our evidence dampens the claim that all candidates universally embrace outsider status, we do find that being a political outsider is not limited to long-shot challengers who, in the mold of Trump, lack all political experience. In fact, incumbents are nearly as likely as challengers to play the part of the outsider. Finally, we find very little evidence of a "Trump effect." Outsider branding appears to be motivated by district-level factors, not leadership from the top of the ticket.

POLITICAL SCIENCE AND THE PHENOMENA
OF THE POLITICAL OUTSIDER

Scholars have focused on the use of outsider rhetoric in the broader context of American politics. While noting its prominence in the 2016 campaign, Rolfe (2016) documents the long lineage of this rhetorical style in American political discourse. Politicians have always campaigned on the tension between insiders and outsiders, between the political class and the populace. Anti-politics has always been part of our politics, but studies suggest that this outsider rhetoric varies systematically in regard to both candidate-level and constituency-level factors. Looking more closely at recent presidential campaigns, Bonikowski and Gidron (2016) define populism as the juxtaposition of a virtuous populace and a corrupt elite. They analyze more than two thousand presidential campaign speeches and find much outsider rhetoric, but they find it varies according to geographic region and the identity of the candidate. Throughout half a century of elections, outsider rhetoric occurs more frequently the further a candidate is from the presidency. For example, Eisenhower used more outsider rhetoric in his first campaign than in his campaign for reelection as an incumbent president. Bonikowski and Gidron also find that Democrats and Republicans use different forms of outsider rhetoric. Republicans use anti-statist rhetoric while Democrats develop a message of economic populism. Moreover, they find a geographic variation. Republicans use outsider rhetoric more in the South while Democrats use it in the Northeast and Midwest. With some exceptions, it is used less frequently among successful candidates.

Looking beyond the presidency, Richard Fenno has developed nuanced interpretations of the ways in which members of Congress relate to their constituents. He argues that each member develops a unique style as he or she builds the trust of his or her constituents. The individual success of members of Congress is juxtaposed with a negative citizen evaluation of Congress as "public enemy" (Hibbing and Thiess-Morse 1995). "Fenno's Paradox" notes the irony of this situation—Congress as an institution faces strong disapproval—while individual Congressional representatives enjoy exceedingly high reelection rates. This paradox creates a powerful incentive for individual members to criticize Congress. Fenno writes "Members of Congress run for Congress by running against Congress. The strategy is ubiquitous, addictive, cost-free and foolproof" (Fenno 1978, p. 168). Fenno suggests that all members of Congress benefit from criticizing the institution to which they belong.

While there are few studies of Congressional outsider rhetoric, several scholars have challenged Fenno's idea of the ubiquitous outsider. Lipinski (2003, 2009) analyzed the official newsletters that members of Congress frank to their constituents. Contrary to Fenno, Lipinski finds that 47 percent of newsletters make predominantly positive statements about Congress and only 17 percent are negative. Interestingly, 28 percent of newsletters make no statement at all about the institution of Congress. Loose (2015) analyzed over 2000 campaign ads and found that only 9 percent mentioned Congress. Three-fourths of these ads mentioned Congress negatively, meaning that only 7 percent of all ads were critical of Congress. Comparing supportive versus outsider ads, Loose finds that challengers and extreme candidates are more likely to criticize Congress. Contrary to Lipinski, she finds no difference between the majority and minority party. Finally, she finds more outsider rhetoric in 2008 than in 2004 or 2006. She attributes this increase to Congress's declining approval ratings in the years preceding the 2008 election.

Some scholars have suggested that gender affects outsider rhetoric, with women more likely to campaign as outsiders. Vavrus (1998) and Shames (2003) suggest that female candidates use gender, even "femininity," in campaign ads as a marker of "outsider" status. Like the "un-cola" in soft drink ads, Shames suggests that female candidates present themselves as "un-candidates." Looking at the official web pages of members of Congress, Gulati (2004) finds that Democratic women are most likely to present themselves as outsiders. Shames also points to the importance of contextual factors which she defines as the "mood" of the nation. In contrast, Niven and Zilber (2001) find no gender differences in their studies of Congressional web sites. Both women and men portray themselves with equal frequency as "zealous" participants in Washington politics. Finally, Vraga (2017) finds that women sometimes resist outsider rhetoric because disagreeing with their party and presenting themselves as "mavericks" can pose electoral risks.

Much of the aforementioned work examines how candidates' messaging strategies are constrained by their own personal characteristics like party, gender, or previous office-holding. A smaller area of focus also suggests that electoral context and constituency makeup ultimately shape rhetorical strategies. Bonikowski and Gidron find a powerful contextual influence in presidential campaigns. Candidates tend to use outsider rhetoric as a way to appeal to their bases. Republicans use it more in the South; Democrats use it in the Midwest or Northeast. Looking at members of Congress, Fenno (1978) sees powerful contextual influences on the ways in which incumbents relate to their constituents. Despite his claims of ubiquitous criticism of Congress, Fenno describes different styles of relating to one's district. He sees it as a mix of contextual, strategic, and personal considerations. While there is criticism of Washington, there is also a discussion of issues and an explanation of Washington activity.

David Mayhew (1974) also highlights a more comprehensive strategic calculus as members of Congress seek reelection. Mayhew sees Congress as being designed to allow individual members to engage in three electorally beneficial strategies. First, credit-claiming commonly means that members will take credit for their Washington success, especially when it means delivering particularized benefits for the district. But Mayhew's other strategies are position-taking and advertising which can be used to develop either an outsider or insider brand. Members of Congress can advertise themselves and choose policy positions that either support or oppose the predominant positions of Congress as a whole. For example, when Barack Obama first ran for the Senate in 2004, he opposed Congress and the president as he took an anti-war position. During the Obama administration, many Republicans highlighted their opposition to the Affordable Care Act just passed by Congress.

Context can help illumine the strategic calculus of both incumbent members of Congress and their challengers. James Glaser (1996) wrote a book that investigates the ways in which racial composition of a district changes the type of racial language used in Congressional campaigns. Looking at Congressional campaigns in the South, Glaser shows that the successful navigation of this contextual difference allowed Democrats to continue to hold southern Congressional seats long after the region shifted to favor Republican presidential candidates. Congressional Democrats created a nuanced and successful southern strategy that was successful well into the 1990s. While racialized language and outsider language are two very different rhetorical devices, Glaser's work suggests that ultimately candidates are responsive to the characteristics of the electorate, and develop messaging strategies accordingly.

MEDIA NARRATIVES AND SOCIAL SCIENCE
EXPECTATIONS ABOUT THE OUTSIDER IN 2016

The aforementioned discussion leads to a number of competing expectations about the political outsider in 2016. First, do members of Congress "run for Congress by running against it," as Fenno held, or is criticism of Congress (and by extension, posturing as a political outsider) a relatively rare strategy, as Lipinski (2003) found? Given the mixed literature, we have no firm expectations; however, we would submit that the 2016 election provides a difficult test for the Lipinski (2003) hypothesis. If candidates in 2016 were still branding themselves as "experienced legislators" rather than "political outsiders" running against a broken Washington, we would expect this dynamic to hold in other years as well.

A related question asks which conditions at the candidate and district level promote the use of outsider branding. As the above literature review suggests, here there are a number of suspects, but no clear consensus. "Challenger status" is perhaps the strongest reason to brand as an outsider, although much of the research has only examined incumbent communication strategies (due to data availability and the like). While incumbents are presumably more constrained to run as outsiders the longer they have served, this remains a question that has not faced empirical scrutiny. Party is another potential predictor. It is reasonable to assume that Republicans, ideologically opposing an active federal government, will be more likely to run as outsiders. However, as Bonikowski and Gidron (2016) make clear, both parties adopt the outsider brand in their own way. In addition to candidate-level predictors, it is also possible that features of the district will influence campaign style. It is well known that candidates tailor messages to appeal to specific constituencies (Chapp 2014) and that past electoral contests provide candidates with cues for how they should present themselves to the public (Parsneau and Chapp 2017). For this reason, it makes sense to look for a "Trump effect," whereby candidates in districts that support the Republican nominee adopt his outsider messaging strategy.

One popular media narrative in 2016 extended the notion of a "Trump effect" in several key ways. According to this narrative, political outsiders in 2016 successfully tapped into latent economic dissatisfaction that had been simmering for some time. Trump brought this dissatisfaction to the surface, and the outsider brand was advanced as an effective way to combat the economic blight born of "same old establishment politics." This, at least, was a popular refrain in media accounts of the Trump phenomena. While it is plausible that the outsider brand thrived in economically downtrodden districts, it is important to note that our review of the literature, from Fenno forward, revealed no theoretic rationale or empirical support for the notion that "running against Washington" will have its biggest impact among low-income citizens. Indeed, while the literature is mixed, there is some basic consensus that outsider politics is a branding choice that is sensible for certain candidates, given constraints imposed by prior office-holding, party, and so forth. In this case, the media's district-centric narrative is juxtaposed with prior research that is more focused on the individual candidate.

A TALE OF TWO ELECTIONS: STUDYING OUTSIDER BRANDING IN 2014 AND 2016

To assess these expectations, we analyzed rhetoric found on Congressional campaign websites. We scraped text from the websites of House of Representatives candidates, and we gathered text from all available websites from the 2016 election cycle (n = 742) and the 2014 election cycle (n = 755). Druckman, Kifer, and Parkin (2009) offer persuasive justification for using campaign websites to study campaign communication. They argue that candidate websites meet three important criteria: namely, they are complete, unmediated, representative sources of information. Content analysis studies often use television advertisements as sources of data, but in comparison to television advertisements, candidate websites offer at least two major advantages. First, candidates are more likely to produce websites than to produce television advertisements, which increases the representativeness of a sample. Second, websites offer much more freedom than television advertisements (both in terms of space and financial cost), which allows candidates to more fully explicate their views (Druckman, Kifer, and Parkin 2009). As a result, campaign websites are a rich source of information about electoral communication.

We restricted our analysis to candidate "Biography" pages because we were interested in examining the personal "brands" and identities that candidates presented to the electorate. Over 95 percent of candidate websites included a Biography page (722 in 2014 and 712 in 2016), and the common features of a Biography page (professional accomplishments, education, community involvement, etc.) offered ample opportunities for candidates to highlight their political experience or lack thereof.

Operationalizing Rhetoric

To operationalize insider and outsider rhetoric, we created custom dictionaries of "insider" and "outsider" phrases. We then used Linguistic Inquiry and Word Count (LIWC) (Pennebaker, Booth, and Francis 2001), an automated content analysis software, to score each web page for rhetorical style. We conducted two separate rounds of dictionary development using two different techniques. In one approach, we began by qualitatively examining biographical material from archetypal insiders and archetypal outsiders. We then used these texts to inductively build initial dictionaries. To build our insider dictionary, we examined official government websites from leaders of the 113th Congress (2013–2014), paying special attention to these politicians' biography pages. These elected officials are "establishment" politicians by almost any definition of the word, and their biography pages provided valuable insight into the ways that experienced legislators discuss their political careers.

We utilized text from 2014 campaign websites to aid us in developing an initial outsider dictionary. We reviewed all 2014 pages that contained classic anti-establishment phrases—specifically, "career politician," "bureaucrat," and "outsider"—and we made note of words and phrases that were frequently used on these pages. These frequent phrases were added to the initial outsider dictionary. Ten volunteer coders then validated these initial word lists. Coders reported whether a phrase framed political experience as an asset or as a liability, and if at least 70 percent of coders agreed on the descriptive connotation of a phrase, it was included in the appropriate final dictionary.

Concerned that this inductive approach yielded an incomplete set of insider and outsider words, we conducted a second round of dictionary development using a more quantitative, data-driven approach. To begin, we turned to past campaign websites from 2008, 2010, and 2012 and developed a database of insider texts and a database of outsider texts. The insider database included biography pages from House leaders, such as the Speaker of the House, the Majority/Minority Leader, and party whips. The outsider database included biography pages from media-identified outsider candidates. Candidates were included in the outsider database if a date-restricted Internet search for "outsider Congressional candidates" yielded a relevant article about a candidate. We used these two databases to identify indicator words—that is, words that were strongly associated with one group of politicians but not the other. We found these indicators by examining the 50 most frequently used words in each database. We selected high face-validity words from the population of indicator words and included these selected words in an initial dictionary. In order to broaden our lists of indicator words, we also drew a random sample of 117 biography pages from the 2008-2012 election cycles and then used text mining strategies to identify additional words that tended to appear alongside our previously identified indicator words. This approach yielded additional high face-validity words that were included in an initial dictionary.

Finally, we validated this set of initial dictionaries using 17 volunteer coders. Coders were asked whether each word described a political insider, a political outsider, or neither/both. We took these responses and excluded "neither/both" responses. A word was ultimately added to the final dictionary if there was at least 70 percent inter-coder agreement on the descriptive connotation of the word *and* if at least seven coders selected a non-neutral response. We then took these validated words and sorted them into our final dictionaries based on which type of politician would use a given word. (e.g., even though our coders said that "career politician" would *describe* a political insider, it would be *used by* an outsider. Therefore, it would be placed in the outsider dictionary.)

Lastly, we merged our validated dictionaries to create our final insider dictionary and our final outsider dictionary. These custom dictionaries were loaded into LIWC, and the program generated two scores for each text—one based on the frequency of insider words and one based on the frequency of outsider words. These scores served as the dependent variables in our subsequent analyses, with most of our efforts focused on the variation in the use of outsider rhetoric.

Predictors of Rhetorical Style

This study seeks, in part, to assess how Donald Trump's powerful outsider rhetoric influenced rhetorical choices in down-ballot races. It seems reasonable that some House candidates may have noted Trump's success in their districts and consciously modeled their rhetoric after his. However, we encounter reverse causation concerns if we attempt to use Trump's district vote share to predict candidate rhetoric. Even though Trump's popularity in a district could presumably lead House candidates to run as outsiders, a House candidate's anti-Washington messages could also make the district electorate more supportive of Trump.

In order to address this reverse causation argument, we use Trump's vote share from the GOP primary as a proxy for district Trump support. There are several advantages to using this measure. Primarily, we avoid aforementioned difficulties with reverse causation. As a general rule, presidential primaries occur well before candidates begin to campaign in earnest. This temporal component ensures that campaign communications themselves are not influencing the degree to a district supported Trump.

It would be possible to object to our independent variable on the grounds that presidential primaries do not attract a representative electorate. Therefore, the critique would go, preferences of the primary electorate should not be generalized to the entire district. This critique has validity, and it should be kept in mind when assessing the findings of this study. However, this critique is surmountable for two reasons. First, politicians and political consultants do not operate in a world of perfect information. They have limited information about voter preferences in a district, and in the absence of better sources of data, it seems reasonable that campaign coordinators would find presidential primaries quite helpful in "taking the pulse" of a district. Therefore, it is likely that *candidates themselves* will (at least at some level) use presidential primary results as a proxy for wider district trends. Secondly, a survey conducted by Druckman, Kifer, and Parkin (2009) found that campaign website designers believe that their sites are visited most frequently by "highly motivated voters." Because presidential primaries attract motivated voters (Norrander 1991), it seems reasonable that candidate websites will be designed with the desires of the primary electorate in mind. Therefore, we still expect primary results to influence the communication strategies of candidate websites.

We obtained this data from Dave Leip's Atlas of U.S. presidential election (2016), which aggregates primary data at the Congressional district level. Trump vote share was available for 342 districts (78.6% of all districts), and we are forced to exclude states that do not have data aggregated at the Congressional district level. However, we do not believe that this exclusion seriously compromises the validity of our study, as there seems to be no reason to suspect that technical decisions about data aggregation indicate the presence of systematic differences between districts.

RESULTS AND DISCUSSION

Our results both confirm and complicate the notion of the political outsider in 2016. While it is clear that some candidates position themselves as outsiders, the outsider motif is still considerably less common than all the tropes associated with being a consummate D.C. insider. In fact, the evidence shows that even Congressional challengers are slow to position themselves as an outsider candidate. Even in 2016, experience is an asset. The evidence also speaks directly to the question of whether Trump—a self-branded political neophyte and anti-Washington outsider—had an effect on how 2016 candidates campaigned. Our answer is that a "Trump effect" was more apparent than real. Drawing on comparative evidence with 2014 campaign rhetoric, we find that district characteristics, not the presence of Trump on the ballot, incentivized candidates to run as outsiders. In short, Trump may have ridden on an outsider wave, but he certainly didn't start it.

Despite media headlines characterizing 2016 as the year of the political outsider, our content analysis comes closer to Lipinski et al.'s (2003) conclusions. Most candidates are not running for Congress by running against it. Figure 10.1 displays the frequency of insider and outsider rhetoric in 2016. Higher rhetoric scores along the x-axis indicate a stronger propensity to use insider terms (like "experienced" or "co-sponsored") versus outsider terms (like "lost touch" as an anti-insider phrase or "fresh face" as a pro-outsider phrase). As Figure 10.1 illustrates, the vast majority of candidates contained very little outsider rhetoric, and indeed, a plurality of webpages (n = 230) contained no outsider words or phrases. In contrast, only a small number of webpages (n=41) avoided insider language completely.

While these differences are striking, it is possible that while outsider rhetoric was low in an absolute sense, it was still high compared to previous electoral campaigns. To address this possibility, Figure 10.2 explores differences between 2014 and 2016 using the same coding scheme. We also differentiate candidates by incumbency status, under the assumption that incumbents would be more likely to avoid using the language of the outsider. The results point to two broad conclusions. First, in terms of Congressional rhetoric, 2016 is virtually identical to 2014. Among both challengers and incumbents, we did not observe any statistically significant shifts in rhetorical style, suggesting the presence of Trump did not alter candidates' strategic rhetorical calculus. Second, the assumption that challengers would be more

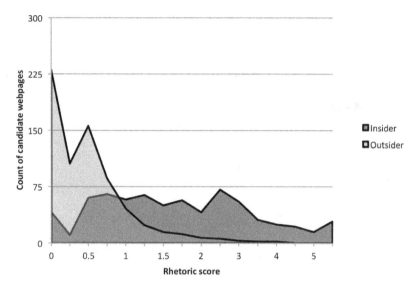

Figure 10.1   Frequency of Insider/Outsider Rhetoric in 2016.

likely to behave like outsiders was only partially met. While incumbents were more adept at using the language of the D.C. insider (the solid grey versus patterned grey bars), both challengers and incumbents were equally likely to use the language of the outsider (the solid black vs. patterned black bars). In short, while Figure 10.2 is not conclusive proof of the absence of a "Trump effect," it does show that on the balance, Congressional campaigns in 2016 looked quite similar to the 2014 midterm elections.

It is worth noting that in both 2014 and 2016, insider rhetoric has a modest negative correlation with outsider rhetoric ($r = -.089$, $p<.05$ in 2014; $-.092$, $p<.05$ in 2016). In other words, candidates generally do not try to "have their cake and eat it too" by using insider rhetoric while simultaneously keeping Congress at arm's length. Rather, candidates devise specific branding strategies, presumably based on strategic calculations about the electorate. A good example here is Dave Trott's (GOP incumbent, MI-11) biography page. Despite incumbency status, Trott emphasizes that he "is not a career Washington politician—instead, he spent his life raising his family and growing his family business in Southeast Michigan" and that "we must get Washington out of the way." Trott's legislative experience is downplayed, noting only that he is a "leading voice" on foreign policy, rather than mentioning specific legislative priorities or committee assignments. Contrast Trott's biography with Tom Emmer (GOP incumbent, MN-6). Like Trott, Emmer was first elected to congress in 2014. However, Emmer's biography makes a point of

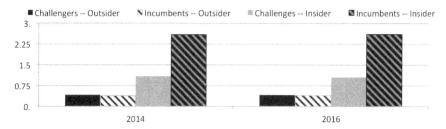

■ Challengers -- Outsider   ◣ Incumbents -- Outsider   ▦ Challenges -- Insider   ◪ Incumbents -- Insider

Figure 10.2   Rhetoric Scores by Year and Incumbency Status.

mentioning prior political experience and his committee appointment on the House Financial Services Committee.[6]

It is also notable that partisan differences (not displayed) are relatively minor and statistically insignificant. Inconsistent with the notion that Republicans would be more likely to embrace the notion of DC-outsider given a small-government ideological outlook, Democrats actually used *more* outsider language, though the difference is not statistically significant. Republicans, in contrast, used significantly more insider rhetoric. However, these differences are more apparent than real and are likely a product of the fact that more Republicans are running for reelection in 2014 and 2016. When we examine insider and outsider rhetoric using a simple multiple regression analysis (not displayed), the partisan differences become statistically indistinguishable.[7]

While this conclusion might seem odd given the parlance of American political discourse, it was not entirely unexpected. Previous research has demonstrated that Republicans and Democrats have each appropriated the outsider label in nuanced ways (Bonikowski and Gidron 2016), and our findings are consistent with this. It is also possible that control of the House dictates outsider posturing, though we cannot test this possibility until Democrats are again in the majority. Based on the data available, then, outsider is a branding choice that need not co-vary with a particular ideological agenda.

On the surface, Figure 10.2 provides evidence that candidate rhetoric in 2016 sounded a good deal like rhetoric in 2014. However, this simple bar chart could be masking important differences in candidate rhetoric. As Lipinski et al. (2003) demonstrate, context matters a good deal in determining who chooses to run as an outsider. Of course, one of the key contextual forces in 2016 was the presence of a political outsider—Donald Trump—at the top of the ticket. One of the key questions in this book is what effect, if any, Trump had on down-ballot races. Accordingly, we now turn to the question of whether Congressional candidates in Trump-friendly districts modified their rhetoric accordingly. This line of inquiry also speaks to broader questions in political science of how presidential candidate leadership influences the tenor of Congressional campaigns.

To test for a "Trump effect" on campaign rhetoric, we regress outsider rhetoric on three key variables: the party of the candidate (to test for partisan differences), Obama's 2012 vote share in the district (as a rough proxy for district partisan lean), and Trump's vote share in the primary election in the district. We specify separate models for incumbents and challengers in each year.

To simplify results, predicted outsider rhetoric scores are displayed in Figure 10.3 (complete regression results available upon request). If one were only to examine 2016 results, one might be tempted to conclude that there was a large (and statistically significant) "Trump effect" among incumbents. As the dashed grey line indicates, if we moved from a Congressional district where Trump received no support to a district that was completely supportive, we would likely see a fourfold increase in outsider rhetoric (from a score of .14 to .55). In other words, in places where Trump performed most strongly in the primary, incumbents were more likely to deploy large doses of outsider rhetoric, suggesting they took a cue from the results of the primary.

However, examining the results from the other three statistical models reveals a more complex pattern that ultimately pushes back against any notion of a "Trump effect." First, for both challengers and incumbents, the relationship between Trump support and outsider rhetoric was as strong in 2014 as it was for incumbents in 2016. The fact that candidates in Trump districts were using outsider language before Trump was a declared candidate suggests that *Trump rode an outsider wave, but he did not begin it.* The seeds of outsider rhetoric were sown long before Trump announced his 2016 candidacy. In addition, the lack of an effect for 2016 challengers is surprising (the slope of the line is negative and not statistically significant), and this further supports the notion that Congressional candidates were not necessarily modeling their rhetoric after Trump's success. Indeed, it is plausible that some candidates intentionally differentiated themselves from Trump by offering a

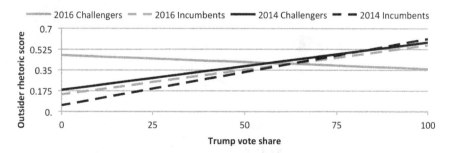

Figure 10.3   Outsider Rhetoric Score by Year and Incumbency Status.

vision grounded in experience rather than anti-establishment politics, though this is merely speculation.

If Trump's presence on the ticket was not responsible for driving outsider rhetoric among Congressional candidates, then why were some candidates embracing the role of the outsider as early as 2014? In other words, can district-level factors explain both Trump's surprising 2016 success and the patterns of outsider rhetoric in 2014? In the wake of the 2016 election, several narratives about Trump's appeal emerged. Some commentators argued that Trump's outsider status was intertwined with a message of economic populism. Trump's outsider branding was popular in white working-class areas that continue to struggle economically, perhaps due to broad changes in the labor market and global economy.[8] Others have persuasively argued that Trump's appeal was more fundamentally rooted in prejudice and an ability to leverage the politics of fear (Shaffner et al. 2016).[9] By this account, "political outsider" branding could be seen as a response to underlying anxiety about demographic change, not a response to economic concerns. To address this, we examine the extent to which Trump vote share—as well as the use of outsider rhetoric by Congressional candidates—covaries with different district-level characteristics.

Results, presented in Figure 10.4, generally run counter to any expectation that candidates run as outsiders when their local economy is flagging. Consistent with recent research by political scientists but inconsistent with many media accounts,[10] Trump actually performed better in wealthier counties ($r = .136$, $p<.001$). District median income also significantly predicted the use of outsider rhetoric in 2014 and 2016 ($r = .121$, $p<.001$ and $r = .162$, $p<.001$, respectively). In contrast to the narrative that economic-fueled

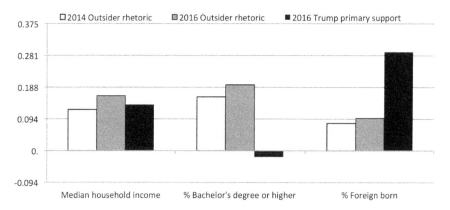

Figure 10.4   Correlation Between Demographic and Political Variables.

discontentment paved the way for the outsider, outsider rhetoric and Trump primary support were both most prominent in well-to-do Congressional districts. Education is another frequently used marker of social class. In both 2014 and 2016, candidates in highly educated districts were also significantly more likely to deploy outsider rhetoric (r=.159, p<.001 and r = .195, p<.001). In this case, however, the pattern of Trump support actually ran counter to the pattern of outsider rhetoric. More educated districts heard more outsider rhetoric from their Congressional candidates, but were less likely to support Trump (though the correlation coefficient here is insignificant). In short, there is no evidence to support the claim that outsider branding—on the part of Trump and Congressional candidates—was a systematic response to the economic conditions or social class of the district.

To capture the phenomena of shifting demographic patterns, we examine how the outsider rhetoric and Trump support are related to the percent of individuals in a district who were foreign born. A similar pattern emerges across all three variables. In both 2014 and 2016, the percent of individuals in a district who were born in outside the United States significantly predicts the use of outsider rhetoric (r = .081, p<.05 and r = .096, p< .05). Percent foreign born is also the single largest predictor of Trump support displayed (r=.292, p<.001), meaning that as counties see higher numbers of foreign-born individuals, Trump support goes up.

Taking Figures 10.3 and 10.4 together, several things stand out. Namely, while it seems unlikely (based on the 2014 results) that Trump led Congressional candidates to embrace the outsider brand, Trump nevertheless had particular appeal in districts where Congressional candidates ran against Washington. Moreover, this rhetoric was not most common in low SES districts. If anything, the profile of a typical district where outsider rhetoric was used is one that is both wealthy and has a high percentage of new immigrants.

These results must be interpreted with several caveats in place. First, we are using county-level data, and so while it is appropriate to talk about county-level patterns, we cannot make individual-level inferences. Second, as discussed earlier, we measure Trump support using his primary vote share to avoid reverse causation concerns. However, as the field of Republican candidates narrowed, Trump was obviously competing against a smaller pool of candidates. Thus, Trump's vote share should be seen as suggestive, not definitive. Third, while the results make it clear that certain demographic patterns are consistent across "outsider" districts, these data do not permit us to make causal attributions. This said, our analysis of "outsider districts" dovetails with broader themes in American politics, and suggests that in many ways, the conventional wisdom surrounding the appeal of the political outsider is incomplete.

THE 2016 ELECTION IN CONTEXT

This chapter set out to hold up one particular rhetorical choice—branding as a political outsider—against the conventional wisdom in the media and in the political science literature. While the outsider trope is just one rhetorical feature among many we could have chosen (campaign negativity and vitriol, issue priming, and racial and gender cues all come to mind), an examination of the outsider brand is both informative and timely. It allows us, for example, to reexamine the notion of "running against Washington" in a context where anti-Washington fervor is perhaps more palpable than ever. It also allows us to test whether candidate leadership at the top of the ticket can become a model for Congressional races. These social scientific questions dovetail with a media narrative that developed throughout 2016. That is to say, was 2016 the year of the outsider, due in large part to widespread economic discontentment and a presidential candidate who effectively tapped this sentiment for the first time? Our answer to this question—based on the rhetorical choices of Congressional candidates—is a clear "no." In practice, outsider rhetoric in the 2016 election defied expectations about who would deploy this trope (and how often it would be deployed).

The data complicate the notion candidates "run for Congress by running against it." While some candidates clearly opt for outsider branding, candidates are far more likely to use some variant of inside-the-beltway language. Whether claiming credit for co-sponsored legislation or delineating one's career in public service, playing the part of a politician is still good politics. What is more surprising, perhaps, is what is *not* predictive of outsider language. Challengers, who are presumably better positioned to claim the mantle of outsider, are only marginally (and insignificantly) more likely to do so. Republicans, who typically eschew federal government involvement as a policy matter, are no more likely than Democrats to claim to be DC-outsiders.

Perhaps most strikingly, candidates did not rely on political cues from the presidential campaign to guide their rhetorical choices. Primary election data provided Congressional candidates with a robust sense of their districts' preference for Donald Trump, who campaigned as the ultimate political outsider. While primary support for Trump was correlated with increased outsider rhetoric, the fact that this relationship was just as strong in 2014 suggests that Trump's success was not used as a cue for the underlying sentiments of the district. From a social scientific perspective, the sum of these findings is problematic: We have a rhetorical pattern with no relationship to incumbency, party, or the presence of a polarizing presidential candidate. The rhetorical pattern does, however, bear a strong relationship with the underlying features of the district. Outsider rhetoric is strongest in relatively well-to-do districts that also have a high percentage of foreign-born residents. This pattern suggests that generalized economic anxiety is likely not the main factor behind a candidate's choice to brand himself or herself as an outsider. One of the most consistent district-level correlates of both Trump support and outsider rhetoric is the percentage of individuals who were born outside the United States. It is possible that rapid demographic change begets anxiety among some voters, which in turn makes an anti-establishment voice more attractive to voters though without more extensive data and testing, it is impossible to know for sure. Thus, while the media's notion that economic dissatisfaction was linked to the political outsider was illusory, results suggest that political science ought to further investigate how district-level factors inform candidates' campaign strategies.

What is clear is that many of the dominant narratives from 2016 were oversimplified. At least in Congressional campaigns, 2016 was not the year of the outsider. Outsider politics are not a simple response to bad economic conditions, nor are they a simple matter of following the lead of a larger-than-life presidential contender.

NOTES

1. Examples cited in http://thehill.com/blogs/ballot-box/presidential-races/254687-candidates-jump-on-outsider-bandwagon

2. http://www.gallup.com/poll/190598/congress-approval-remains-low.aspx

3. http://www.cnn.com/interactive/2016/politics/unprecedented/

4. http://www.pbs.org/newshour/bb/makes-2016-election-unique-history/

5. https://www.nytimes.com/2016/01/19/upshot/why-2016-is-different-from-all-other-recent-elections.html

6. In our dataset, Emmer's "insider" rhetoric score was at the 99th percentile and he had an "outsider" score of 0. Trott had an "insider" score of 0, and his outsider score was at the 89th percentile.

7. Analysis available from authors upon request.

8. For representative examples, see http://www.denverpost.com/2016/01/29/ciruli-2016-is-the-year-of-the-outsider-in-presidential-politics/; http://www.economist.com/news/briefing/21689539-primary-contest-about-get-serious-it-has-rarely-been-so-ugly-uncertain-or;

9. For other representative examples, see https://www.washingtonpost.com/news/monkey-cage/wp/2016/05/26/these-9-simple-charts-show-how-donald-trumps-supporters-differ-from-hillary-clintons/?utm_term=.294370fe0869; https://www.washingtonpost.com/news/monkey-cage/wp/2016/08/01/trump-is-the-first-republican-in-modern-times-to-win-the-partys-nomination-on-anti-minority-sentiments/?utm_term=.9c5623be41c6

10. For example, https://www.washingtonpost.com/news/monkey-cage/wp/2017/06/05/its-time-to-bust-the-myth-most-trump-voters-were-not-working-class/?utm_term=.845ff23fe25b;

REFERENCES

Bonikowski, Bart, and Noam Gidron. 2016. "The Populist Style in American Politics: Presidential Campaign Discourse, 1952–1996." *Social Forces* 94(4): 1593–1621.

Chapp, Christopher B. 2014. "Economic Appeals in Unequal Communities: Stump Speeches in the 2012 Presidential Election," In *The American Election 2012: Contexts and Consequences*, edited by Ward Holder and Peter Josephson, 81–95. New York: Palgrave.

Druckman, James N., Martin J. Kifer, and Michael Parkin. 2009. "Campaign Communications in U.S. Congressional Elections." *American Political Science Review* 103(3): 343-66.

Fenno, Richard. 1978. *Homestyle: House Members in Their Districts.* Boston: Little, Brown and Co.

Glaser, James M. 1996. *Race, Campaign Politics, and the Realignment in the South.* New Haven: Yale University Press.

Gulati, Girish J. 2004. "Members of Congress and presentation of self on the World Wide Web." *Harvard International Journal of Press/Politics*, 9(1): 22–40.

Hibbing, John R., and Elizabeth Theiss-Morse. 1995. *Congress as Public Enemy: Public Attitudes toward American Political Institutions.* Cambridge: Cambridge University Press.

Leip, David. 2016. "Dave Leip's Atlas of US Presidential Elections." Accessed June 27,2017. http://uselectionatlas.org/.

Lipinski, Daniel. 2009. *Congressional Communication Content and Consequences.* Ann Arbor: University of Michigan Press.

Lipinski, Daniel, William T. Bianco and Ryan Work. 2003. "What Happens When HouseMembers "Run with Congress"? The Electoral Consequences of Institutional Loyalty." *Legislative Studies Quarterly* 28(3):413–429.

Members "Run with Congress"? The Electoral Consequences of Institutional Loyalty." *Legislative Studies Quarterly* 28(3):413–429.

Loose, Krista. 2014. "Talking about Congress: The Limited Effect of Congressional Advertising on Congressional Approval." *MIT Political Science Department Research Paper No. 2014-30.*

Mayhew, David. 1974. *Congress: The Electoral Connection.* New Haven: Yale University Press.

Niven, David and Jeremy Zilber. 2001. "Do Women and Men in Congress Cultivate Different Images? Evidence from Congressional Web Sites." *Political Communication,* 18(4): 395–405.

Norrander, Barbara. 1991. "Explaining Individual Participation in Presidential Primaries." *Political Research Quarterly* 44 (3): 640–655.

Parsneau, Kevin and Christopher B. Chapp. 2017. "Partisan Extremity in the 2014 Midterm Elections: How Primaries and Incumbency Influence Polarized Position-Taking on Campaign Websites." In *Political Communication & Strategy: Consequences of the 2014 Midterm Elections*, edited by Tauna S. Sisco, Jennifer C. Lucas, Christopher J. Galdieri. Akron, OH: University of Akron Press.

Pennebaker, James W., Martha E. Francis, and Roger J. Booth. 2001. Linguistic Inquiry and Word Count. Mahway: Lawrence Erlbaum Associates.

Rolfe, Mark. 2016. *The Reinvention of Populist Rhetoric in The Digital Age Insiders & Outsiders in Democratic Politics* (Rhetoric, Politics and Society). Singapore: Springer Singapore : Imprint: Palgrave Macmillan.

Schaffner, Brian F., Matthew MacWilliams, and Tatishe Nteta. 2016. "Explaining White Polarization in the 2016 Vote for President: The Sobering Role of Racism and Sexism." Paper presented at the Conference on The U.S. Elections of 2016: Domestic and International Aspects, IDC Herzliya Campus, January 8-9, 2017.

Shames, Shauna. 2003. "The "Un-Candidates": Gender and Outsider Signals in Women's Political Advertisements." *Women & Politics* 25(1-2): 115–47.

Vavrus, Mary. 1998. "Working the Senate from the Outside In: The Mediated Construction of a Feminist Political Campaign." *Critical Studies in Mass Communication,* 15(3): 213–235.

Chapter 11

The Trump Effect and Gender Norms in the 2016 Senate Elections

Robert G. Boatright, Valerie Sperling, and Sean Tatar

It is not uncommon for congressional candidates to distance themselves from their party's nominees.[1] Yet in 2016, merely avoiding mentioning the presidential nominees' names was not enough. In Arizona, Senator John McCain faced a primary opponent who argued that the 80-year-old senator was too physically weak to do his job well. This alleged weakness carried over to his voting record too—McCain's primary opponent criticized him for being insufficiently conservative and for being a career politician. After surviving that primary challenge, McCain faced a new round of advertisements that alleged that he was too weak to stand up to Donald Trump. Although McCain sought to distance himself from Trump and only reluctantly admitted that he supported Trump's campaign, his Democratic opponent was not satisfied with this. Nor is there evidence that she would have let things go even if McCain had more forcefully condemned Trump. In Illinois, as a point of comparison, another embattled Republican incumbent, Senator Mark Kirk, did officially break with Trump, only to face ads that pointed out that he was a "flip flopper" who supported Trump until it became politically unpopular to do so.

Although McCain did win reelection, his opponents' campaigns suggest that impugning his masculinity was a good strategy. Both McCain's primary opponent and his general election opponent, we should add, were women (as was Mark Kirk's general election opponent in Illinois). While allegations of weakness are stereotypically made about women, such claims are often made about men as well. And in the context of Trump's many troubling pronouncements, these claims could easily be linked to the presidential race. There was, it seems, no solution for congressional candidates—there was little to be gained from talking about Clinton or Trump, but there also was no easy way to feign ignorance of the unpleasantness of the campaign.

With regard to gender, the 2016 election had several unique characteristics. First was the presence of a female presidential candidate, which had the effect of injecting gender-related content into any references to the presidential race. Just as important was the overt misogyny of the Donald Trump campaign—a misogyny that arguably went far beyond what would exist in a race between a female candidate and a more conventional male opponent. Finally, given the first two points, there also appeared to be a consensus among candidates for lower office that there was little to be gained (and potentially much to lose) by connecting themselves to the Trump campaign. To understand the effect of the presidential race on campaigns for lower office, it is necessary to explore the actual content of these campaigns with an eye toward the way that gender norms were wielded in both positive and negative advertising.

In this chapter we explore the content of advertising in competitive Senate races in 2016. We provide a brief summary of research on advertising effects, with a particular focus on how gender and gender norms are used to frame political candidates. We then describe the characteristics of the year's competitive Senate elections. Using a dataset of all advertisements run in these races by the candidates, their parties, and nonparty organizations, we explore when and how the presidential candidates were discussed, and we discuss how gender-related phrases and images were presented in campaign ads. In doing so, we illustrate how such words and images were used to present male and female Senate candidates, and how consistently Democrats and Republicans (and their allies) made use of gendered content both to foster support for their candidates and to undermine their opponents. Among other things, we find that Senate campaigns made an effort to use particular moments in the presidential contest (such as the Access Hollywood revelation) to release ads that distanced their candidates from—and linked their opponents to—Trump-style misogyny. This was the case for both male and female candidates; Democratic women were impugned in attack ads for failing to protect women from the kinds of abuses that Trump bragged about committing, while Democratic and Republican men alike tried to show themselves as caring souls who took seriously the task of protecting women from mistreatment.

CAMPAIGN ADVERTISING AND TELEVISION

Televised campaign advertisements have been fodder for academic inquiry for many years. Herrnson (2012, 90) estimates that advertising expenses constitute one-third of the typical Senate campaign budget, a figure that is undoubtedly much higher in competitive races. Even as television has declined as the principal source of information for Americans, the volume of campaign advertising has steadily increased. This is the case in part because of the Supreme Court's 2010 *Citizens United v. Federal Election Commission* decision, which loosened restrictions on advertising by nonparty organizations and paved the way for the establishment of "Super PACs," which are permitted to raise contributions in unlimited amounts from individuals or other organizations. The establishment of this new type of organization has facilitated the infusion of large sums of money into election-related advocacy, and television advertisements have been by far the main way in which this advocacy has been conducted.

Gender-related themes are common in television advertisements, whether they are presented overtly or more subtly. References to gender, to gender stereotypes, and to political issues that have gendered connotations are a part of elections regardless of the actual sex of the candidates. Even though recent research (Dolan 2014) has established that women are no longer at a disadvantage at the ballot box in America (except perhaps at the presidential level), and that party affiliation dwarfs gender when voters are making their choices (Dolan and Lynch 2016), candidates, the media, and voters still expect men and women to conform to certain gender norms. However, the stereotypical characteristics of masculinity overlap with popular expectations about political leadership ability. In other words, campaigns try to use gender to their advantage, but female candidates can be expected to have a more complicated path to navigate in that regard. As Dittmar (2015, 32) writes, "Candidate gender is tied to voters' perceptions of suitability for office and likability, whereby female candidates face conflicting demands to fit a masculine ideal while upholding femininity, while expectations of masculinity and men are complementary."

Ad-makers are highly conscious of gender norms, and they make an effort to appeal to viewers through the strategic use of gender stereotypes and assumptions that viewers make about masculinity and femininity. Political advertisements for candidates (whether sponsored by campaigns or by outside groups) are a prime vehicle for the expression of gender cues. However, scholars exploring gender and political advertising disagree about the degree to which male and female candidates run for office differently, and whether particular differences in ads reflect a gender-based calculus or can be more easily reduced to other factor such as party affiliation.

One area in which researchers have sought to identify patterns in political ads is the appearance, behavior, and characteristics that are typically associated with masculinity and femininity. Some analysts find differences in men's and women's ads that are rooted in and reinforce gender norms. For instance, as befits the expectation that properly feminine women make the effort to be likeable, women are shown to smile more than men in candidate ads (Bystrom, et al. 2004). However, when it comes to *exhibiting* or *countering* gender stereotypes about what is masculine and what is feminine the analysis of ads is particularly vexed, since candidates of both sexes apparently are under pressure to conform to their gender-stereotypical traits and to counteract them. Kahn (1993, 491) found that women running for Senate seats emphasize "male" traits (like strength and toughness) more than men do, given the prevailing societal stereotypes that might discourage people from regarding women as sufficiently tough or strong to succeed in office. Bystrom, et al. (2004) likewise found that candidates are portrayed in ads in ways that would counter viewers' gender stereotypes, such that men include their families in ads more often than women do (women not wanting to be overly associated with family, and men not wanting to be seen as uncaring), and women emphasize "toughness and strength" more frequently than men, while men emphasize "sensitivity and understanding." Likewise, Sapiro, et al. (2011, 114) noted a "counter-stereotype" effort, wherein women candidates' ads highlighted toughness more than men's did. Dittmar's interviews with candidates and campaign personnel confirm that female candidates' campaigns labor "to assure voters that women candidates meet the masculine credentials required for political office" (2015, 88). However, female candidates have to be careful not to run afoul of voters' expectations of sufficiently feminine tone. The ideal for female candidates is to "demonstrate the masculine credential of toughness while upholding the feminine likability viewed as important to women candidates' electoral success" (Dittmar 2015, 89-91).

Research also suggests that norms of masculinity dictate different behavior for men running against women than for men running against men. Kahn (1993, 491) found that men were less likely to attack a woman opponent in ads because this could seem like "beating up on" her, an act that truly "masculine" men are rhetorically taught to despise (though the frequency of domestic violence suggests this lesson is not particularly well internalized). Dittmar's research among campaign consultants (2015, 40) confirms that they avoid having male candidates go "too negative" against women opponents, as this makes the male candidate appear "as a bully instead of a gentleman." Women's attack ads likely reinforce the message of "toughness" that seems central to all political contests. However, consultants also remain wary of women going too negative, since this can violate the "likeability" or "niceness" expectation that voters have about women candidates (Dittmar 2015, 143).

Below we will discuss how the ads from the Senate races we examined support or undermine several of the claims addressed here about gender and advertising, looking specifically the use of gender-related words, visual cues, and context.

CONTEXT AND METHODOLOGY

The U.S. presidential election, because it featured a male and a female candidate, unavoidably introduced gender-related themes into Senate campaigns whenever it was mentioned. That is, we would contend that it is not possible to think about advertisements that connected a Democratic candidate to Hillary Clinton without introducing gender-related ideas into the advertisement—the Democratic candidate in question was being compared to a female presidential candidate. This is, of course, the case with any comparison between a candidate and Donald Trump as well—in an advertisement that sought to connect a candidate with Trump, that candidate was being connected to a male presidential candidate. Yet because of the frequent media accounts of misogynistic statements made by Trump, such a connection was not merely between said candidate and a male presidential candidate. Rather, it would be between the candidate and a male presidential candidate who was understood to have made degrading statements about women.

Such effects are obviously different according to the sex of the Senate candidate in question—for instance, comparing a male candidate with Clinton might make that candidate appear weak, while comparing a female candidate with Clinton might not have the same effect. Similarly, comparing a male candidate with Trump might serve to connect that candidate to Trump's offensive statements, but connecting a female candidate to Trump might send a very different sort of message.

Given the way the 2016 presidential election dominated much of the news cycle, we also would contend that many advertising themes might plausibly have been related to the presidential campaign even without explicit reference to the candidates. A reference to immigration policy, for instance, might cause viewers to think about the presidential candidates and their stances even without a direct reference to Clinton or Trump. Similarly, gender-related cues might be seen in that light. A male Republican's efforts to present himself as a supporter of women's issues, or merely to show that candidate in the presence of female politicians or constituents, might serve to distance him from Donald Trump even without any explicit condemnation of some of Trump's gender-related comments.

Of course, we cannot rerun the 2016 election with different presidential candidates, so we cannot conclusively argue that all gender cues were necessarily related to the presidential election. It is quite possible that some candidates might effectively be portrayed in gendered fashion regardless of the larger electoral context; such an approach might, in addition, be more effective for some candidates than others. Indeed, Conroy (2015, ch. 6) has found that the media during presidential election campaigns maintains the idea that "masculine" qualities are to be preferred in presidential candidates, and will frame presidential elections as contests between a more masculine and a more feminine candidate even when both candidates are male.

Ad timing is also important, in that changing perceptions of the likely outcome of the presidential race may have influenced advertising content. At moments when Donald Trump was under fire for boorish or sexist behavior, did advertisements appear that linked other Republican candidates to such behavior, or distanced them from such behavior? In short, did gender matter differently at different times in the campaign? We know that negative advertisements are more common in the early fall than they are in the final days of the campaign or the early phases of it, so we cannot be certain that such appeals are not simply part of the regular cycle of campaigning. Yet the early October media coverage of the most vulgar gender-related event of the presidential campaign—the release of the Access Hollywood recording of Trump's musings about his treatment of women—suggests that if advertisers are reacting to gender-related issues in the presidential campaign, then gender-related claims should increase at this time.

As of early 2016, most of the better known political handicappers agreed that there were 12 Senate general election campaigns that were likely to be competitive. At that time, only two of these races (Colorado and Florida) did not have clear primary frontrunners in both parties. Conveniently, five of these races pitted two men against each other, while six featured women running against men, and one featured two women running against each other. Less conveniently, only two of these races (Indiana and Nevada) were open seat races, and all of the female/male races featured Democratic women running against Republican men. We can, then, consider how well Republican men defended themselves against campaign themes raised by Democratic women, but we cannot say anything about how the dynamics of the Trump/ Clinton race might have influenced Republican women incumbents' efforts to ward off male Democratic challengers. Ten out of these 12 races (all but Indiana and Illinois), in addition, took place in states that received some attention from the presidential candidates.

Table 11.1 shows characteristics of these races. We will leave it to the reader to decide whether the nuances of any state or candidate determined some of the themes in the campaigns. Not all of these races ended up being particularly competitive. Democratic groups abandoned Iowa early, and the Ohio race was written off by Democrats by August. Meanwhile, Missouri, a state that was not expected by prognosticators to be close, ended up featuring a spirited race. Such variations suggest that candidates can matter in making races competitive.

We thus have a presidential race between a male and a female candidate, and a set of Senate elections that featured varying combinations by sex. Our

Table 11.1 Senate Elections Considered in this Chapter

State	Party, Status	Republican (M/F)	Democrat (M/F)	Outcome
Arizona	R Inc	John McCain (M)	Ann Kirkpatrick (F)	53-41 R
Colorado	D Inc	Darryl Glenn (M)	Michael Bennet (M)	50-44 D
Florida	R Inc	Marco Rubio (M)	Patrick Murphy (M)	52-44 R
Illinois	R Inc	Mark Kirk (M)	Tammy Duckworth (F)	55-40 D
Indiana	R Open	Todd Young (M)	Evan Bayh (M)	52-42 R
Iowa	R Inc	Charles Grassley (M)	Patty Judge (F)	60-36 R
Nevada	D Open	Joe Heck (M)	Catherine Cortez Masto (F)	47-45 D
New Hampshire	R Inc	Kelly Ayotte (F)	Maggie Hassan (F)	48-48 D
North Carolina	R Inc	Richard Burr (M)	Deborah Ross (F)	51-45 R
Ohio	R Inc	Rob Portman (M)	Ted Strickland (M)	58-37 R
Pennsylvania	R Inc	Patrick Toomey (M)	Katie McGinty (F)	49-47 R
Wisconsin	R Inc	Ron Johnson (M)	Russ Feingold (M)	50-47 R

analysis of these races focuses on four questions about this set of Senate campaigns:

- Were the presidential candidates discussed differently in the male/male races than in the female/male races?
- Were other gender-related cues presented in a different fashion in the male/male races than in the female/male races?
- Did the presentation of gender-related cues change according to the competitiveness of the presidential race?
- Were gender-related cues presented differently in the lone female/female race than in other campaigns?

Answers to these questions will not offer proof that the presidential race *caused* gender or gender-related themes to be presented in any particular way, but they can enable us to identify patterns in how candidates confronted running in the shadow of the Clinton/Trump race.

In order to answer these questions, we conducted an analysis of all advertisements aired in these races by the candidates, parties, or by outside groups. We used data provided by the Political TV Ad Archive, a website funded by the Knight Foundation, the Democracy Fund, and other groups which collected all television advertising in the presidential election and in 10 Senate elections in 2016. We supplemented the advertising data provided by the Political TV Ad Archive with our own content codings. We sorted advertisements according to candidate characteristics, the type of sponsor (that is, candidate committees, 501c groups, party committees, and so on), and the time of the first airing of the advertisement.

Our unit of analysis is the individual advertisement, not the ad airing. That is, we can present data about, for instance, how many different advertisements in a particular race mentioned Hillary Clinton, but we do not seek to measure how many times advertisements that mentioned Clinton were aired. Our goal is to provide an overview of the ways in which gender and the presidential candidates were discussed. We are interested in describing the range of approaches that were present, not in describing which approach was most prevalent. Were we to discuss the number of advertisements aired that, for instance, discussed Trump or Obama, our interpretation of what mattered might be shaped by a single particularly effective advertisement that ran many times, or by a single idiosyncratic advertiser. Considering each advertisement, on the other hand, allows us to investigate whether ideas about how a particular topic might be discussed spread across candidates or groups. We can look at which ideas, words, or methods of framing were popular.

For each advertisement, we measure the following characteristics:

- Were the two presidential candidates discussed in the advertisement? We also coded references to Barack Obama here, in an effort to help us think about whether the intent was to frame the candidate as being a Democrat, as opposed to framing the candidate in gendered terms.
- We coded instances of the following gender-related words (and variations on them): brave, care, compassionate, courage, fight, independent, insider, man, outsider, patriot, protect, strong, tough, weak, woman.

In the discussion below, we draw primarily upon these codings, yet at times we also refer to other themes or characteristics of the advertisements in question.

USE OF THE PRESIDENTIAL CANDIDATES
IN SENATE ADVERTISEMENTS

Figure 11.1 breaks down references to the presidential candidates by state. This figure shows that mentioning Donald Trump was a popular strategy in three different races—those in Arizona, Illinois, and New Hampshire. All references to Trump in these states are made by Democrats and are critical. These three states are noteworthy because the incumbents in these races (John McCain, Mark Kirk, and Kelly Ayotte) did the most of any incumbents here to distance themselves from Trump. Kirk renounced his support for Trump, and McCain and Ayotte both gave rather tortured explanations about their dissatisfaction with Trump (Kane 2016; Phillips 2016). References to Clinton were most common in Indiana—the state here where she performed the worst

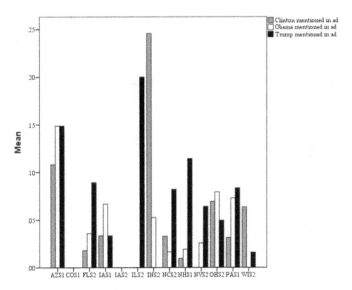

Figure 11.1   Presidential Candidate References by State.

in the general election—and Arizona. The two least competitive races here—those in Colorado and Iowa—were the two races where the presidential candidates were mentioned the least.

Another way to look at references to the presidential candidates is to consider the sex of the candidate who is advantaged by the advertisement. Figure 11.2 compares advertisements aired in female-male races to ads run in male-male races (collectively, all of the races except New Hampshire). The left-hand side figure compares these election types with regard to mentions of the candidates by Democrats. It is clear that Democratic women (and their allies) sought to tie their opponents to Trump, referring to him in more than 20 percent of the ads that were cut, as compared to less than 10 percent of the ads by, or on behalf of, Democratic men. Clinton and Obama were not mentioned at all by male Democratic candidates, and were mentioned a very small number of times in ads by or for Democratic women. In contrast, Republican ads (in the right-hand side figure) were more than twice as likely to mention Clinton if the Democratic opponent was a man than they were if the Democratic was a woman. References to Obama were constant across types. In the female-female New Hampshire race, more than 20 percent of the Democratic ads mentioned Trump, while fewer than 5 percent of the Republican ads mentioned either Clinton or Obama. The lesson, it seems, is that Democratic men appeared weaker when connected to Clinton, while Democratic women had greater credibility in connecting their Republican opponents to Trump.

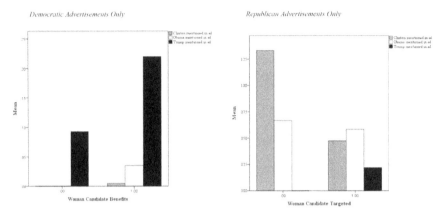

Figure 11.2   **Presidential Candidate References by Candidate Sex.**

Virtually all of the references to the presidential candidates in Senate ads were negative—they were attempts to link the opposing candidate to an unpopular presidential nominee. The conventional wisdom in campaign advertising literature is that entities other than the candidate (such as interest groups or party committees) are more likely to "go negative" than are candidates. This gives candidates the ability to maintain distance from negative campaigning. The candidate references in 2016 did not necessarily conform to that logic, however.

Finally, Figure 11.3 shows two different measurements of when the presidential candidates were discussed. Ads were sorted according to the week in which they first aired; the figure shows the percentage of ads run in each week that mentioned each presidential candidate, and the number of ads from that week that mentioned the candidates. As expected, critical coverage of Trump spikes in October, when there was the most ammunition to use against Trump and when he was furthest behind in the polls. Clinton and Obama are common ad targets in the late summer, but by the fall, most Republican ads were paying little attention to them. This is consistent with the expectation that Republican advertisers expected Trump to lose, and were at least hopeful that voters would split their tickets.

We can thus consider whether the presidential candidates were discussed, and who discussed them, in order to gauge how Senate campaigns were shaped by Clinton and Trump. But are these gender effects? On the one hand, the timing of these references suggests that these are calculations about whether the candidates can use the presidential race to their advantage; the same logic might have applied to any prior election. On the other, there are unmistakable patterns in how Clinton was selectively used against male Democrats, and how Trump was selectively used by female Democrats.

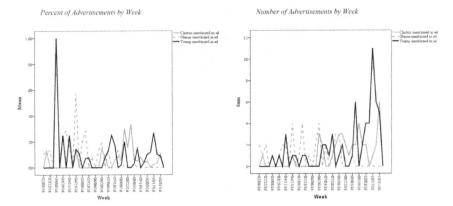

Figure 11.3   **Timing of Senate Ads Featuring the Presidential Candidates.**

These patterns are instructive, then, but they provide only a starting point for looking at the actual language and visual cues that were used in campaign advertisements. To do this, we need a more nuanced look at the ads themselves and at the characteristics of the individual campaigns and candidates as portrayed in gendered terms in the advertisements.

GENDER-RELATED WORDS AND CUES

In this section we explore the use of gender-related words and cues to illustrate the way that voters are invited to support or oppose candidates based on gender norms. Many of these themes would have played out as they did regardless of who the presidential candidates were. At the same time, it is possible that gender cues in 2016 were received differently by viewers than they would have been in previous presidential years. We present some of the more obvious gender cues in the 2016 Senate races below, along with speculation on their relationship to the presidential election campaign.

While much scholarship on campaign advertising refers to positive and negative ads, Benoit (2014, 33) argues that any given ad can contain both positive and negative themes. Using societal norms about femininity and masculinity in an ad can help establish a negative impression easily. With a few words or images a male candidate can be made to seem a "weak man" and a woman candidate can likewise be painted as weak (insufficiently masculine) or as being too maternal or as violating other feminine expectations such as likeability. While gender may not be at the center of the ad, ads frequently draw on these widespread and recognizable gender norms.

Gendered Words and Advertising

One way to analyze the use of gender norms in ads is to examine the language used to describe candidates and their actions. To that end, we tallied instances where candidates used words that have traditionally been held to be gender-normative.[2] In general, Republican ads tended to use more gender-normative language. Looking specifically at four words (and their variants)—strong, weak, fight, and protect—we found that these gender-normative terms were used in approximately 38 percent of Republican ads and in 31 percent of Democratic ads. One might assume this is because in 11 of the 12 races studied, the pro-Republican ads were run for the benefit of male candidates; this may have resulted in the addition of language emphasizing masculinity to portray their strength to the audience, or (in negative ads) to allude to the weakness of their opponent. In the New Hampshire race, the only one featuring two female candidates, 28.8 percent of the Republican ads used this gender-normative language while only 8.5 percent of the Democratic ads did so. The percentages here were below the average for each party, but the partisan tilt was the same.

This distinction seems to be more a matter of gender than partisanship, however. 36.7 percent of the Republican ads aired in male-versus-female races featured gendered language, while 27.2 percent of Democratic ads in such races used this language. In contrast, in male-versus-male races, 41.2 percent of Republican ads used gender-normative language while 40.7 percent of Democratic ads used such language. Men, it seems, are more likely to use gender-normative language than are women, and they are more likely to use it against other men than they are to use it against women.

Looking solely at usages of "toughness" words (tough, fight/er/ing, protect, strong, courage, warrior) in the "pro" ads issued in the 12 races we examined, we found that the two women in the all-female New Hampshire race used these words (about themselves) 54 percent of the time, and that, by contrast, women running against men used them 69 percent of the time (i.e., in Arizona, Pennsylvania, Nevada, North Carolina, Illinois, and Iowa). In other words, women used "toughness" words considerably more often when running against men than against women. While we cannot generalize from the Ayotte-Hassan race to woman vs. woman races more generally, it is possible that women feel the need to assert their toughness more when running against men, against whom they have to prove their "masculine" credentials more so than when running against a woman. And while the literature on the use of gender-normative language seems to have reached consensus that women use "toughness" language more than men in political advertisements, according to our dataset men and women used these "toughness"—connoting words to describe themselves in equal measure—61 percent of the time.

Although we noted above that there were few significant differences between candidates, parties, and groups in their propensity to refer directly to the presidential candidates, candidates and groups differ in more predictable ways in their use of gendered terms. Group-sponsored ads were more likely to use directly gender-normative language (strong, weak, fight, protect) for the purposes of attacking a candidate; for instance, by calling the opposing candidate "weak." Candidate-sponsored ads were more likely to use gender-normative language in a positive way by arguing that the candidate will "protect" voters or that the candidate is a "fighter." Group ads that call candidates "weak" on national security issues, such as the Iran nuclear treaty, were particularly common.[3]

It has generally been found that group-sponsored attack ads tend to be more negative than those sponsored by candidates' campaigns directly (Fowler and Ridout 2012, 59). Although it is hard to quantify the ways in which this interacts with gender, it seems apparent to us that group-sponsored ads play upon gender themes in a more negative fashion as well. A noteworthy example of the candidate/group distinction can be seen in the Nevada Senate race. There were three pro-Republican PAC ads that criticized Democrat Catherine Cortez Masto for the slow processing of thousands of backlogged rape kits during her time as attorney general. These ads referred to Masto as "incompetent," but also neglectful, and, by comparison to other attorneys general, unconcerned with the identification and punishment of rapists, thus making her "unacceptable" for Nevada.[4]

These ads also show that women's *issues* can be mobilized to attack a candidate in gendered terms. The PACs sponsoring the Nevada ads may have calculated that this issue would be particularly damaging to a female candidate. While male candidates should be "tough" on rape, one might expect that female candidates would be even tougher, given that rape disproportionately affects women. These ads are designed to alarm female viewers in particular, while making the targeted candidate appear weak. By attacking a female candidate, Cortez Masto's opponent likely hoped to undermine her credibility with women by showing that she was "weak"—even on a "women's" issue like rape.

Indeed, while gendered words like "strength" and "weakness" are common in political ads, advertisers have found a wide range of ways in which to cue viewers' attention to gender norms. As scholarship on these issues suggests, in positive ads candidates can be shown as embodying gender norms appropriate to their sex and also in ways that counter sex-stereotypes. In attack ads, candidates can be undermined by implications that they are violating expectations for proper feminine and masculine behavior.

Gender Norms and the Response to the Trump Candidacy

The presence of an overtly misogynist presidential candidate in the race highlighted the ways in which proper masculine behavior (or its absence) could be used to support or undermine male Senate candidates. In particular, the release of the Access Hollywood tape of Donald Trump's 2005 conversation with Billy Bush on October 7, 2016 provided campaigns and their allied PACs with an ideal opportunity to portray male candidates in terms that would implicitly link or contrast those candidates to Trump's misogynist statements. Candidate ads soon reflected the Access Hollywood scandal, both directly and indirectly. In some cases, male Republican Senate candidates were condemned directly as Trump supporters, or indirectly as sexists similar to Trump, and also as weak for failing to condemn Trump.

In this vein, an ad released on October 24 by the Deborah Ross for Senate campaign in North Carolina embraced the tactic of condemning her opponent, Richard Burr, for his support of Trump while also painting Burr as a sexist. In the ad, a female narrator quoted Burr as saying, "I'm gonna support Donald Trump" even after Trump had "bragged about sexually assaulting women." The narrator further explained that Burr had been "exploiting victims of sexual assault to falsely attack Deborah Ross," implying that even if Burr had not assaulted women himself (as Trump apparently had), he, too, was willing to exploit those women for his own purposes. Burr, the narrator concluded, "puts politics and himself ahead of us."[5] In contrast, Ross had released a self-narrated ad 10 days earlier that highlighted her legislative "fight" to "protect" female victims of assault, as versus her opponent's "no" vote on the Violence against Women Act.[6] Meanwhile, in Ohio, the Strickland for Senate campaign posted an attack ad within a week of the Access Hollywood fiasco. Here, Republican Rob Portman was described—again by a female narrator—as a "coward" because he had been afraid for so long to repudiate Trump publicly despite Trump's "history of degrading women." The ad compared Portman—who finally reversed his position after having "panicked" (a non-manly behavior)—unfavorably to past "leaders" who had shown "courage" by turning in a timely fashion against such figures as George Wallace and Joseph McCarthy.[7]

Other campaigns took the opportunity of the Access Hollywood scandal to release ads that *contrasted* their male Republican candidates to Trump. These ads emphasized the candidates' status as family men, and, who, especially, had acted to protect women from sexual or other gender-related assault. For instance, an ad aired by the Marco Rubio campaign at the end of October used a similar tactic to highlight Rubio's status as a man who looks out for women's safety, and who is, himself, a true family man. The ad features Rubio's wife, Jeanette, who explains that "of all the things Marco has done, the one thing" she is "most proud of" is his authorship of the "Girls Count Act," which mandates that states receiving U.S. aid issue birth certificates to female children as an anti-trafficking measure. By pointing to Rubio's concern about the trafficking of girls, and showing Rubio surrounded by his family members, the ad contrasts his normative status as a married man to Trump's philandering.[8]

Women's campaigns had linked male Republicans to Trump before the Access Hollywood scandal as well. Cortez Masto, for instance, posted an ad in September that spliced footage of Joe Heck repeatedly asserting his support for Trump with footage of Trump voicing racist opinions about Mexicans and imitating a disabled reporter.[9] This method of interspersing Trump's words with Republican Senate candidates' statements of support was common in Democratic ads; the intent, it seems to us, was to show that Republican male candidates were too weak to condemn Trump's statements. In early July an attack ad aimed at Pat Toomey by Katie McGinty's campaign made an effort to portray the Pennsylvania Republican as cowardly. In the ad, Toomey was said to be representative of Congressional Republicans who were trying to "hide out" until after the election, having ducked into an elevator rather than answer reporters' questions about Trump's "incendiary" speech on Muslim immigration and his unsympathetic response to the attack on the Pulse nightclub in Orlando.[10] Meanwhile, Democratic women sought to contrast themselves to their male Republican opponents by showing they were not afraid to stand up to Trump. In North Carolina, Democracy for America launched an ad narrated by a Latina woman who pointed out that when a presidential candidate calls Latinos "criminals and rapists," North Carolina needs "a fighter of our own, and for Senate, that person is Deborah Ross." Arguing that "Deborah Ross isn't afraid of Donald Trump," the ad's unspoken suggestion was that Ross was braver and thus more manly than Richard Burr.[11]

Republicans running against male Democrats also used Hillary Clinton to illustrate their opponents' purported weakness. For instance, in an amusing mid-September ad by Republican candidate Todd Young, an actor playing Democrat Evan Bayh is instructed by his campaign staff before an interview to "pretend" he's in Indiana, and to claim not to know Hillary Clinton, in an effort to escape his Washington "insider" reputation. Meanwhile, a male narrator points out that while in Washington, Bayh "got comfortable doing Hillary Clinton's bidding." Having "left us, to work for them," the narrator continued, Bayh had returned, but could no longer be trusted.[12] Other attack ads against Bayh returned to the theme of his relative weakness, due to his Clinton connections. A U.S. Chamber of Commerce ad launched at the end of August contrasted Bayh to Young. While the female narrator criticizes Bayh's vote for Obamacare ("one of the biggest government overreaches in modern U.S. history") and explains that the policy resulted in thousands of dropped insurance policy for "Hoosiers," he is pictured in a celebratory still photo with a grinning Hillary Clinton. Upbeat music then accompanies the introduction of Young, who is "fighting back, fighting Obamacare; he fought for his country as a Marine, and now he's ready to do it again."[13] A Young campaign ad on August 10th echoed the same message of Young as a "fighter" for Indiana. Reminding viewers of Young's military background, the male narrator emphasized that Young was "the only one with a backbone to stand up against the Clinton-Obama agenda," leaving unstated the implication that Bayh could not compete with Young's masculinity and military resolve and properly resist a Clinton presidency.[14]

Even without direct reference to the presidential race, ads pursued the use of gender norms to bolster their chosen candidates and criticize their opponents. Whether these ads should be construed as indirectly or implicitly related to the presidential race or not is hard to say, since campaigns have long made use of gender norms even when neither an overt misogynist nor a female candidate was running for president.

Showing Masculinity

Central to masculinity is the notion of strength. And while candidates can certainly refer to themselves as "fighters" or use other language lauding their own strength, candidate ads also incorporate testimony from other "strong men" on that subject. For example, in May the non-profit group US Chamber of Commerce ran an ad supporting Pat Toomey that featured former Philadelphia Eagles player Vince Papale. After introducing himself as a "fighter" for his former NFL team, Papale argued that Toomey "fights for Pennsylvania because he's one of us"—implying that Toomey is not only not a Washington insider, but that he might even belong on Papale's virtual "team" of tough Philadelphians.[15]

The opposite side of the "strength" coin, however, is the absence of strength—that is, weakness. One attack ad theme witnessed in the Senate election played on the male gender norm of protecting women. Just as Heck's and Rubio's campaigns sought to highlight their candidates' protective role in relation to women (and others who might need protection, such as children), negative ads sought to show their failure to carry out that role. A Patrick Murphy ad from mid-October on gun violence (in the wake of the Pulse nightclub massacre in Orlando) featured the tearful mother of one of the shooting victims, who mused, "I cannot understand how Marco Rubio could go back to Washington, DC, and do nothing," suggesting that Rubio had failed to do his part to protect future potential victims of such attacks. By contrast, she noted, "I don't think Patrick Murphy is afraid to take on the toughest problems, like gun violence, in this country." The ad closed with a short clip of Murphy strolling next to the woman, nodding compassionately at her as she spoke. Murphy was shown to be both caring and "not afraid" to act—and therefore a better man than Rubio on several counts.[16]

Since female politicians are also expected to be able to carry out the male protective function, attack ads directed at female candidates can critique them for failing at the "masculine" task of protecting others, and failing to protect women in particular. Deborah Ross was subjected to multiple attack ads relating to sex offender registries and the accusation that she had not protected North Carolina's families. An October 26 ad by a non-profit, the NRA Institute for Legislative Action, showed a neatly coiffed and feminine-appearing Ross, wearing pearls and a pink v-necked sweater, describing herself as "lobbyist, lawyer, legislator." Against a threatening musical soundtrack, a male narrator summarized Ross's activities as North Carolina director of the American Civil Liberties Union, stating that Ross had lobbied to prevent public access to sex offender registries, had "tried to get leniency for a sex predator," and "voted against your gun rights." The ad ended with a caption stating, "Deborah Ross/Too Dangerous."[17] The Burr campaign had released a similar ad on October 13, decrying Ross's poor record on domestic violence and sex offenders, issues on which one might expect a Democratic female candidate to take a harder line.[18]

Showing Femininity

In addition to condemning women for insufficient masculinity, attack ads against women can criticize the candidate's lack of proper femininity. A July ad by the National Republican Senatorial Committee against Pennsylvania's Katie McGinty lifted images of children watching television from a Clinton ad, making it appear as though the children instead were watching a clip of McGinty on television. The clip showed McGinty referring to Pat Toomey, saying, "He's an asshole, dammit!" and thus appearing lacking in the politeness stereotypically associated with women—particularly in the context of an audience of children.[19] A similar ad by the same PAC aired two weeks later, starting with the same clip, but then showing segments of McGinty's speech at the Democratic Convention, blurring her mouth and bleeping out her words every few seconds as if she had liberally peppered her speech with foul language (which she had not done in reality).[20] The purpose was to undermine McGinty's feminine image, replacing it with one most unladylike, and, of course, to draw parallels between McGinty's statements and the offensive statements by Donald Trump that were a staple of Democratic advertisements in Pennsylvania.

A woman candidate can be blamed for her husband's failures to live up to proper gendered behavior expectations, as well as for her own ostensible lapses. Donald Trump and others repeatedly raised the question of Hillary Clinton's husband's infidelity as though it somehow represented a failure on her part. Along these lines, in the Senate campaign in New Hampshire, a

Super PAC favoring Kelly Ayotte emphasized Democrat Maggie Hassan's purported failure to protect women by highlighting accusations of misconduct against her husband. In a late-October (post-Access Hollywood) ad, the PAC, Granite State Solutions, claimed that Hassan's husband, the principal of Phillips Exeter Academy, had covered up a male teacher's sexual misconduct at the school. The ad further condemned Hassan for accepting campaign contributions "from the sexual predator," and closed by wondering, "How could she not have known?"[21]—a question that had also been asked of Hillary Clinton with reference to her husband's alleged affairs.[22] Ayotte, in stark contrast, had been portrayed by another supportive Super PAC early in the race (in February) as a "typical mom who worries about her children … and our kids' safety," and who therefore worked for "strong terrorist detention policies" and other protective measures. The ad summed Ayotte up as a "mom who keeps us safe."[23]

From a political advertising perspective, the ideal woman candidate can demonstrate that she has the necessary masculine and feminine characteristics to meet society's normative gender expectations. One April ad by the Democratic Senatorial Campaign Committee, narrated by a female bartender struggling to make ends meet, portrayed Katie McGinty as a woman of the people with working-class origins who "gets it," and who would "fight for equal pay for equal work" and "protect social security and Medicare." This "fighting" and "protecting" language signaled the "masculine" characteristic of protecting those who need defense; that it was a hardworking woman (in the perhaps traditionally male occupation of bartending) who endorsed her only reinforced the message.[24] A McGinty campaign ad showed McGinty with her own parents, as well as with constituents' families, explained that she was the ninth of ten children, and stressed that she would "put middle-class families first," casting her again in the role of family protector.[25] A similarly themed advertisement showed McGinty calling herself a "fighter," and also presented her as the "mother of three daughters," suggesting that she was a gender-balanced candidate; tough and "masculine" enough to "fight" for families, as well as possessing traditionally feminine credentials as a daughter and mother.[26]

This effort to present female candidates as sufficiently but not overly masculine and feminine occurs not only when women run against male opponents. New Hampshire's campaign presents this study's only race pitting two women against each other. While both women's campaigns (and the groups allied with them) ran ads lauding Hassan's and Ayotte's strength and status as fighters, as well as attack ads calling each other weak on "safety" issues, and violating feminine norms by not "caring" or "protecting" sufficiently, both campaigns also ran ads that reinforced their status as mothers closely tied to their families. In an October ad by the Ayotte campaign, Ayotte was pictured walking outdoors with her arms around her mother and her daughter, talking about how her own mother's hard work continues to inspire her as a Senator. At the end of the ad, Ayotte's daughter echoes the message, saying that her own mother had taught her that with hard work, "you can do anything." The ad focused purely on the feminine. Ayotte wears pink lipstick and a pink sweater; she is shown in two other pink tops (a blazer and a sleeveless blouse) in the ad, and her mother wears a pink polo shirt. It is possible that this ad was introduced to try to distance Ayotte from her tortured efforts to break—without really breaking—with Trump following the Access Hollywood fiasco, thought it may simply have been an end-of-campaign effort to end on a positive note.[27] Maggie Hassan's campaign, too, released a "family" ad at that time, narrated by Hassan's daughter, Meg, who, like Ayotte's daughter, lauds her own mother's success at teaching her the importance of "working really hard with your community to get things done."[28]

The ads in New Hampshire diverged from other states' ads in intriguing ways, but it is difficult to determine whether these differences had to do with the unique gender matchup or with New Hampshire's political culture. Without delving overly into the state's circumstances, it should be noted that New Hampshire at the time of the election had a woman governor, two female Senators, and one of the House seats was held by a woman and the other would be after the election. Perhaps the novelty of women as candidates has worn off in New Hampshire, and accordingly, gender cues take on a different form.

CONCLUSIONS

In this chapter we have explored the effects of the presidential race on the use of gender-related language and themes in Senate campaigns. Many of the qualitative statements above suggest that gender norms in the 2016 election were not radically different than in prior years—and this is not an unexpected finding. Female candidates sought to portray themselves as being "tough," and male candidates were at times shown by their opponents to be less masculine than they might have liked. Women faced the challenge of being attacked both on being insufficiently feminine—that is, for lapses in their voting or actions on issues that might be seen as being of particular importance to women—but also for being insufficiently masculine. Yet given the highly polarized nature of voting in 2016—not a single state that voted for Trump elected a Democrat to the Senate, and not a single state that voted for Clinton elected a Republican—it is hard to say that this made a difference in the election outcome.

It is, however, clear that the expectation that Donald Trump would lose the election had a substantial effect on the nature of advertising in 2016.

The consequences of this are clear both in our quantitative measurements of the presidential candidates' appearances in advertisements and in our analysis of gender-related themes in the ad content. Democrats sought to use Trump against their Republican opponents, but they did so in different ways. Female Democrats were more willing to draw connections between their male Republican opponents and Donald Trump, and female Democrats were able to make their male opponents look weak by tying them to Trump. Male Democrats were less willing and able to do this, although many of the male Democrats here were running in states that were more favorable for Trump. Republicans, in turn, made great efforts to present themselves as being sympathetic to women's issues, and at times to question their female opponents' commitment to those same issues. In a few instances the same pattern played out even in competition between two male candidates. Hillary Clinton played a more peripheral role—she was often linked by male Republicans to their male Democratic opponents, but it is hard to know if this was a matter of gender or simply an effort to harm Democrats in Republican-leaning states.

We found few significant differences here between candidate advertisements and ads by other types of organizations. Our unit of analysis here was the individual advertisement, not the individual ad airing, so it is possible that super PAC or party ads that linked the senate and presidential candidates were much more ubiquitous than candidate ads which did the same. However, the willingness of candidates to use the presidential candidates, and Trump in particular, in their own ads indicates either that the candidates saw Trump as being unpopular enough that they could directly target him, or that conventional beliefs about the differences in advertising strategy and coordination between different campaign organizations were not particularly relevant in 2016.

There is, of course, much room for further research—particularly as it applies to races featuring two women candidates. In all likelihood, we will see again in 2018 and 2020 how Donald Trump is used in Senate campaign advertisements. In the grand scheme of things, we may never get another chance to gauge the effects of our natural experiment here—the effect a female presidential candidate and a male candidate with a propensity for particularly misogynistic statements can have on Senate races. However, it is likely that future female presidential candidates will continue to find that their campaigns' choices are confined to a narrower band of acceptable behavior than those of their male opponents. One evident lesson of the Trump campaign is that the latitude for the behavior of male candidates for the highest possible office is strikingly vast. One has only to imagine Hillary Clinton, Kelly Ayotte, or Deborah Ross mocking a disabled reporter, labeling Mexican immigrants as "rapists and criminals," or, heaven forbid, bragging about going up to attractive men and kissing them without warning, to understand that no woman running for political office would be able to do even one of these things without being pilloried, and would certainly not be rewarded with an electoral victory. Whether or not the use of gender norms in advertising changes election outcomes, our analysis suggests that gender-normative expectations for male and female behavior shape candidates' words and actions in campaigns as well as shaping popular perceptions of candidates' appropriateness for office. In short, as Trump's campaign and subsequent election show, the collective justification of misogynist words and actions under the rubric of "boys will be boys" will continue to make behavior that is completely unacceptable for women (because it violates feminine gender norms) seem almost entirely unproblematic for men.

NOTES

1. The authors wish to thank the Patron-Cohen Endowed Faculty Research Fund at Clark University for supporting this project.

2. These words included brave, care, compassionate, courage, fight, independent, insider, man, outsider, patriot, protect, strong, tough, weak, and woman.

3. For example, see this National Horizon Super PAC attack ad against Katie McGinty from November 2, 2016: https://archive.org/embed/PolAd_KatieMcginty_4tup8, accessed March 12, 2017.

4. See: https://archive.org/embed/PolAd_CatherineCortezMasto_nl3l2; https://archive.org/embed/PolAd_CatherineCortezMasto_bt3p3; https://archive.org/embed/PolAd_CatherineCortezMasto_bri70, all accessed March 12, 2017.

5. https://archive.org/embed/PolAd_RichardBurr_DonaldTrump_8ufnn, accessed June 21, 2017.

6. https://archive.org/embed/PolAd_RichardBurr_DeborahRoss_oxl3e, accessed June 21, 2017.

7. https://archive.org/embed/PolAd_RobPortman_6zp7m, accessed June 21, 2017.

8. https://archive.org/embed/PolAd_MarcoRubio_5qsld, accessed June 21, 2017.

9. https://archive.org/embed/PolAd_JoeHeck_DonaldTrump_uo6dq, accessed June 21, 2017.

10. The ad can be seen here: https://archive.org/embed/PolAd_PatToomey_DonaldTrump_61lsu, accessed March 12, 2017. Trump responded to the attack by blaming the Obama administration for its weakness, and praising his own prediction of future attacks by "radical Islamic" terrorists (https://www.nytimes.com/2016/06/15/us/politics/donald-trump-shooting-response.html?_r=0).

11. https://archive.org/embed/PolAd_DonaldTrump_DeborahRoss_s6e7m, accessed June 21, 2017.

12. https://archive.org/embed/PolAd_EvanBayh_HillaryClinton_5110l, accessed June 21, 2017.

13. https://archive.org/embed/PolAd_EvanBayh_ToddYoung_7ccsm, accessed June 21, 2017.

14. https://archive.org/embed/PolAd_ToddYoung_EvanBayh_fu2sz, accessed June 21, 2017.

15. https://archive.org/embed/PolAd_PatToomey_3gpf5, accessed June 21, 2017.

16. https://archive.org/embed/PolAd_PatrickMurphy_MarcoRubio_0i1f5, accessed June 21, 2017.

17. https://archive.org/embed/PolAd_DeborahRoss_zhcl6, accessed June 21, 2017.

18. https://archive.org/embed/PolAd_DeborahRoss_bow0y, accessed June 21, 2017.

19. https://archive.org/embed/PolAd_KatieMcginty_0uudt, accessed June 21, 2017.

20. https://archive.org/embed/PolAd_KatieMcginty_5qhug, accessed June 21, 2017.

21. https://archive.org/embed/PolAd_MaggieHassan_8vhv7, accessed June 21, 2017.

22. See, for example, Lowry 2016.

23. https://archive.org/embed/PolAd_KellyAyotte_0oqif, accessed June 21, 2017.

24. https://archive.org/embed/PolAd_KatieMcginty_e8wyq, accessed June 21, 2017.

25. https://archive.org/embed/PolAd_KatieMcginty_7z8h9, accessed June 21, 2017.

26. https://archive.org/embed/PolAd_KatieMcginty_0m39b, accessed June 21, 2017.

27. https://archive.org/embed/PolAd_KellyAyotte_g2erm, accessed June 21, 2017.

28. https://archive.org/embed/PolAd_MaggieHassan_0zthl, accessed June 21, 2017.

REFERENCES

Benoit, William L. 2014. *A Functional Analysis of Political Television Advertisements*. Lanham, MD: Lexington Books.

Bystrom, Dianne G., Terry Robertson, Mary Christine Banwart, and Lynda Lee Kaid, eds. 2004. *Gender and Candidate Communication: Videostyle, Webstyle, Newstyle*. New York: Routledge.

Conroy, Meredith. 2015. *Masculinity, Media, and the American Presidency*. New York: Palgrave Macmillan.

Dittmar, Kelly. 2015. *Navigating Gendered Terrain: Stereotypes and Strategy in Political Campaigns*. Philadelphia, PA: Temple University Press.

Dolan, Kathleen and Timothy Lynch. 2016. "The Impact of Gender Stereotypes on Voting for Women Candidates by Level and Type of Office." *Politics & Gender* 12 (3): 573–595.

Dolan, Kathleen. 2014. *When Does Gender Matter? Women Candidates & Gender Stereotypes in American Elections*. New York, NY: Oxford University Press.

Fowler, Erika Franklin, and Travis N. Ridout. 2012. "Negative, Angry, and Ubiquitous: Political Advertising in 2012." *The Forum* 10: 51–56.

Herrnson, Paul S. 2012. *Congressional Elections*, 6th ed. Thousand Oaks, CA: Sage/Congressional Quarterly.

Kahn, Kim Fridkin. 1993. "Gender Differences in Campaign Messages: The Political Advertisements of Men and Women Candidates for U.S. Senate." *Political Research Quarterly* 46 (3): 481–502.

Kane, Paul. 2016. "John McCain Abandons his Support of Donald Trump." *Washington Post*, October 8.

Lowry, Rich. 2016. "Yes, Hillary was an Enabler." *National Review*, May 27. Accessed June 21, 2017. http://www.nationalreview.com/article/435941/hillary-clinton-enabled-bill-clintons-abuse-women-her-own-standards.

Phillips, Amber. 2016. "Kelly Ayotte's Donald Trump Agony Continues." *Washington Post*, October 4.

Sapiro, Virginia, Katherine Cramer Walsh, Patricia Strach, and Valerie Hennings. 2011. "Gender, Context, and Television Advertising: A Comprehensive Analysis of 2000 and 2003 House Races." *Political Research Quarterly* 64 (1): 107–119.

Part IV

ELECTION ADMINISTRATION: DID ELECTION ADMINISTRATION IMPROVE IN 2016?

Chapter 12

Election Administration in 2016

A Tale of Two Cities

Charles Stewart III and Terri Susan Fine

At a presidential election rally on October 17, 2016 in Green Bay, Wisconsin, Republican nominee Donald Trump claimed: "Remember, we are competing in a rigged election .... They even want to try and rig the election at the polling booths, where so many cities are corrupt and voter fraud is all too common" (Collinson 2016).

Three weeks after Donald Trump won the majority electoral vote despite losing the popular vote, the president-elect tweeted on November 27, 2016: "In addition to winning the Electoral College in a landslide, I won the popular vote if you deduct the millions of people who voted illegally" (Trump 2016).

On May 11, 2017, over three months after taking office, President Trump signed Executive Order 13799 establishing the "Presidential Advisory Commission on Election Integrity." In that executive order, President Trump established the mission of the commission as:

Sec. 3. Mission. The Commission shall, consistent with applicable law, study the registration and voting processes used in Federal elections. The Commission shall be solely advisory and shall submit a report to the President that identifies the following:

(a) those laws, rules, policies, activities, strategies, and practices that enhance the American people's confidence in the integrity of the voting processes used in Federal elections;

(b) those laws, rules, policies, activities, strategies, and practices that undermine the American people's confidence in the integrity of the voting processes used in Federal elections; and

(c) those vulnerabilities in voting systems and practices used for Federal elections that could lead to improper voter registrations and improper voting, including fraudulent voter registrations and fraudulent voting (Trump 2017).

Together, Donald Trump as nominee, as president-elect, and as president used three communication approaches (speech, social media, executive order) to indicate his distrust of election procedures.

Analysts suggest that Trump's actions are unprecedented as the allegations emerged at odd times. The statement at the Wisconsin rally occurred before the election took place and after voters in several states had already participated in early voting. The added concern of a rigged system placed increased pressure on election administrators who already expected high turnout because the presidential election was an open seat race.

Trump was not the only one alleging election-related irregularities. Democratic Party activists supporting U.S. senator Bernard ("Bernie") (I-VT) for the Democratic presidential nomination filed a class action lawsuit "alleging the Democratic National Committee worked in conjunction with Hillary Clinton's 2016 campaign to keep Bernie Sanders out of the White House" (Riotta 2017). Sanders' supporters claimed that the Democratic National Committee (DNC) failed to fulfill Article 5, Section 4 of its charter requiring:

> In the conduct and management of the affairs and procedures of the Democratic National Committee, particularly as they apply to the preparation and conduct of the presidential nomination process, the chairperson shall exercise impartiality and evenhandedness as between the presidential candidates and campaigns. The chairperson shall be responsible for ensuring that the national officers and staff of the Democratic National Committee maintain impartiality and evenhandedness during the Democratic Party.[1]
>
> The lawsuit claimed that the DNC and its chair, U.S. Representative Debbie Wasserman Schultz (D-FL) engaged in "deceptive conduct, negligent misrepresentation and fraud" (Riotta 2017). The class action suit included allegations that favoring former U.S. senator and former U.S. Secretary of State Hillary Clinton over Sanders resulted in donations made to the DNC by Sanders supporters were misdirected and misappropriated which contributed, in part, to Clinton enjoying advantages leading to her nomination. The Democrats' failure to uphold its impartiality clause, according to litigants, extended benefits to Clinton to which she was not entitled. The DNC defended its actions on the grounds that the charter did not have the force of law; rather, the charter language represents a "political promise" and not a legal obligation to remain neutral (Riotta 2017).

The criticisms leveled by Trump and by Sanders supporters may have colored how voters perceived the electoral system both as to their confidence in the election and perceptions of their voting experience. These allegations, made on a national scale, may be reflected in how voters perceived their election experience all of which took place in their local community.

This chapter focuses on efforts made by local election administrators to improve voter experiences in polling places in response to criticisms leveled about the 2012 presidential election. These criticisms included that lines at polling places were too long and that voters were inconvenienced. These efforts will be framed in terms of trying to build confidence in elections in general by improving the experience that voters have when they go to vote. This approach is implicitly a test of a proposition that has emerged in academic scholarship suggesting that election officials have control over certain aspects of the voting process. If election officials focus on those aspects over which they do have control, such as polling place congestion, they can make progress in instilling confidence in the election process.

We start by reviewing the two sides of voter confidence. The first side is fostered by the contestation of the candidates themselves. The result of an election produces winners and losers, and those affiliated through their partisanship to the winners end up feeling better about the process than do those affiliated through their partisanship to the losers. The second side is the direct experience of voters. When voters have a positive experience at the polls, they will think better of the process. We have evidence about each from the 2016 election.

Second, we discuss the recommendations of the Presidential Commission on Election Administration (PCEA) about improving polling place experiences. We produce two contrasting case studies of jurisdictions that attempted to improve polling place practices and, as a consequence, reduce lines in 2016. One will be Urbanity, Massachusetts and the other Magnolia County, Florida.[2]

Both jurisdictions saw significant efforts made to improve voter experiences, with positive results in terms of wait times. In Magnolia County, voters responded by becoming much more confident that their votes were counted as intended (a good proxy for confidence in the process). The same was not true in Urbanity. Thus, while in these cases, undertaking efforts to improve polling place practices were made in response to PCEA recommendations, it is not clear that confidence, in fact, was improved uniformly.

Evidence of voter confidence was analyzed through public opinion polls. These polls showed that voter confidence was higher in 2016 compared with 2012 while partisan identification related to voter confidence in general as well as how voters perceived the possibility that election interference had taken place.

Results from the 2016 Survey of the Performance of American Elections are presented below. The Survey of the Performance of American Elections (SPAE) is based on the responses to an Internet survey of 200 registered voters in each of the 50 states and the District of Columbia. Individuals were asked about their experience voting whether they voted in person on Election Day, took part in early voting in person or voted absentee. Non-voters were also included in the survey (Stewart 2017).

Voters were asked "How confident are you that your vote was counted as you intended?" The results indicate that voter confidence is high although it has varied between 60 percent and 70 percent since 2000. The lowest voter confidence was expressed in 2012, when 61 percent responded that they were "very confident" that their vote was counted as intended while 70 percent responded in the same way in 2000. While voter confidence is generally high, there is evidence that there are factors affecting it.

Partisanship plays an important role in how the public perceives elections including confidence that one's vote will be counted as cast (Abramowitz and Webster, 2016). As shown in Figure 12.1, there were some partisan differences in voter confidence in 2016 although these differences were much smaller compared with other years going back to 2000. Partisan differences have not demonstrated a clear pattern over time as Democrats were generally less confident in 2000 and 2004 while Republicans expressed less confidence than Democrats in 2008 and 2012. Over time and across elections there has been reasonably high confidence in elections although partisan differences continue.

Events surrounding the 2016 election also raised concerns about computer "hacking." Hacking, in the context of the U.S. election, involves external entities accessing computer systems not intended for them in order to manipulate hardware or software so that information not intended for the public is released to the public, information and records are manipulated for a specific purpose, or something else. Concerns about hacking in the 2016 election first

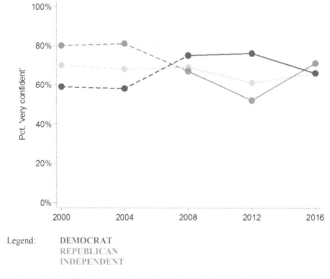

Figure 12.1   How Confident Are You That Your Vote Was Counted as Intended?

emerged in mid-June 2016 when the *Washington Post* reported that "hackers working for the Russian government accessed the Democratic National Committee's computer system, stealing oppositional research on Donald Trump and viewing staffers' emails and chat exchanges" (Nakashima 2016). Since that time news reporting of computer hacks has continued and remain unresolved as of this writing.

Partisan differences in perceptions of the integrity of the election were also revealed in how the public viewed the possibility of computer hacking in the election at the national and local levels. The first reports of hacking on the Democratic National Committee may have played a role in Democrats more than Republicans viewing hacking as a "major problem" even though it was the Republican nominee who claimed at several junctures during the election season that the system was rigged or otherwise unfairly biased against him.

Table 12.1 shows that Democrats were more than twice as likely to agree that computer hacking was a major problem in the national election compared with their concerns about computer hacking at the local level. One-quarter of the public, regardless of party, were not sure whether hacking was a problem.

These results speak to voter trust in election administration. The criticism leveled by Donald Trump suggested that concerns about election integrity were a national problem while first reports, and the continued focus of ongoing election administration concerns, have focused on compromising the Democratic National Committee as an organization and compromising specific Democratic candidates such as Hillary Clinton. Concerns about

Table 12.1 Percent of Democrats and Republicans Who Considered Computer Hacking a Problem

	Major Problem	Minor Problem	Not a Problem	Not Sure
Percent Democrats who considered computer hacking a problem nationwide in the 2016 election	24	25	27	24
Percent Democrats who considered computer hacking a problem locally in the 2016 election	15	18	43	24
Percent Republicans who considered computer hacking a problem nationwide in the 2016 election	10	38	29	23
Percent Republicans who considered computer hacking a problem locally in the 2016 election	5	22	49	24

Source: Charles Stewart III, *Survey of the Performance of American Elections*, 2017.

computer hacking were much lower when the question was asked about local elections although Democrats were still more likely than Republicans to consider computer hacking a major problem at the local level.

These response differences further indicate that Americans believe that while computer hacking may be a national election–related problem, that problem has not trickled down to local-level election administrators. These differences in how partisans perceive the decentralized nature of election administration may be linked to an enduring trust based on individual experiences with that system. After all, in some communities, federal, state, and local election schedules may mean that voters interact with their local election administrators at least once each year. For example, presidential election years may warrant three interactions (presidential nomination vote, congressional/state nominations, and general elections) with local election administrators. These frequent experiences, if positive, may foster an enduring trust in election administration.

Still, less overall concern with computer hacking at the local level compared with concerns about computer hacking at the national level do not mean that the public was not concerned about local election administration. The public did express concerns about illegal voting-related activities that were shaped by their partisan affiliation. All of these voting-related activities took place solely at the local level.

As shown in Table 12.2, Republicans more than Democrats expressed concern about illegal voting-related activities. For example, Republicans far more than Democrats asserted that voters voted multiple times, impersonated other voters and voted absentee illegally. Republicans more than Democrats further claimed that election officials tampered with voted ballots and with election returns although the differences were not as great compared with the other activities outlined. These results suggest greater party differences when considering those illegal activities for which poll workers are primarily responsible (e.g., allowing voting among those who should not be voting) compared with responsibilities associated with elected election administrators (e.g., handling election returns).

Table 12.2　The Frequency That Illegal Election Activities Occur

Activity	Democrat	Republican
Voting multiple times	15%	31%
Tampering with voted ballots	18%	24%
Voter impersonation	16%	32%
Voting by non-citizens	15%	41%
Illegal absentee voting	19%	35%
Officials tampering with returns	18%	20%

Source: Charles Stewart III, *Survey of the Performance of American Elections*, 2017.

These party differences are notable in that Democrats are more likely to see election-related tampering from an external, unidentified source (e.g., computer hacking) while Republicans are more likely than Democrats to claim that poll workers (those who check in-voters and confirm their eligibility to vote) play a role in illegal election activity off.

These results suggest that a deeper examination of voter confidence is warranted giving focus to local-level election administration. Voters' direct knowledge of election administration through their experience at the polls may be related to their confidence in the electoral process as a whole. A positive voting experience may build higher confidence in the system overall while the opposite may also be true. Voters having a negative experience at the polls may view the big-picture election–related confidence issues (such as concerns about computer hacking in the election at the national level) as a greater concern.

Voter experience at the polls appeared to affect voter confidence. As shown in Table 12.3, the more difficult that voters perceived their experience at the polls the less confident that they were that their vote would be counted as cast. These differences in voter perception reveal how important a voter's experience is in fostering confidence in democratic processes.

As shown in the table, almost twice as many persons indicating that they experienced no problems stated that they were very confident that their vote would be counted as intended. Those experiencing minor or major problems were far less likely to express their confidence that their vote would be counted compared with those experiencing no problems at all. As well, the length of time that voters waited in line also affected their perceptions. Almost three-fourths (71%) of voters who did not wait expressed confidence in their vote while those numbers reduced, albeit slightly, among those waiting for longer periods.[3] These differences suggest that voter perceptions of their own experience may shape how they view the larger electoral system as voters generalize from their own experiences to broader questions about elections. These results are also reflected in how voters assessed poll worker performance at their own polling places. Voters working with poll workers whom they saw as excellent were far more likely to express confidence

Table 12.3 How Confident Are You That Your Vote Was Counted As You Intended?

How well the voter's polling place was run	*Percent very confident that their vote was counted as intended*
Very well/no problems	71%
Acceptable/minor problems	47%
Not well/minor problems	33%
Terrible/major problems	38%

Source: Charles Stewart III, *Survey of the Performance of American Elections*, 2017.

that their ballot would be counted compared with others whose experience did not meet that same standard. Voters suggesting that they had a negative experience, whether it be the amount of time that they spent waiting in line, their perception of how their polling place was run, and the evaluation of poll worker performance, were less likely to express confidence that their vote was counted as cast.

These results suggest that there may be factors associated with election administration that play a role in these opinions as voter confidence that their vote was counted as cast may be affected by their perception of how the polling place was run, the performance of individual poll workers, or how long these voters waited at their polling place.

One of these factors, voter wait times, was addressed by President Barack Obama on March 28, 2013 when he signed Executive Order 13639. E.O. 13639 formed the Presidential Commission on Election Administration (PCEA). The PCEA was formed, in part, to address overly long lines at the polls on the November 6, 2012 general election day.

The PCEA was established "in order to promote the efficient administration of Federal elections." E.O. 13639 identified 11 areas of concern including "the number, location, management, operation and design of polling places" (Obama 2013). The PCEA released a lengthy report in 2014 outlining best practices for election administrators, giving specific attention to voter experiences including poll wait times. The commission called for greater attention to polling place congestion because long wait times suggest a fundamental mismatch between the number of voters and the resources allocated to accommodate them (see Fine and Stewart 2017).

The 2016 presidential contest was the first general election that took place after the PCEA was formed.[4] The 2016 election created opportunities to identify ways that voter experiences had improved since the PCEA recommendations were released as well as possible opportunities for further improvement as many election officials were concerned about repeating the long lines and congestion evident in 2012.

The PCEA established a benchmark of 30 minutes as the maximum wait time before voters cast their ballot. Recognizing that long lines often occur because of a fundamental mismatch between the number of voters and the resources to accommodate them, the PCEA called for greater attention to polling place congestion. It also encouraged the development of computer-based tools that could assist election officials to better understand where inadequate polling place resources might lead to unreasonably long lines.

Nationwide results suggest that there was some improvement in the length of time that voters waited at polling places. The percentage of persons experiencing no lines remained about the same (36% in 2012 vs. 38% in 2016) while the percentage of voters waiting more than 30 minutes declined by 4 percent (13% to 9%). Overall, the average wait time declined from 13 minutes to 11 minutes while in no state was the average wait time over 30 minutes (see Figure 12.2). These data suggest that efforts at improving wait times bore fruit as voter turnout was higher in 2016 (60.2%) compared with 2012 (58.6%) and wait times were lower (Wilson 2017).[5]

Still, these national- and state-level improvements, while heartening, do not provide insight as to what led to these improvements nor do these results speak to the unique characteristics of local election administration.

Election administration provides a good example of how federalism works. Article I, Section 4, Clause 1 of the *U.S. Constitution* provides that "The Times, Places and Manner of holding Elections for Senators and Representatives, shall be prescribed in each State by the Legislature thereof; but the Congress may at any time by Law make or alter such Regulations." The *Constitution* extends to the states the responsibility for regulating election administration unless Congress decides otherwise (e.g., the Voting Rights Act of 1965 bans literacy or citizenship tests as a condition of voter registration; until then, states could choose whether or not to require such tests). States

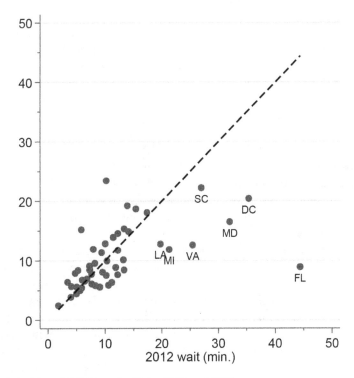

Figure 12.2 Voter Wait Times by State: 2012 and 2016.

extend election administration responsibilities to localities (cities, counties) which are then responsible for implementing federal and state election law when they administer elections. Local election administrators are responsible for fulfilling these laws within the political and geographic boundaries of their districts such as identifying polling place locations, designing ballots, staffing polling places, overseeing the selection of election equipment, training poll workers to use that equipment and other responsibilities.

Thus, while the PCEA was established based on national concerns associated with election administration, running elections is an entirely local concern. It is important, then, that we investigate how local election officials administered the 2016 election to see if, where and how election administration unfolded in the first post-PCEA presidential election.

In the next section, we describe election administration in Magnolia County and Urbanity in 2016 while we also compare differences between election administration in 2012 and in 2016 in those same communities.

Magnolia County, Florida, is a large urban/suburban central Florida county. Magnolia County, Florida, was the fifth largest election jurisdiction (of 67) in Florida and the 37th largest election jurisdiction in the United States. Voters check in using electronic poll books that were developed by the county. Voters on Election Day and during early voting use a paper ballot which is then scanned using an optical scanner. Florida has an early voting option and a large percentage of Magnolia County voters vote before Election Day, both early in-person and by mail (absentee). In 2016, 46 percent of voters voted in-person during the early voting period, 29 percent voted by mail, and 25 percent voting on Election Day. In 2012, 27 percent voted in-person during the early voting period, 29 percent voted by mail, and 44 percent voted on Election Day. These participation statistics indicate that early voting occurred at a much higher rate in 2012 compared with 2016 while in-person voting on Election Day was much higher in 2016 compared with 2012.

Magnolia County implemented several changes between 2012 and 2016 as a means to reduce Election Day in-person voting wait times. The elections supervisor introduced "line walkers," a polling place position involving an individual walking through voter lines armed with tablets linked to the Magnolia County Supervisor of Elections voter rolls to make certain that waiting voters were in the correct polling place and were registered to vote. Individuals who showed up at the incorrect polling place were redirected to the correct polling place and avoided waiting in line only to find out that they had to go elsewhere to vote. Time spent completing ballots was helped when the state reduced the number of amendments on the ballot compared with 2012.[6] The county increased personnel in order to grow the number of check-in stations so that wait time would be reduced at check-in. The supervisor of elections also increased capacity by emphasizing the use of the "Help Desk Oath

Person," a position normally reserved for individuals requiring additional administrative support such as address changes, directions to correct polling places, and other interventions. Additional booths and scanners were also in use in polling places with anticipated higher traffic.

The county election supervisor also decreased the number of persons assigned to any polling place by increasing the number of precincts from 227 to 247 while also encouraging early in-person and absentee voting through public service announcements and providing information about early voting sites, including days and times of operation, on sample ballots sent to each registered voter. The election supervisor also increased the number of early voting locations compared with 2012 which remained open for longer hours. The results discussed earlier indicate the effectiveness of these efforts as the percent voting on Election Day was nearly 20 percent lower between 2012 and 2016.

Overall wait times decreased between 2012 and 2016. Overall, nearly two-thirds of Magnolia County voters reported in 2012 that they waited more than 30 minutes to vote while just 12 percent of voters recalled waiting more than 30 minutes in 2016. Breaking down these results between those voting early in-person compared with those voting in person on Election Day also showed differences. Almost 60 percent of those voting early in-person in 2012 reported waiting more than 30 minutes to vote while 15 percent of those voting early in-person in 2016 reported waiting more than 30 minutes in 2016. On Election Day, 67 percent of voters reported waiting more than 30 minutes while 9 percent reported waiting 30 minutes or more in 2016.

Voter confidence patterns also increased between 2012 and 2016. In 2012, one-half (51%) of Florida voters indicated that they were confident that their votes were counted as cast while 12 percent of Magnolia County voters expressed the same viewpoint. In 2016, 55 percent of Florida voters expressed that they were "very confident" that their vote counted as cast while 46 percent of Magnolia County residents did so. Overall, the percentage of Florida residents indicating that they were confident that their vote counted as it was cast increased by a small amount between 2012 and 2016 while a large increase was revealed among Magnolia County voters.

Urbanity, which serves as the county,[7] covers 48 square miles and has a population of 673,184. It is the largest city in New England and the 23rd largest city in the United States by population and the sixth largest Combined Statistical Area in the United States. The Urbanity City Council has a strong mayor-council government. There are nine city council districts. The two members of the U.S. House of Representatives representing Urbanity are both Democrats. Almost 400,000 of Urbanity's residents are registered to vote.

Like Magnolia County, Urbanity also made election administration changes between 2012 and 2016. Urbanity grew its administrative capacity by increasing the number of check-in stations at polling places. Urbanity also increased the number of booths and ballot scanners to avoid a bottleneck at key points in the voting process. The Urbanity Elections Commission also increased the number of election precincts which decreased arrival rates. As well, the Urbanity Elections Commission encouraged early voting which resulted in 19 percent of voters voting early in Urbanity.

Changes in the percentage of persons waiting over 30 minutes declined between 2012 and 2016. Overall, combining early in-person voters with Election Day Voters, in 2012, 24 percent of voters waited more than 30 minutes while 11 percent waited over 30 minutes in 2016. Among Election Day voters only, 5 percent waited more than 30 minutes to vote in 2016 while 34 percent waited more than 30 minutes to vote among those voting early.

Voter confidence declined in Urbanity between 2012 and 2016. In 2012, just less than three-fourths of Urbanity voters (and Massachusetts voters overall) indicated that they were "very confident that their votes counted as cast." That percentage declined to about one-half in 2016 showing that, despite efforts to make voting easier, voting confidence did not increase between 2012 and 2016 in Urbanity while it did in Magnolia County across the same two elections.

The Presidential Commission on Election Administration sought to reduce wait times to 30 minutes or less in light of the difficulties that voters experienced in 2012. Both Magnolia County, Florida, and Urbanity, Massachusetts, streamlined various election procedures at polling places to reduce polling place congestion and improve voter experiences.

Despite national findings suggesting that a better, smoother, and shorter polling place experience relates to voter confidence such that spending less time in line will increase confidence that one's ballot will count as it was cast, these results were not consistently revealed in Magnolia County and Urbanity. Magnolia County voters appeared to have a better voting experience and also expressed higher confidence levels while Urbanity voters did not express the same viewpoints. Urbanity voters showed a confidence decline while Magnolia County voters expressed more confidence with the post-PCEA election changes.

Voter confidence is one indicator of system legitimacy. The more that voters express confidence that their vote will be counted as cast, the more legitimacy that they accord the election system as a whole. Voter confidence, which may be related to voter experience at the polls, is also filtered through partisanship.

Of the greatest concern, of course, is overall system legitimacy. Concerns about election-related hacking, claimed on a national scale, could very well affect voter confidence in local-level election administration. Here, in investigating these two cities, we see clear reasons why voter confidence should have increased between 2012 and 2016. The PCEA recommendation of a 30-minute benchmark for voter wait times has now been met for most voters in both places even though voter confidence was not affected in the same way between them.

Perhaps these results speak to a bigger picture. Pre-election allegations of election irregularities by candidate Donald Trump have been reinforced with Executive Order 13799 by now-President Trump. The partisan differences evident through which individuals perceive election legitimacy may affect voter confidence and expectations regardless of their experience at polling places. In essence, what voters experience may be colored by preconceived claims that they learn about regarding national-level allegations before they arrive at their polling place. Partisan beliefs associated with the individuals making those claims may also affect how voters perceive local-level election administration as well as their expressed confidence that their vote will be counted as cast. Consequently, there are limits to the effect of improvements in polling place administration in expressed voter confidence.

NOTES

1. Democratic National Committee Charter, Article 5, Section 4.

2. We honor a promise made to the county supervisor of elections and city elections commission to not divulge the names of the city or county in any research reports produced for public consumption.

3. There appears to be no meaningful pattern between voter confidence and wait times as 64 percent of those expressing confidence that their vote would be counted as intended waited less than 10 minutes, 60 percent of those waiting 10–30 minutes expressed confidence while two-thirds of those waiting more than 30–60 minutes expressed confidence. Sixty-three percent waiting over an hour agreed that they were confident. See Charles Stewart, *Survey of the Performance of American Elections*, 2017.

4. The congressional midterm election in 2014 also created opportunities to see if and how PCEA recommendations, if implemented, might have been effective in improving polling place administration. However, results from 2014 would have limited comparability to 2012 because congressional midterm elections tend to exhibit low voter turnout. Low voter interest, less media attention, high incumbent re-election rates, and high numbers of uncontested elections typical of midterm congressional elections tend to depress voter turnout.

5. The 2016 election was an open seat race, which tends to increase turnout compared with those races when an incumbent is seeking re-election.

6. In Florida voters decide whether or not to amend the state constitution; there are six ways to place an amendment on the state ballot. Of these, all but one method allows proposed amendments to be longer than 75 words. Amendments proposed by a joint session of the state legislature are not subject to word limits. Ballots that include amendments are longer than those without amendments while amendments proposed by the state legislature are longer than amendments proposed by some other means.

7. The county government was disbanded in 1999.

REFERENCES

"2016 Presidential Campaign Hacking Fast Facts." 2016. *CNN Library*, Accessed June 22, 2017. http://www.cnn.com/2016/12/26/us/2016-presidential-campaign-hacking-fast-facts/index.html.

Abramowitz, Alan I. and Steven Webster, 2016. "The Rise of Negative Partisanship and the Nationalization of U.S. Elections in the 21st Century." *Electoral Studies* 41: 12–22.

"The American Voting Experience: Report and Recommendations of the Presidential Commission on Election Administration." 2014. Accessed May 24, 2017. http://web.mit.edu/supportthevoter/www/.

Collinson, Stephen. 2016. "Why Trump's Talk of a Rigged Vote is So Dangerous." *CNN*, October 19. http://www.cnn.com/2016/10/18/politics/donald-trump-rigged-election/index.html.

Democratic National Committee Charter, Article 5, Section 4, Democratic National Committee.

Fine, Terri Susan, and Charles Stewart. 2017. "Assessing Recommendations of the Presidential Commission on Election Administration in a Central Florida County" In *Races, Reforms, & Policy: Implications of the 2014 Midterm Election*, edited by Tauna Sisco, Jennifer Lucas, Christopher Galdieri. Akron, OH: University of Akron Press.

Nakashima, Ellen. 2016. "Russian Government Hackers Penetrated DNC, Stole Opposition Research on Trump." *Newsweek*, June 14.

Obama, Barack. 2013. "Executive Order 13639—Establishment of the Presidential Commission on Election Administration," March 28. Online by Gerhard Peters and John T. Woolley, *The American Presidency Project*. http://www.presidency.ucsb.edu/ws/?pid=103416. Accessed May 24, 2017.

Riotta, Chris. 2017. "Was the Election Rigged Against Bernie Sanders? DNC Lawsuit Demands Repayment for Campaign Donors." *Newsweek*, May 15.

Stewart, Charles. 2017. *Survey of the Performance of American Elections*, Harvard Dataverse, V1, UNF:6:/Mol52fZ59fx6OsPWIRsWw==.

Sances, Michael and Charles Stewart. 2015. "Partisanship and Confidence in the Vote Count: Evidence from U.S. National Elections since 2000." *Electoral Studies* 40: 176–188.

Trump, Donald. 2016. "In addition to winning the Electoral College in a landslide, I won the popular vote if you deduct the millions of people who voted illegally." November 27. 12:30p.m. Tweet.

Trump, Donald. 2017. "Executive Order 13799—Establishment of Presidential Advisory Commission on Election Integrity," May 11. Online by Gerhard Peters and John T. Woolley, *The American Presidency Project*. http://www.presidency.ucsb.edu/ws/?pid=124262. Accessed May 24, 2017.

Wilson, Reid. 2017. "New Report Finds that Voter Turnout in 2016 topped 2012." *The Hill*, March 16.

Index

About the Contributors

Matthew D. Atkinson is an assistant professor in the Department of History and Political Science at Long Beach City College. He received his doctorate in Political Science from UCLA and his scholarship has been published in the *Journal of Politics, British Journal of Political Science, Political Research Quarterly, Quarterly Journal of Political Science*, and *PS: Political Science & Politics*.

Julia R. Azari is an associate professor of political science at Marquette University. She is the author of *Delivering the People's Message: The Changing Politics of the Presidential Mandate* (Cornell, 2014) and the coeditor of *The Presidential Leadership Dilemma: Between the Constitution and a Political Party* (SUNY, 2013). She holds a PhD from Yale University and is an active political science blogger.

Tyler Benning is a recent graduate of St. Olaf College. He majored in Political Science and Biology, and plans to pursue a degree in medicine. His political interests include voting behavior, American Constitutional law, and legislative procedure.

Robert G. Boatright is a professor of Political Science at Clark University and the director of Research at the National Institute for Civil Discourse. His research focuses on the effects of campaign and election laws on the behavior of politicians and interest groups, with a particular focus on primary elections and campaign finance laws and practices. He is the author or editor of six books, including *The Deregulatory Moment? A Comparative Perspective on Changing Campaign Finance Laws* (University of Michigan Press, 2016); *Getting Primaried: The Causes and Consequences of Congressional Primary*

Challenges (University of Michigan Press, 2013); and *Interest Groups and Campaign Finance Reform in the United States and Canada* (University of Michigan Press, 2011). He received a PhD from the University of Chicago and a BA from Carleton College.

Mark D. Brewer is a professor of Political Science and member of the Honors College faculty at the University of Maine. His research interests focus generally on political behavior, with specific research areas including partisanship and electoral behavior at both the mass and elite levels, the linkages between public opinion and public policy, and the interactions that exist between religion and politics in the United States. Brewer is the author or editor of a number of books and articles in academic journals, with the most recent being *Parties and Elections in* America, 7th edition (with L. Sandy Maisel, Rowman & Littlefield, 2016), *Polarization and the Politics of Personal Responsibility* (with Jeffrey M. Stonecash, Oxford University Press, 2015), *The Parties Respond*, 5th edition (with L. Sandy Maisel, Westview Press, 2013), *Party Images in the American Electorate* (Routledge, 2009), and *Dynamics of American Political Parties* (with Jeffrey M. Stonecash, Cambridge University Press, 2009). He is also the editor in chief of the *New England Journal of Political Science*.

Christopher Chapp is an associate professor of Political Science at St. Olaf College, where he teaches classes on American politics and research methodology. He received his undergraduate degree from the University of Wisconsin—Madison, and his doctorate from the University of Minnesota. He is the author of *Religious Rhetoric and American Politics: The Endurance of Civil Religion in Electoral Campaigns*, published by Cornell University Press. His research has also appeared in journals such as the *American Political Science Review* and *Communication Monographs*. His primary research interests are American political behavior, political communication, and religion in politics.

Jack D. Collens is an assistant professor of political science at Siena College in Loudonville, NY. He is a graduate of the University of Georgia, where he earned a PhD in political science, and Louisiana State University, where he earned bachelor's degrees in political science and Spanish. His research and teaching focus on American political institutions and elections, American political development, political communication, and research methods.

Darin DeWitt is an assistant professor of Political Science at California State University, Long Beach. He received his PhD from UCLA and his work is published in *Celebrity Studies*, *PS: Political Science & Politics*, and *Urban Affairs Review*.

Terri Susan Fine, PhD, is a professor of political science at the University of Central Florida. She is the recipient of 10 undergraduate teaching excellence awards and one university-wide award each in faculty leadership, professional service, scholarship, and academic advising. In addition to publishing several chapters in books, her work has been published in *Presidential Studies Quarterly, Polity, Women and Politics,* the *Journal of International Women's Studies, State Politics and Policy Quarterly,* the *Journal of Policy Practice, White House Studies,* and *Perspectives on Political Science,* among others. She also serves as the content specialist for the Florida Joint Center for Citizenship which takes an active role supporting the implementation of the Sandra Day O'Connor Civic Education Act enacted in Florida in 2010.

Christopher J. Galdieri is an Associate Professor of Politics at Saint Anselm College in Manchester, New Hampshire. He received his undergraduate degree from Georgetown University and his doctorate from the University of Minnesota. Before coming to Saint Anselm, he taught for two years at St. Olaf College in Northfield, Minnesota. His research has appeared in Politics and Policy, the New England Journal of Political Science, the Columbia Journalism Review, and several edited volumes. He is writing a book about carpetbagger Senate candidates.

Dan Hofrenning is a professor of Political Science at St. Olaf College where he teaches classes in American politics including campaigns and elections, environmental politics, and the intersection of religion and politics. As a scholar, he has written a book (*In Washington But Not of It* published by Temple University Press) and numerous articles about a range of topics including religion, campaigns, lobbying, and issues of pedagogy. As a media commentator, Hofrenning has written op-ed pieces and provided commentary for a range of print, radio, and television outlets across the country. The *StarTribune* has been the most frequent place for his commentary, but he has also commented for Minnesota Public Radio, the *New York Times, Los Angeles Times,* MSNBC, NBC Nightly News, CNN, and BBC Worldwide Radio. He has been part of the Political Science panel on the Twin Cities Public Television show, *Almanac.*

Steven Katz is a graduate student in the Psychology program at Rutgers, studying the contributions made by specific emotions to political decision-making. He is writing his thesis on the effects of emotions expressed in political advertisements in senatorial races, and hopes to investigate the moderating effects of partisanship on emotional political messages. He has contributed to a presentation, Specific Emotions in Negative Campaigning: A Role for

Contempt? at the International Society of Political Psychology, and presented graduate posters at the Eastern Psychological Association.

Chad Kinsella is currently an assistant professor of political science at Ball State University where he focuses on teaching state and local government and public administration. His research focuses primarily on electoral geography but he also examines state and local government, federalism, and pedagogy.

Jennifer Lucas is a professor of Politics as Saint Anselm College, where she teaches courses on gender and politics, congressional politics, and public policy. She earned her BA from Providence College and her PhD from the University of Maryland, College Park, and has served as the co-editor of the *Journal of Women, Politics, & Policy.*

Seth Masket is professor of political science at the University of Denver and director of the Center on American Politics. He is the author, most recently, of *The Inevitable Party: Why Efforts to Kill the Party System Fail and How They Hurt Democracy* (2016: Oxford University Press). He teaches and studies political parties, state legislatures, and campaigns and elections. His research has appeared in the *American Journal of Political Science*, the *Journal of Politics*, the *British Journal of Political Science*, *State Politics and Policy Quarterly*, and other peer-reviewed publications. Masket is a regular contributor at Vox's "Mischiefs of Faction" blog, as well as *Pacific Standard,* and *FiveThirtyEight.*

Kyle Mattes is an associate professor of political science at Florida International University in Miami, FL. He has published articles about negative campaigning, candidate strategy, and voter decision-making in journals including *Political Psychology* and the *Journal of Politics*. His book with David P. Redlawsk, *The Positive Case for Negative Campaigning*, is available from the University of Chicago Press.

Kevin J. McMahon is the John R. Reitemeyer Professor of Political Science at Trinity College in Hartford, Connecticut. His book, *Nixon's Court: His Challenge to Judicial Liberalism and Its Political Consequences* (University of Chicago Press, 2011), was selected as a 2012 *CHOICE* Outstanding Academic Title and won the Supreme Court Historical Society's Erwin N. Griswold Prize in 2014. His first book, *Reconsidering Roosevelt on Race: How the Presidency Paved the Road to Brown* (University of Chicago Press, 2004), won the American Political Science Association's Richard E. Neustadt Award for the best book published that year on the American presidency. He is also the coauthor/coeditor of three books on the presidency and presidential elections and author of numerous book chapters and journal articles.

Elizabeth P. Ossoff, PhD, is a professor of Psychology. Her research interests include politics and the media, and the psychology of gender. She focuses on the psychology of political behavior, from the perspective of voter and candidate. She has published articles on voter reaction to attributes of political candidates and the role of gender in how women see their political roles. Her recent projects include the impact of the label of parent and party on male and female candidates. She has also looked at the role of late-night television, such as SNL and the Daily Show in framing young voters' impressions of political candidates. She teaches courses in advanced research techniques, Social Psychology, the Psychology of Gender, Political Psychology, and Psychology of the Media. She received her BA from Colby College and her MS and PhD from Tufts University in General Experimental Psychology with a specialty in Social Psychology.

Richard J. Powell is a professor of Political Science and director of the Cohen Institute for Leadership & Public Service. He is the author of numerous journal articles and book chapters on presidential-congressional relations, presidential communications, presidential and congressional elections, and state politics. He has also coauthored *The 2012 Presidential Election: Forecasts, Outcomes, and Consequences* (Rowman & Littlefield, 2013), *Legislating Without Experience: Case Studies in State Legislative Term Limits* (Lexington Books, 2007) and *Changing Members: The Maine Legislature in the Era of Term Limits* (LexingtonBooks, 2004). In 2010, he was a Fulbright Lecturer at Zhejiang University in Hangzhou, China.

David P. Redlawsk is the James R. Soles Professor and Chair of Department of Political Science and International Relations at the University of Delaware. He received his PhD and MA from Rutgers University, and holds an MBA from Vanderbilt University and a BA from Duke University. His research focuses on campaigns, elections, the role of information in voter decision making and on emotional responses to campaign information. He has received several grants to support his research from the National Science Foundation, and served on the Board of Overseers for the American National Election Studies from 2009 to 2013. His newest book is *The Positive Case for Negative Campaigning*, with Kyle Mattes, published in 2015 by the University of Chicago Press.

Elizabeth Hahn Rickenbach, PhD, is an assistant professor of Psychology at Saint Anselm College. Her work has been published in *The Gerontologist*, *Psychology and Aging*, the *Journal of the American Geriatrics Society*, and the *Journal of Population Aging*. Her research interests are related to gerontology and in particular, the role of stress and coping across the adult lifespan and adaptation to age-related normative and non-normative changes. Her recent work includes research examining how individuals adjust to retirement. She teaches courses in Developmental Psychology, Gerontology, and Research Methods. She received her BS in Human Development from Pennsylvania State University and a PhD in Aging Studies from the University of South Florida.

Ira J. Roseman is a professor of Psychology at the Camden campus of Rutgers University. His widely cited model of the emotion system (e.g., Roseman, 2001, 2011, 2013), encompasses 17 emotions, including anger and contempt. He was an early student of emotion in political communication (Roseman, Abelson & Ewing, 1986) and has studied anger and contempt in individual experiences, social relations, negative advertising, and voting behavior.

Tauna S. Sisco is an associate professor of Sociology at Saint Anselm College, in Manchester, NH. Her work has appeared in *Feminist Media Studies*, *Journal of Women, Politics, and Policy*, and includes two edited books on national midterm elections titled *Races, Reform, & Policy* and *Political Communication & Strategy* both published with The University of Akron Press (2017). Her work also includes the Homeless Access Survey 2009–2013, a five-year collaborative partnership with the New Hampshire Department of Health and Human Services, Bureau of Housing and Homelessness, to assess the needs and access of New Hampshire adult homeless population. Her research interests include gender and political sociology, media studies of social problems, and rhetoric of ambivalence of public policy concerning the homeless. Originally from Indiana, she received her PhD from Purdue University.

Valerie Sperling is a professor of Political Science at Clark University. Her research interests center around Russia and include gender politics, social movements, patriotism, and the European Court of Human Rights. She is the author of *Organizing Women in Contemporary Russia* (Cambridge University Press, 2000); *Altered States: The Globalization of Accountability* (Cambridge University Press, 2009); and *Sex, Politics, and Putin: Political Legitimacy in Russia* (Oxford University Press, 2015), which won the Association for Slavic, East European, and Eurasian Studies (ASEEES) Davis Center Book Prize for the "outstanding monograph on Russia, Eurasia, or Eastern Europe in anthropology, political science, sociology or geography," as well as the Association for Women in Slavic Studies (AWSS) Heldt Prize for the "Best book in Slavic/Eastern European/Eurasian Women's Studies." She received a PhD from the University of California, Berkeley, an MA in Russian Area Studies from Georgetown University, and a BA from Yale University.

Charles Stewart III is the Kenan Sahin Distinguished Professor of Political Science at MIT, where he has taught since 1985, and a fellow of the American Academy of Arts and Sciences. His research and teaching areas include congressional politics, elections, and American political development. Since 2001, Professor Stewart has been a member of the Caltech/MIT Voting Technology Project, a leading research effort that applies scientific analysis to questions about election technology, election administration, and election reform. He is currently the MIT director of the project. Professor Stewart is an established leader in the analysis of the performance of election systems and the quantitative assessment of election performance. Professor Stewart also provided advice to the Presidential Commission on Election Administration. His research on measuring the performance of elections and polling place operations is funded by Pew, the Democracy Fund, and the Hewlett Foundation. He recently published *The Measure of American Elections* (2014, with Barry C. Burden). Professor Stewart received his BA in political science from Emory University, and SM and PhD from Stanford University.

Atiya Kai Stokes-Brown is an associate professor of Political Science at Bucknell University. She received her PhD in Political Science from the University of Maryland, College Park and her teaching and research interests include American Politics, Racial/Ethnic Minority Political Behavior, Latino Politics, Women and Politics, Campaigns and Elections, and Congressional/State Politics. Dr. Stokes-Brown has numerous publications broadly centered on the political incorporation of women and racial/ethnic groups into the American political system, and issues of representation. She is the author of *The Politics of Race in Latino Communities: Walking the Color Line* (Routledge, 2012, 2014) and her work has appeared in several peer-reviewed journals including the *Journal of Politics, American Politics Research, Politics and Policy,* the *Journal of Elections, Public Opinion, and Parties, Social Science Quarterly, National Political Science Review,* and *Political Research Quarterly.* She is also the author of several peer-reviewed book chapters.

Sean Tatar graduated from Clark University in May 2017 with a Political Science major and a minor in Women's and Gender Studies. She is currently earning her Master of Public Administration (MPA) at Clark.

Joseph E. Uscinski is an associate professor of political science in the College of Arts & Sciences, University of Miami. He earned his PhD at University of Arizona, his MA at University of New Hampshire, and his BA at Plymouth State College. He is coauthor of *American Conspiracy Theories* (Oxford, 2014).

Emily O. Wanless earned her bachelor's degree from Clemson University (political science major) and her master's degree in political science from the University of Montana. She holds a PhD in political science from the University of Georgia. Her teaching and research interests include American politics, institutions, and elections. Most recently, she served as an adjunct faculty for the University of Georgia's Department of Political Science, School of Public and International Affairs. Ahead of the 2018 South Dakota legislative session, Wanless was chosen by South Dakota lawmakers to head the Initiative and Referendum Task Force, which will examine potential changes to the initiated measure, constitutional amendment, and referred law processes.

Aidan Zielske is a current senior at St. Olaf College. She is majoring in Political Science and plans to pursue a degree in law. She is an avid reader of nonfiction about the Supreme Court.

CPSIA information can be obtained
at www.ICGtesting.com
Printed in the USA
LVHW091606150421
684631LV00003B/392

9 781498 566636